Theodore Roosevelt was the biggest character in US history, as William Allen White declared: "an overgrown personality." Rick Marschall has collected a broad sampling to help us understand the many elements of the man—the erudite and the exuberant, the dogged and the aphoristic, the warm boyish TR and the serious scholar and shrewd political leader. TR attracted devoted followers and harsh critics, then and now. You can't understand TR without taking in the contradictions, the flaws, the virtues, and the amazing scope of the man. Enjoy this book!

—*Kathleen Dalton*, author, *Theodore Roosevelt, A Strenuous Life*

If you love Theodore Roosevelt as I do, Rick Marschall's new book is a must-have, must-read. I wish I could memorize every TR quotation that Rick has uncovered. A fast-paced, can't-put-it-down book! It will be my first choice to share with family and friends who love TR...or who need to know him.

—*Bernadette Castro*, former Commissioner, New York State Office of Historic Preservation; member, Theodore Roosevelt Association Advisory Board

Capturing the prism of a fellow like Theodore Roosevelt is a mega-task requiring an artist's eye and a writer's nose! Rick Marschall makes it look so easy! Wonderful insights into a complex subject! TR must be grinning from ear to ear!

—*Feather Schwartz Foster*, author, *The First Ladies* and *Mary Lincoln's Flannel Pajamas*; and the POTUS-FLOTUS blog, www.featherschwartzfoster.blog.

The real Theodore Roosevelt leaps off the pages of Rick Marschall's new book, *The Most Interesting American*. It allows those who actually knew Theodore to speak about the man, giving readers an insightful look into the man behind the legend. In this case, the man more than lives up to the legend. It is a BULLY! of a book.

—*Michael F. Blake*, author, *The Cowboy President: The American West and The Making of Theodore Roosevelt* and *Go West, Mr. President: Theodore Roosevelt's Great Loop Tour of 1903.*

Who better to paint a picture of who TR was as a statesman, family man, historian, rancher, and buddy than the contemporaries who experienced him in real time? Rick Marschall has assembled more than 150 of those voices who reveal what TR was like. *The Most Interesting American* adds the personality to the historical accomplishments we know so well. This is a unique portrait and a solid addition to the ongoing study of the Colonel.

—*Terrence Brown*, former Executive Director,
Theodore Roosevelt Association; illustration historian
and Director, Society of Illustrators, 1984–2006.

They say that the next life lasts for an eternity, and a good thing too: the wait to see the Colonel will be long indeed. If you want a sneak peek at what awaits you and a chance to spend time with those in line ahead of you—Jacob Riis, John Burroughs, William Allen White, and others—read Rick Marschall's *The Most Interesting American*. Interesting Theodore Roosevelt was, but also, we learn, uncommonly kind, decent, and gentle; and imbued with a common touch that belied his blue-blood background. Well done, Rick, and if you get there before me, save me a spot in line, won't you?

—*Duane G. Jundt*, Theodore Roosevelt Center
at Dickinson State University

The Most Interesting American is a fascinating and entertaining collection of insightful, fun, and often profound quotations about Theodore Roosevelt. They bring TR to life. Having served on the Executive Committee of the Theodore Roosevelt Association at the request of Jim Roosevelt, TR's cousin and the godfather of my oldest son, and having rescued the only remaining archival TR film footage from decomposing into nitroglycerine, I was pleasantly surprised by the many first-hand revelations in *The Most Interesting American*. I recommend it highly.

—*Dr. Ted Baehr*, Chairman, Christian Film and Television
Commission; Editor-in-chief, *Movieguide*

If you really want to know "The Colonel," as those close to him called him, there is no better resource than those who actually knew him and knew him well. Here are their first-hand thoughts and impressions, collected in a single pithy and easy-to-read volume. Rick Marschall has met and spoken to Roosevelt family members (including TR's ever- entertaining and rowdy daughter, Alice) and scoured thousands of articles and books to assemble *The Most Interesting American*. If you admire TR, this is a book you should have in your library.

—*Rod Sullivan*, Editor, The Roosevelt Dynasty: Family,
Fitness & Faith on Facebook.

Rick Marschall truly lifted TR out of the dusty and cliched old history books. It is as if we the readers are there in TR's time. TR becomes once again a fully realized person, foibles and all, seen through others' eyes—those of his generation, be they friend or opponent. We finally meet a truly interesting man—TR.

—*Maureen R. Trainor Nestor, M.Ed*, Admin of the
Theodore Roosevelt Facebook Group

THE MOST INTERESTING AMERICAN

PERSONAL ENCOUNTERS, QUOTATIONS, and FIRST-HAND IMPRESSIONS of THEODORE ROOSEVELT

COLLECTED and ANNOTATED by
RICK MARSCHALL

Post Hill
PRESS

A POST HILL PRESS BOOK

The Most Interesting American:
Personal Encounters, Quotations, and First-Hand Impressions
of Theodore Roosevelt
© 2023 by Rick Marschall
All Rights Reserved

ISBN: 978-1-63758-632-7
ISBN (eBook): 978-1-63758-633-4

Cover design by Cody Corcoran
Interior design and composition by Greg Johnson, Textbook Perfect

Post Hill Press
New York • Nashville
posthillpress.com

Published in the United States of America
1 2 3 4 5 6 7 8 9 10

For my grandson
Lewis Theodore McCorkell

*May these impressions of a great man
inspire you as they have long inspired me
and uncountable others.*

CONTENTS

Introduction

"There is a sweetness about the man you can't resist."
"Nominate him by acclamation? Hell, we'll nominate him by assault!"
"Death had to take him in his sleep. If he had been awake,
there would have been a fight."

Statements like these attest to the force of Theodore Roosevelt's personality, magnetism, and appeal. And they were spoken by political enemies—a Democrat president, a bitter party rival, and a vice president of the other party.

Equally compelling are awe-struck descriptions of TR by friends and acquaintances:

> I curled up in the seat opposite, and listened and wondered, until the universe seemed to be spinning around. And Theodore was the spinner. —*Rudyard Kipling*

> Review the roster of the few great men of history, our own history, the history of the world; and when you have finished the review, you will find that Theodore Roosevelt was the greatest teacher of the essentials of popular government the world has ever known. —*Elihu Root*

> Roosevelt possesses the quality that Medieval philosophers ascribed to the Deity—he was Pure Act. —*Henry Adams*

These are samples of the assessments of Theodore Roosevelt that I have collected in the following pages. You will learn that an acquaintance said that, after a meeting with TR, he felt like he needed to return home and wring the man's personality from his clothes. The newspaper columnist and author Irvin S. Cobb famously said that "you have to hate the Colonel an awful lot to keep from loving him." Even opponents uttered colorful, and usually awe-struck, descriptions of Roosevelt. And, needless to say "of course," his children adored him. Latter-day rumors and armchair psychologists claim to detect a resentment or rivalry between TR and his first-born, Alice. But she was merely obstreperous by nature (and DNA?) and many times proved her fealty to her remarkable father—even politically, to the dismay of her Old-Guard husband Nick Longworth. I had the exquisite privilege of meeting "Princess" Alice (as she was widely and adoringly called for her imperious celebrity), and TR virtually lived in her through her spirit, colorful language, and brilliant blue (of course) eyes.

Many history buffs, and even casual readers of American history, might know some of these quotations, and more. If a parlor game commenced, the things that people said about Theodore Roosevelt, as well as the famous phrases and quotations of his own, would last long into the evening. Except for two forgotten volumes compiled after Roosevelt's death in 1919, no one book has dedicated itself exclusively to anthologizing what others thought, said, and wrote about him.

This is *not* a parlor game, however. Yes, there was the sheer fun of the man, an exceptional man, arguably the Most Interesting American. And, a century after his death, we propose to rescue him from that form of personal obscurity. A president; the author of more than forty books; America's usher into the twentieth century; a world-class naturalist; an iconic cowboy and war hero. The *pince nez* spectacles, toothy grin, and bushy mustache. The face on Mount Rushmore, several postage stamps, and the focus of movies. Can Theodore Roosevelt ever become obscure?

My vision for this book is to rescue TR from the ironic side-effects of the recent and overdue scholarly interest in the man. More has been written about Theodore Roosevelt than any other American except Abraham Lincoln, in the estimation of some historians. After numerous biographies, there have been, increasingly, studies of (for instance) Roosevelt and sports; Roosevelt's lawsuits; Roosevelt and his crusade to save the environment; Roosevelt's relations with foreign leaders, congressional opponents, authors, and hunting companions; Roosevelt's views on religion and race…

Introduction

It is meet and right so to do. He was a consequential man, and he did consequential things, so no detail is inconsequential. To understand such a person's smallest aspects is to better understand that person (beyond facts and dates and lists of accomplishments), which allows us to more deeply understand the society and the country…and often to understand ourselves, the heirs of his consequences, better too.

Theodore Roosevelt lived at the cusp of the American Century. It seems a miracle of Providence that he "happened" when he did. TR's America was burgeoning as a new world power replete with inventions and technology and swelling with (welcomed) immigrant populations; it was suddenly the most prosperous nation and largest exporter (and importer) of the world's agricultural and manufactured goods. TR and the American Century were meant for each other.

It is, in fact, hard to imagine a robust United States of the time without the colorful and visionary leader that Roosevelt was. Consider a Theodore Roosevelt who might have been president in, say, the Era of Good Feelings, the tranquil decades before the Civil War. *That*, as a parlor game, would be a rough challenge. TR's nature, however, was to enliven any office, any job, any challenge he might have faced. When he was elected vice president, for instance, he regretted its almost institutional irrelevance. Indeed, many vice presidents before and since have regarded the office as a political graveyard.

What contemporaries and historians have neglected in this matter is the factor of…Roosevelt's personality. After a few days of presiding over the Senate, TR engaged a Supreme Court justice to tutor him in Constitutional matters and the heritage of the office. Can anyone doubt that, if Vice President Roosevelt had served four years, that "warm bucket of spit" (the allusion of a later VP, John Nance Garner, describing the job) would be extremely different today, a more vital office in the Executive Branch?

Roosevelt frequently asserted his religious beliefs and the nation's spiritual heritage, yet he also was fiercely private about such matters, and demanded that America be tolerant in the extreme. Such anomalies about an otherwise well-examined man, whether the intervening century seems long or short, confronted me as a historian. TR has the reputation of being exuberant…yet he only reluctantly, and infrequently, yielded to the nascent form of moving-picture "newsreels." Recordings of his voice are few; he generally delivered only campaign appeals. His "Tennis Cabinet" of informal advisers was well known, and—when the weather permitted—he played matches daily...yet he considered being seen by the public in his tennis whites undignified. So they never did.

In many ways, therefore, this very public man was very private. And there is the challenge to the Roosevelt canon.

Contemporary America has come to know TR for *what* he did—setting aside millions of acres of public lands and creating the Panama Canal (whose construction and many surmounted obstacles were very personal triumphs), as well as his association with landmark legislation and regulatory reforms, and his negotiations in labor disputes and foreign wars. Adding to such matters, and digging deeper, we have the scholarly research into Theodore Roosevelt's accomplishments.

But I have come to realize—and the impetus for this book—that America is in danger of losing knowledge of the *essence* of Theodore Roosevelt. His accomplishments in the fields aforementioned, and many more, reserve an exalted place for TR in American history. What we have had stolen, however, or somehow hidden, is the Theodore Roosevelt who was vital, ebullient, wise, forceful, courageous, impulsive, humorous, knowledgeable, persuasive, just plain fun, and...interesting.

Logically, his unique personality assisted the advancement of so many accomplishments. But these qualities are known to people in the 21st century mostly by implication and third-hand descriptions. Historians virtually have to ask their students and readers to accept on trust these aspects of Roosevelt's personality. It is surprising that his legacy as an individual—the actual impression Americans have of the man—is derived from cartoons, mostly of a political nature. Photographs left an impression, too, unavoidable when Americans were drawn to this man of action. So we have cartoons and a few photos of TR speaking, gesticulating, laughing, riding, greeting crowds, chopping wood, and rowing. But the eyewitness records of this effervescent personality? "Take our word for it."

There is actually a wide divide, then, between his secure status in history texts, and the popular conception in cartoons and caricatures. I previously have addressed these aspects of Roosevelt's life in my book *Bully!: The Life and Times of Theodore Roosevelt* (a biography illustrated exclusively with 250 vintage cartoons; 2011, Regnery History), and in the exhibition and book *TR in '12*, documenting the material culture of his Bull Moose campaign (with Gregory Wynn; 2012, Theodore Roosevelt Association and National Park Service).

The "divide" will be bridged in this book. America needs TR (and TR deserves) to live again as he did when he strode across the landscape. How did his family and friends regard him? How did strangers assess him? How did reporters and writers describe this dynamo? What did his political supporters and opponents say about him? *What was he like?* Not in musty history books, but as a man people saw and knew. I have combed contemporary letters, articles, diaries, quotations, and memoirs to re-establish a vivid portrait of Theodore Roosevelt.

Some of the assessments and passages were written on assignment— reporters, for instance, on the campaign trail—but many impressions, long and short, assure us that many views are entirely unselfconscious. Thus, reality comes through…not that the personality of Theodore Roosevelt easily could be contained.

So you will meet Theodore Roosevelt the man vicariously in these pages. I have determined to avoid, as much as possible, his own words (those have been collected through the years, in everything from Cyclopedias to small gift books) as well as history-class data. TR shied away from introspection anyway, and the recitation of legislative battles or specimen-lists from the safari are pertinent elsewhere. I invite readers not to be eavesdroppers, but to share the visceral feelings of those fortunate souls who met and knew Roosevelt.

Be prepared to cut through some stereotypes, such as they are. The effusive, ebullient, grinning whirlwind of a man, as much a "common man" as any could be, who was called by the public and known to posterity as "Teddy"…strongly disliked to be called Teddy. "Any man who uses that name does not know me," he said. We know him, and will know him better through this book, so we will respect his wishes. "Theodore," even; "Colonel" always, after the Spanish-American War; or simply "TR" will be the names we use for the Most Interesting American.

* * *

A basic biographical tour will set the context. Theodore Roosevelt lived from 1858 to 1919, almost neatly spanning the period between the Civil War and World War I. Those wars defined many things in America and were cathartic in many ways, but they also served as bookends to a remarkable period of fecundity. Those years roughly encompassed the Industrial Revolution, the Gilded Age, and the Progressive Era.

TR was not a bundle of contradictions but virtually the opposite: a polymath; cognoscente; a mental dervish with multiple interests, passions, specialties, and friendships. He likely was the most intellectual of American presidents; certainly he was the most intellectually accomplished. Roosevelt routinely read a book every day, and his memory's retention was astonishing; he often remembered meeting someone, even when it was a casual introduction, from previous decades…and that person's family, interests, and job.

Of all American presidents, it might be said of Theodore Roosevelt, in his obituary, serving as president of the United States would not necessarily be the first accomplishment listed. If public service had not beckoned, TR would yet be remembered as a leading expert in fields of natural history—birds, protective coloration, mammalian migrations. He was the author of history books, some of which are still standard texts today. And…he will be remembered by much more, as this book will share, category by colorful category.

Several presidents, and many notable men and women, famously have overcome youthful burdens like poverty, meager education, and prejudice. It is a distinguishing characteristic of Roosevelt that he overcame, in a sense, his privileged and patrician origins. TR transcended the obligations of American aristocracy. He fulfilled the expectations of his class, prosperous New Yorkers who helped settle New Amsterdam. His father, Theodore ("the best man I ever knew"), was a philanthropist and reformer.

As TR matured he did not rebel against his family's status—even as he resented others in his social world who were indolent and "malefactors of great wealth"—but did not let it define him. A sickly boy, he built his body and became known for his strenuous prowess. He entered local politics when it was a saloon-keeper's province. In 1884, both his wife and his mother died when he was twenty-five, in the same house on the same day, of different causes (his wife Alice of Bright's disease; his mother of typhus). He sought solace in the West and re-made himself as a rancher-cowboy with large herds and two ranches.

He returned from the West to run for mayor of New York City, re-married his childhood sweetheart Edith with whom he would have five more children, wrote a series of histories, served in Washington as a reforming Civil Service Commissioner, and then worked hard in the mid-1890s to rid the New York Police Department of corruption as Commissioner. His first book, on the Naval War of 1812, attested to his interest that led to appointment as Assistant Secretary of the Navy. When war with Spain over atrocities in Cuba loomed, Roosevelt risked insubordination by ordering Admiral Dewey's fleet to Manila. But when war was declared, Dewey decimated the entire Spanish Pacific fleet with no American casualties. Famously, when war was declared, TR organized a volunteer regiment comprised largely of cowboys and society types from Roosevelt's East Coast clubs and society.

The Rough Riders, so called by an adulatory public, captured Cuba's San Juan Hill... and America's imagination. Mere months after TR returned from the war, he was elected governor of New York State. After two years of controversies and reform, he was named to the Republican presidential ticket with William McKinley. Upon a landslide election victory for the ticket and the subsequent assassination of McKinley, Roosevelt became the youngest president in history at forty-two (a distinction he retains).

He was president for the remainder of that term, and by a larger majority than McKinley's, elected in 1904. In addition to the accomplishments of his administration, reform became his watchword, and he contended with Congress, his own Republican Party, major corporations, and "trusts" (monopolies), malign foreign governments, corruption... and even random annoyances like authors of false narratives in nature books. He crusaded, unsuccessfully, for "Simplified Spelling" reforms. He wrote a scholarly essay on ancient Irish sagas. He discovered an obscure poet, Edwin Arlington Robinson, and publicized the future Pulitzer-Prize winner. He encouraged his publisher to issue the little-known English book *The Wind in the Willows*, of which Roosevelt was a devoted fan. His interests could not be contained.

After his presidency, Roosevelt arranged an enormous African safari, in part on behalf of the Smithsonian Institution. Thousands of specimens were discovered and collected, studied and sent to America, many still on display there and at New York's American Museum of Natural History.

Following this long expedition he toured the capitals of Europe to tumul-tuous welcomes. He also delivered major addresses, for instance, at the Sorbonne in Paris, his famous "Man in the Arena" speech.

After an unprecedented ticker-tape parade through Manhattan upon returning to the United States, he grew increasingly concerned that the initiatives of his presidency and the programs of political, social, and economic reforms he championed were being sabotaged by his chosen successor William Howard Taft and the emboldened reactionaries of the Republican Party. After Roosevelt's probity was questioned over his resolution of the Panic of 1907 and private exploitation was revealed in Alaska's public lands during Taft's watch, TR yielded to appeals and chal-lenged Taft for the 1912 nomination.

The political fight between old friends grew personal and ugly. It seemed clear, especially evident in numerous primaries, that Roosevelt was the choice of the GOP rank and file, but President Taft's forces controlled the convention. TR and his delegates bolted the convention and established the Progressive Party. The Democrats nominated a very different brand of Progressive (differences and long-term implica-tions that have been misunderstood, or lost, to subsequent history and politics). Woodrow Wilson achieved a plurality of votes—but the "Bull Moose" candidate Roosevelt trumped the incumbent Taft, who carried only two states.

After his election defeat, Roosevelt delivered an address as newly elected President of the American Historical Association, and left for South America for a series of lectures. While there, he was persuaded to join an expedition whose purpose was to discover the source of the never charted, always mysterious, and surely dangerous River of Doubt. TR accepted the challenge, of course; it represented "my last chance to be a boy." He arranged to share whatever scientific results that would arise from the expedition with the American Museum of Natural History, of which his father was a co-founder.

The party, with TR's son Kermit a member as of the African safari, soon was confronted by severe challenges: near-starvation rations, a surprising lack of edible animals or vegetation in the jungles, attacks by hostile tribes, piranha-infested waters, and dangerous cataracts and major waterfalls that obliged the party often to carry their canoes and provisions on lengthy detours. Roosevelt injured himself in an attempt to save a loose canoe and developed a fever of 105 degrees. For days he was delirious. He lost fifty pounds and never fully recovered from his jungle fever.

Soon after this latest return to his homeland, the Great War commenced in Europe. The issues that appertained generally consumed Roosevelt for the rest of his life…even if, at first, his advocacies virtually were ignored and largely rejected by an American public determined to look inward and stay there. For months he was practically a lone voice on the American scene, arguing at first for awareness of international events, then a policy of preparedness, then—by accepting the Allies' versions of circumstances and events—intervention. So devoted to these positions was he that in 1916 he declined a second nomination of the Progressive Party—sealing its doom—in order to defeat Wilson and the administration's virtually pacifist agenda.

Wilson was re-elected, by a hair, and Roosevelt almost immediately was touted as a GOP candidate in 1920. Today, little recognized by historians is the consequential role of TR until his death in 1919. The TR of these years often is described as a scold, peppering President Wilson on wartime policies even after America's declaration in April of 1917. However, after a year many draftees were still drilling with broomsticks, while European allies pleaded for America's immediate help. During this period, Theodore Roosevelt became the closest America has ever had to a "shadow president," a situation more common in parliamentary systems. Roosevelt prodded; he questioned and challenged; he spoke independently at training camps; he made policy suggestions, including for post-war programs. When President Wilson spoke, the press immediately sought Roosevelt's reaction. TR raised a hundred thousand men above draft age willing to volunteer while the Army trained (Wilson vetoed the possibility, even as the French President pleaded for "Teddies" to join his forces). His role as a "counter" to the President during these years was unprecedented and has not been replicated by another political figure.

The youngest of Theodore and Edith's children, Quentin, was killed in the war. A pioneer aviator, he was downed in a dogfight and buried with elaborate honors and ceremony by the German enemy as "a gallant aviator, who died fighting bravely against odds, [and] because he was the son of Colonel Roosevelt…esteemed as one of the greatest Americans," in the words of a witness.

All the Roosevelt children, including daughter Ethel and her doctor husband served in the war with distinction, his sons Ted and Archie sustaining severe wounds.

TR himself was in poor health at war's end, his tested and tortured body much older than its sixty years when he died of an embolism while sleeping. He was too sick anyway to deliver a speech he wrote, and it was read at Madison Square Garden on his behalf. In a sense, it was his final will and testament to the American people. In it, he required America to embrace unity and reject division along ethnic and class lines. "There is room for one language…and one soul-loyalty, and that is loyalty to the American people."

Those are the highlights of a busy life. The public reacted in uncountable ways to his uncountable activities and initiatives. Those reactions are recorded in history books, engraved on statuary (despite ungrateful legatees denigrating such heroes), and depicted in popular culture. What follows, lest it be forgotten in the shuffle of passing time and micro-scholarship, is how the Most Interesting American, Theodore Roosevelt, was perceived, assessed, and described—and loved—by his American people.

(Brief identifications of men and women I have quoted and who encountered TR are listed at the end of the book.)

Rick Marschall

"Hurrah for Teddy!" by Charles Dana Gibson

CHAPTER 1

The Personality of the Man

The essence of the man Theodore Roosevelt:
The imprint he left on America

Theodore Roosevelt met many people during his busy life. In various political offices, it was natural that a variety of citizens wanted to greet him, and since he was notable in so many arenas—bestselling author, cowboy and rancher, explorer and naturalist—celebrity-seekers were also drawn to him.

But of TR's many distinctions, perhaps the most distinctive was his personality itself. He savored exchanges with everyday folk, no less than with the famous. In the middle of his tour of European capitals after the African safari, he privately complained that if he met another Royal he would bite him!

He loved train travel, and through his life, TR crisscrossed the United States many times. Invariably he asked for railroad crews or restaurant staffs to assemble so he could greet each one, not just for *Hellos* or *Thank Yous*, but to inquire about backgrounds and families. More remarkable was the frequent occurrence that, two or three decades later, at chance encounters, Roosevelt recalled the person's face, name, and whatever information had earlier been shared.

This facility was more than eidetic memory or photographic memory. These rare abilities are closely related gifts of retention, both of which Roosevelt seemed to possess—eidetic memory generally enables a person to recall images and faces; photographic memory can extend to words on many pages, an abundance of dates and facts, and "seeing" rather than remembering things. TR's astonishing recall plausibly was also born of a passionate interest in people. Unlike many politicians whose motto might be akin to the *Peanuts* character who stated, "I love humanity; it's people I can't stand," Roosevelt had genuine, broad sympathies.

These characteristics, these sympathies, form only one aspect of a multi-faceted gem. The passages in this chapter have been gathered to do what friends and acquaintances endeavored to do—a rather unique challenge: to describe Roosevelt the man in something approximating the totality of his personality. That is, not as a specialist in his pursuits, or "wearing one of his hats," but it attempts, often breathlessly, to describe the experience of simply being with him.

His own sisters never tired of being with him, nor, more precisely, did they ever really lose the fascination of contact. All through his life, both strangers and intimates confessed to feeling "the very fun of the man" or "almost feeling that one had to go home and wash the personality" out of their clothes or "having to hate the Colonel an awful lot to keep from loving him."

Eyewitness accounts follow. The variety of spectators—friends and casual—and the endless assortment of circumstances enable us to gain an appreciation and even to imagine ourselves as eyewitnesses too.

William Hard, journalist and reformer, wrote:

> He was life's lover and life's scorner. He explored it forever and was forever ready to leave it. He was not simply life's energy. He was not simply, beyond any other living man, life's eternal forthright force. He was the irrelevant curiosity of it and the vagrant wandering of it and the finding of great magics in it and the perpetual amazement of it and its laughter. He was everything in it, but its tears. Tears he put aside…. He did not make life an end. Life for him was nothing but openings beyond, openings to effort and chance and to the joy of effort and chance, joy everlasting.
> So to be with him was not simply to live more strivingly. It was to live more abundantly. A primrose by the river's brim became a

prodigious episode in the migration of flowers. A shy child coming into the room became a romp and a riot. A dusty book chanced on in the garret became a gigantic pitiless controversy among scholars past and present and to be.... Everything became something else. There ceased to be any such thing as the commonplace.... He made Theodore Roosevelt the most interesting thing in the world. He seemed to do so. But when one had gone away from him one found that what he had really done was to make the world itself momentarily immortally interesting. He was the prism through which the light of day took on more colors than could be seen in anybody else's company....

He had a genius for the whole of life, but he had an even greater genius for the wholesome. With him one seemed to roam the world without limit and yet to return without soil. To be sophisticated to the very verge of the ultimate human abyss and yet to be as clean as a clean animal—that was his most extraordinary achievement and his most extraordinary legacy in the possibilities of the art of living....

So he himself still lives. I see him striding on and beating the mist back with swinging elbows; and in the space beyond is the gravity of Washington and the fierceness of Jackson and the melancholy of Lincoln and all the riches of men in which we Americans are already so rich; and he turns his head on his shoulder; and he looks back; and I cannot hear him speak; but I can hear the thing that was his mark and the symbol of his meaning; I can hear the click of teeth with which he girded himself to all denial of things in himself that weaken and to all conquest in himself of things beyond; and I can hear him laugh. And to the gravity of Washington and the fierceness of Jackson and the melancholy of Lincoln I see added the timeless gaiety of Roosevelt.

* * *

I believe that Theodore Roosevelt's greatest contribution to his country and his time was personality—was Theodore Roosevelt himself. —*Lawrence F. Abbott*

John Morley, the British statesman, told me, "The two things in America which strike me as most extraordinary are Niagara Falls and President Roosevelt." —*John Hay*

He is a superman if ever there was one! —*Arthur Conan Doyle*, after a visit to the United States.

I have held through a generation my first flash of Theodore Roos-evelt—a tallish yet stockily built man, physically hard and rugged, obviously fighting down the young man crescent of his vest; quick speaking, forthright, a dynamo of energy. Given to gestures and grimaces, letting [his voice] run the full gamut from bass to falsetto. He seemed spiritually to be dancing in the exuberance of a deep physical joy of life. —*William Allen White*

When I first met Colonel Roosevelt, I cannot pretend that I expected him to be attired in the khaki of the cavalry or to be heavily armed, but I did expect him to be—what shall I say? —to be more like the cartoons; to be, somehow, wilder looking…. I had not expected Colonel Roosevelt to look like a conservative banker of Amsterdam or The Hague. And that was what he made me think of as he sat behind his desk in one of the editorial offices of the *Metropolitan Magazine*.

The only sign there was about him that afternoon of the much pictured Rough Rider was the broad-brimmed, putty-colored hat which he laid upon his desk as he came in, and even that was but a modified version of the out-and-out cowboy hat, such as they wear around Medora.

Though I missed the cartoon costume, I was not to be cheated of the smile. It met all specifications. As the Colonel advanced to greet me he showed his hard, white teeth, wrinkled his red weather-beaten face, and squinted his eyes half shut behind the heavy lenses of his spectacles, in suggestion, as it seemed to me, of a large, amiable lion which comes up purring gently as though to say: "You needn't be afraid. I've just had luncheon"…

For the rest, his torso is like a barrel, his neck thick, short, and full of power…his mustache is now quite gray, but he has not aged and will not age. He has simply ripened, matured. He is fifty-seven years old…looks forty-seven, and evidently feels as men of thirty-seven wish they felt.

I had been there but a moment when reporters came to find out what he had to say about the criticisms of his speech which had been printed in the morning papers. The Colonel remained seated at his desk while he dictated the first few paragraphs of a statement which the reporters wrote down word for word…He arose and paced slowly back and forth, thinking out his remarks very carefully, speaking in a measured tone, enunciating with a kind of exaggerated distinct-ness which is always characteristic of him, forming each syllable elaborately with his mobile lips, the workings of which cause his mustache to gyrate at times in a curious manner. All these mannerisms are manifested in his most casual conversation, but when he is making a "statement" or dictating a letter they become extreme.

At other times, I studied carefully the Colonel's mode of speech. Each syllable leaves his mouth a perfectly formed thing; his teeth snap shut between the syllables, biting them apart, and each important, each accented syllable is emphasized not merely vocally, but also with a sharp forward thrust of the head which seems to throw the word clattering into the air. When he utters the first personal pronoun it sounds like *I-ye-e-e-e-*, with the final *e* trailing off like the end of an echo. —*Julian Street*

He stood in 1912, when he was in the midst of his most important activity. A stocky man of five feet ten or eleven, long-legged, short-bodied, never pursy, though at times too heavy. He kept himself well trained physically; and electric energy seemed to exude from his body and emphasize his personality. His walk was a shoulder-shaking, assertive, heel-clicking, straight-away gait, rather consciously rapid as one who is habitually about his master's business. He shook hands vigorously with a powerful downward pull like a pumper, with a firm but never rough handclasp. His shoulders sloped a little off the square line, and his head often, perhaps generally, was thrust forward from the neck, a firm short pedestal for his face; indeed, his neck was a sort of muscular part of his face, which jammed his head forward without ever requiring a stoop of the shoulders. His countenance was dominated by a big, pugnacious nose, a mustache dropped to cover a sensitive mouth in which a heavy underlip sometimes protruded, indicating passion.

Occasionally he used the loose lip as a shutter, purposely to uncover a double row of glittering teeth that were his pride. He knew that his display of teeth was effective as a gesture of humor or of rage. His slightly cleft chin could shoot out from a broad jaw, and when he was excited he worked his jaw muscles with an animal ferocity. They swelled and undulated in his moments of excitement, furnishing a physical outlet for his inner stress. Even in his thirties, when youth was still strong upon him, he had a wide, high brow, and to the end kept his hair intact. Probably his hair did not retreat a fraction of an inch in all his life. It was always stiff hair, inclined to curl, fairly close-cropped, always trimmed, and gave his countenance an aspect of virility so real that, looking at Roosevelt's hair, one could understand how Delilah thought she would sap Samson's strength by shearing him. Roosevelt's eyes always peered through glasses, generally nose glasses when he was indoors or in civilized environment, and the glasses often gave a glint to his face which was absent when he took them off; for his grayish-blue eyes were the least ferocious features in his face....

Every faculty, every purpose, every impulse, every physical and spiritual inch of him was over-engined. Yet his qualities were coordinated. He made, with all his Cyclopean features, a well-balanced man and mind. If he was a freak, God and the times needed one.
—*William Allen White*

[As a Harvard student, Roosevelt volunteered to teach Sunday School during all his college years.]

There is this incident connected with young Roosevelt's teaching of the mission class. He had quite a scene in the school. It seems that a boy named Joe came into the class one Sunday with a black eye. The teacher naturally asked him how he got it. He told him that a boy had pinched his sister in Sunday School and that he had given the boy a good licking, but had himself got the black eye in the encounter. The teacher, Roosevelt, said, "You did exactly right. Here's a dollar I want you to take, as a mark of my appreciation of your courage in defending your sister."

The mission class belonged to a high Episcopal church and the Sunday School authorities were rather shocked by this militant teacher of theirs. They were afraid that the doctrine he preached was rather too strenuous; besides, the young Harvard student got tangled in the ritual service at times and, altogether, both the officers and the young teacher thought it would be just as well for him to offer his services to another Sunday School. So he took up a class in a Congregational mission Sunday School and remained an intensely popular and efficient teacher till the day of his graduation.
—*Ferdinand Iglehart*

Of course over-nice people objected to the Roosevelt manner. They preferred the punctilios of hypocrisy which certain other Presidents had felt constrained to use under the rules of the political game. Such bald candor as Roosevelt's had not been seen in the White House since Jackson's time. Roosevelt succeeded because in all his demands of the party he asked for no improper thing. There was his strength.

He had moral sense as well as moral courage. His moral sense kept him from tripping. — *William Allen White*

Once on returning from his ranch...he found that some horse thieves, in making their escape, had taken his boat. They felt sure that this would make them safe from pursuit because there was no other boat. [Roosevelt's ranch hand] Bill Sewall, however, built a rude craft in great haste, and on this he and Mr. Roosevelt and another man started down the Little Missouri. They floated probably for one hundred and fifty miles before they saw the camp of the fugitives.

Mr. Roosevelt, unseen, stole ashore and upon the camp. When near enough he cried, with his weapon pointed, "Hands up, or I will shoot!" The only man about the place was asleep, so it chanced, and, thus rudely awakened, he was in great alarm. He rolled over and over on the ground in his anxiety not to be shot. He proved to be no more than a poor tool of the robbers and could hardly make himself understood in English. The thieves, two in number, made their appearance towards dark. They were in the stolen boat. Mr. Roosevelt and one of his men crept down by the river, where they sprang from their hiding as the outlaws drew near, and covered them with their guns. There was nothing for the men in the boat to do but to throw up their hands and surrender.

Nearly a week was required to take the captives to the county seat, a distance of two hundred miles. The boats stuck in the ice-jams and were almost upset. Each night a fire was built on the river bank and the two culprits were compelled to lie on opposite sides of it, while Mr. Roosevelt sat on watch until midnight and the rest of the night was divided between his two assistants. —*Hermann Hagedorn*

[Roosevelt recounted a story from his ranching days in his address at the Sorbonne in Paris, "Citizenship in a Republic," the message that has come to be known as the "Man in the Arena" speech, April 23, 1910. Condensed from TR's moral illustration:]

There were no fences. The cattle wandered free, the ownership of each being determined by the brand…. By the custom of the country, mavericks were branded with the brand of the man on whose range they were found. One day I was riding on the range with a newly hired cowboy, and we came upon a maverick.

We roped and threw it; then we built a little fire, took out a cinch-ring, heated it on the fire; and the cowboy started to put on the brand. I said to him, "It's so-and-so's brand," naming the man on whose range we happened to be. He answered: "That's all right, boss; I know my business."

In another moment I said to him: "Hold on, you are putting on my brand!" To which he answered: "That's all right; I always put on the boss's brand."

I answered: "Oh, very well. Now you go straight back to the ranch and get what is owing to you. I don't need you any longer."

He jumped up and said: "Why, what's the matter? I was putting on your brand." And I answered: "Yes, my friend, and if you will steal *for* me you will steal *from* me."

He could wash his clothes, and cook his meals, and in his Wild West days he went into frontier society. He attended the balls, and danced with the women, and opened one cowboy ball with the wife of a small stockman, dancing the lancers with her, opposite her husband, who not long before had killed a notorious bad man in self-defense. —*Carleton Case*

One day a quick-shooting cowboy named Jim was telling a disgusting story when Mr. Roosevelt came up, looked him straight in the eye and said, "Jim, I like you, but you are the nastiest-talking man I ever heard." The cowboys were accustomed to see gun-play in such cases, and were surprised when Jim hung his head in shame and apologized. After that they were good friends. —*Christian Reisner*

In all my experience I have never known anything like that man's vigor. Usually when I treat a patient as I have been treating Roosevelt I feel that some of my vital force has gone out of me into the patient and I come away slightly relaxed or exhausted. I suppose all physicians have the same feeling, in similar circumstances. But I have been treating Colonel Roosevelt now for several days; and each time, instead of coming away relaxed, I have come away invigorated, as though some kind of vital energy had passed from *him* into *me* instead of from *me* into *him*! —*An English throat surgeon who treated TR at Chequers, the estate of Sir Arthur Lee, after Roosevelt's European tour, 1910. Reported by Lawrence F. Abbott*

Among soldiers he was greeted as a soldier; among statesmen, as a statesman; among pioneers and woodsmen, as a hunter and naturalist; among scientists, as a scholar and explorer; among men of letters, as a writer and historian; among preachers, as a teacher of morals; among kings, as a man of royal prerogatives; among plain men and women, as a fellow citizen and democrat; and—last, but far from least—among children, as a protector and sympathetic companion. His personality was a unique and unprecedented combination of many qualities, any one of which, carried to a high development, makes what we call a great man. —*Lawrence F. Abbott*

I find that the President fills a good deal of the minds of those around him. He is mental and physical energy personified, and you find yourself caught up in his whirl and go skimming through space with him without any will power either to stop the machinery or even to slow it up. —*Archie Butt*

[After assuming the presidency] he spoke in the East and in the West, and for the first time the people of many of the States heard him speak and saw his actual presence. His attitude as a speaker, his gestures, the way in which his pent-up thoughts seemed almost to strangle him before he could utter them, his smile showing the white rows of teeth, his fist clenched as if to strike an invisible adversary, the sudden dropping of his voice, and leveling of his forefinger as he became almost conversational in tone, and seemed to address special individuals in the crowd before him, the strokes of sarcasm, stern and cutting, and the swift flashes of humor which set the great multitude in a roar, became in that summer and autumn [1902] familiar to millions of his countrymen; and the cartoonists made his features and gestures familiar to many other millions. —*William Roscoe Thayer*

He never wrote an article that he did not, before publication, submit to one of us, and he almost invariably accepted our suggestions, sometimes with regard to verbal expressions and sometimes with regard to change of ideas or views of the article. I do not mean to give the impression that he altered his mind frequently. On matters of principle he could be as fixed as adamant. But in methods of putting a principle into effect he habitually sought counsel and was eager to adopt suggestions. Not only did he contribute to our pages articles over his own name, but his wide experience, his comprehensive knowledge of men and affairs, and his unique ability as an interpreter of political and social movements found expression in our own editorials through the comments and suggestions which he made at the weekly conferences. —*Lawrence F. Abbott*

Senator Shelby M. Cullom of Illinois once discovered the loyalty of the Colonel to his field comrades when he was President. The Senator had called at the White House and was told that the President was engaged.

"Who's there?" he asked of the doorkeeper.

"Somebody who says he was in the Rough Riders," was the reply.

"Well," observed the legislator as he turned away, "What chance have I, then? I'm only a Senator." —*Newspaper clipping*

It was the first time in the history of the United States that an ex-President had chosen journalism as his professional career on returning to private life. After leaving *The Outlook* in 1914, Mr. Roosevelt became editorially associated with the *Metropolitan Magazine*, and, still later, an editorial contributor to *The Kansas City Star*. Thus he was engaged in active journalism for ten years from the time he ceased to be President in 1909 until his death. Indeed, he wrote editorials for *The Kansas City Star* almost up to the very hour of his death, for one of his last acts, the evening before he suddenly and unexpectedly passed away, was to correct the proof of a *Star* editorial. His success as a journalist is only another striking illustration of his almost unmatched versatility. Historians say that he might have been a historian; biologists and zoologists, that he might have been a scientific naturalist; soldiers, that he would have made a great professional soldier. It is equally clear that if the environment of his early life had so influenced him he might have become a great newspaper editor. He had the instinct for news and the faculty for interesting the public in it. He also had what is more important, but too often lost sight of in modern journalism: definite views as to the moral standards which ought to apply to the trade or profession of newspaper men as rigorously as the ethics of the medical profession or the obligations of the Hippocratic oath apply to doctors. —*Lawrence F. Abbott*

I know that Theodore Roosevelt took the Bible as the standard of individual character and national virtue, for he told me so, and I believe that God was in him and back of him in his miraculously great personality and service for his country and the world. —*Ferdinand Iglehart*

After his nomination Theodore Roosevelt, [Jake] Hess…and I went out on a personal canvass. It was the custom in those days to visit the gin-mills, the stores, and places of business. The first place we happened to go into was the lager-beer saloon on Sixth Avenue, near Fifty-Fifth Street kept by a German named Fischer. Hess introduced Mr. Roosevelt to the proprietor as the candidate for Assembly.

Mr. Fischer says to him: "Well, Mr. Roosevelt, the liquor interest has not been getting a square deal. We are paying excessive taxes. I have no doubt that you will try to give us some relief when you get up to the Legislature." (One of the grievances of Mr. Fischer was that the license was too high.) Mr. Roosevelt asked him: "Mr. Fischer, what is the license now?" Mr. Fischer named the figure—what he had to pay—and Mr. Roosevelt says, "Well, that's not right. I don't think you pay enough. I thought it would be at least twice as much!"

After that we hustled him out and told him that he had better see to the college boys and his friends on Fifth Avenue, the society folks; that Hess and I would do the other end. —*Joe Murray*

[*In 1883, TR hunted in the Dakota Territory and stayed with Lincoln Lang and his father, Badlands ranchers. It was during that visit, and the*

Langs's description of the country, that Roosevelt conceived of becoming a cattle rancher in the Badlands. He initially offered them employment, but when they declined, he turned to his friends from Maine and established two cattle ranches near Medora.]

Altogether he was with us some ten or twelve days upon that first occasion. When he left, we were genuinely sorry to see him go. As he rode away in the wake of the wagon bearing the head and hide of his kill, well do I recall father saying to me: "There goes the most remarkable man I ever met. Unless I am badly mistaken the world is due to hear from him one of these days," a prophecy which in large part he lived to see verified. —*Lincoln A. Lang*

Roosevelt…was not a philosopher; he was simply human. He took the hard knocks of life, not with resignation but with a kind of boyish zest and joy. When attacked he hit hard in return, but without bitterness or rancor. And, in spite of his not-infrequent conflicts with Congress, his opponents had a kind of subconscious fondness for him even when they were exchanging blows. —*Lawrence F. Abbott*

Once he told me that he had made many mistakes; but just to himself as to others, he quickly added: "If I had not been willing to risk making mistakes I would have accomplished nothing worth while." —*William Draper Lewis*

Jacob A. Riis, once an emigrant tramp, though of a fine Danish family, was being entertained at Christmas breakfast in the White House when he happened to mention his sick mother in Denmark longing for her boy. Mrs. Roosevelt, with tender solicitude, said, "Theodore, let us cable over our love to her."

And then said Mr. Riis: "Consternation struck my Danish home village when a cable from the President of the United States was received, which read:

"The White House, December 25, 1902.
"Mrs. Riis, Ribe, Denmark. Your son is breakfasting with us. We send you our loving sympathy.
"Theodore and Edith Roosevelt."

—*Christian Reisner*

You know how he looks. To my mind, he is as handsome a man as I ever saw; and I know I am right, for my wife says so too, and that settles it…. By handsome I do not mean beautiful, but manly. Stern he may, indeed, appear at times, though to my mind nearly all his portraits do him hideous injustice in that respect. I have seen but two that were wholly himself. One was a pen sketch of him on horseback at the head of his men, climbing some mountain ridge. There he had on his battle face, the dark look I have seen come in the middle of some pleasant chat...I knew then that he was alone and that the burden was upon him, and I felt always as if, upon some pretext, any pretext, I would like to get him away where he could be by himself for a while. The other, curiously, was an old campaign poster from the days when he ran for Governor.... It was the only picture of him I ever saw that had the smile his friends love. —*Jacob Riis*

Roosevelt had this magnetic force of personality in a very marked degree. It surrounded him as a kind of nimbus, imperceptible but irresistibly drawing to him everyone who came into his presence—even those who believed they were antagonistic or inimical to him. It is impossible in a sketch of this character to make a complete analysis of Roosevelt's magnetic personality or to achieve a full and rounded portrait with a careful and accurately studied perspective. —*Lawrence F. Abbott*

The politicians of the old order and the high caste in his first presidential years felt that Roosevelt's audacity was a sign of weakness, forgetting that audacity for the right is golden, and that mere impudence, for the sake of winning, is brass. —*Jacob Riis*

The President takes up a good deal of one's time, but he is always so uniformly courteous and considerate that it becomes a pleasure to serve him. I rather suspect you of smiling when you read that he is considerate and courteous, but such is the case. Instead of rushing around with a Bowie knife between his teeth and a pistol and big stick in his hands, he moves softly but swiftly. It is the quickness of the man's physical movements which gives one the impression of bounding in and out of the rooms, as I have so often seen him described by the ever-interesting correspondents. —*Archie Butt*, writing about his duties as Aide to the President

I happened to be sitting in a box [at the March 1912 Carnegie Hall "The Right Of the People To Rule" speech] and could look down upon the people who filled every available seat in the body of the hall. I noticed William Barnes of Albany, the well-known leader of the "Old Guard" faction in the Republican Party, a typical reactionary, who had fought Roosevelt in the gubernatorial campaign of 1910 and who was later to engage in a bitter libel suit with him as a result of their political antagonisms. But Barnes rose and applauded with the rest. A friend told me that when Barnes later in the evening at one of the clubs was twitted for this public tribute to his arch-enemy he replied: "Why, I was on my feet before I knew it. Roosevelt, confound him, has a kind of magnetism that you cannot resist when you are in his presence!" —*Lawrence F. Abbott*

One day while I was seated in his private office, which was a fairly good-sized room, his secretary announced Senator Carter of Montana. The Senator was shown into the room. He was dressed, as I recall it, in a gray frock coat. His round face, surmounted with red hair, shone with pleasure.

To my intense amazement Mr. Roosevelt leaped out of his chair, seized the Senator by the hands and they began dancing back and forth across the room, chanting the following doggerel in unison:

"Oh, the Irish and the Dutch, They don't amount to much, But huroo for the Scandinoo-vian!"

After Senator Carter had left, Mr. Roosevelt, amused at the look of surprised interrogation on my face, volunteered the following explanation: "Tom Carter is a good friend of mine, although we have often disagreed radically on political principles and issues. He is something of a standpatter and I am afraid he sometimes thinks I am something of a visionary crank. Some years ago, during a political campaign, he and I were scheduled to speak on the same occasion in a town of the Northwest. When we came out of the hall and were walking along the boardwalk of the little village to our hotel we met a huge Swede or Norwegian who was somewhat exhilarated from pouring too many libations in honour of the Republican party. As he zigzagged his way along the narrow sidewalk, we had to step aside to avoid a collision. He was singing at the top of his lungs that song about the Irish and the Dutch. Now Senator Carter is Irish and I am Dutch and we thought it was a very good joke on us. So every time we have met since, unless there are too many people about, we are apt to greet each other as we did just now. It has become a kind of ritual." —*Willis J. Abbot*

Yesterday I played tennis with the President again, but this time got licked by him. I think after he trains down a bit he will improve very much. You know there has always been known what is termed the Kitchen Cabinet. Well, the Washington wags have added a "Tennis Cabinet" to Mr. Roosevelt's official family. The Tennis Cabinet is supposed to be that coterie which plays tennis with the President and between plays, gives him points on people and things. If some of them could see how little talking there was at these alleged tennis cabinet meetings and how much real work, they would be surprised. In fact the only way for one to make himself solid with this man when doing anything is to do it hard. —*Archie Butt*

[During the last year of Secretary of State John Hay's life, when he was usually confined to his bed, TR would visit him every Sunday on his walk home from church back to the White House. In Oyster Bay, he had a similar routine:]

My aged mother was cheered every Sunday after church during the summer [in Oyster Bay] because the President of the United States had time to call upon her. My mother was a Quakeress, very devout and an earnest student of the Bible, and, like Theodore, she used her imagination in the study of it. They always had vigorous discussions about Bible incidents, verses, and interpretations. Each would frequently convince the other. —*W. Emlen Roosevelt*

The truth is that Theodore Roosevelt was more kinds of a man than biographical literature has heretofore attempted to embody in one person. No one of his associates, no one of his interpreters, quite saw every side of him. —*Lawrence F. Abbott*

The great courage of Mr. Roosevelt and his lack of fear were shown after he was shot in Milwaukee on October 14, 1912. When he had recovered from his wound he was told that he was foolhardy to make a speech after he had been shot. "Why," said Roosevelt in reply, "you know I didn't think I had been mortally wounded. If I had been mortally wounded I would have bled from the lungs. When I got into the motor I coughed hard three times and put my hand up to my mouth; as I did not find any blood I thought I was not seriously hurt and went on with my speech." —*Carleton Case*

TR wrote to Henry Cabot Lodge about the incident, with a description of the gun; and confession that, after all the dangers he faced in the Badlands, hunting, on the Police Force, on the battlefield—coming through safely, courting death—he felt after being shot

like the old lady who discovered a burglar under her bed and exclaimed: "There you are! I've been waiting for you for thirty years!"
—*Newspaper clipping*

An old comrade in arms approached him and said: "Mr. President, I
have been in jail a year for killing a gentleman."

"How did you do it?" asked the President, inquiring for the
circumstances.

"Thirty-eight on a forty-five frame," replied the man, thinking
that the only interest the President had was that of a comrade who
wanted to know with what kind of a tool the trick was done. His
reference to this joke, in a telegram to a Western friend immediately
after he was shot in Milwaukee, mystified so many people... that he
had to explain it.

"Probably a .38 on a .45 frame," he telegraphed. —*Carleton Case*

People have come to believe that because Roosevelt wrote so much,
and that often under the most unfavorable conditions, he must
therefore have dashed off his articles for the press with little or no
effort. Nothing is further from the truth. No one was more pains-
taking or conscientious than Roosevelt was in his literary work. I had
frequent evidence of this, especially in the upper Paraguay. Here it
often happened that he received different and contradictory reports
regarding the habits of certain animals, but he would not put in
writing his own opinions about the disputed questions until he had
thoroughly investigated the subject and had satisfied himself that he
had arrived at the truth....

Sometimes his observations were penned after he had returned
from a long and tiresome hunt in the jungle. Any other man would
have thrown himself into his hammock and taken a rest. But not so
our Nimrod. He would refresh himself by a plunge into a stream, if
there was one nearby or by a copious ablution in his portable bath,
and then he would forthwith seat himself at a folding writing table,
which he always carried with him, and set down the experiences of
the day while they were still vividly before his mind. He would thus
continue to write for an hour or two, or even several hours, according
to the time at his disposal.... —*Father John Augustine Zahm*

The newspaper men were all knit to him by genuine affection. A
taxicab driver overheard one newspaperman at Sagamore Hill say

to another on the day of the funeral, "Brace up, Bill, we'll soon be in town."

"Shut up, you fool," blubbered the other. "You're crying yourself just as hard as I am." —*Christian Reisner*

Boys admire President Roosevelt because he himself "is a good deal of a boy." Some men have claimed that Mr. Roosevelt never has matured; but this is saying no more than that he has not stopped growing, that he is not yet imprisoned in the crust of age. To him the world is still young and unfinished. He has a boy's fresh faith that the things that ought to be done can be done. His eyes are on the future rather than on the past." —*Jacob Riis*

It is not an insignificant thing that while he was accused of proceeding rashly along unconstitutional lines as a political executive, both during his governorship of the State of New York and his Presidency of the United States, no legislative act that he advocated and signed and no executive act that he performed without legislative cooperation has ever, I believe, been declared unconstitutional by any court. —*Lawrence F. Abbott*

His party was taken for an automobile drive around [Knoxville], which included a trip through some exposition grounds. A Wild West show was performing there at the time, and its members paraded for the entertainment of the Roosevelt party. As the cowboys were riding by on their broncos, one of them turned in his saddle and shouted:

"Hello, Teddy! Remember the Lazy Y?"

I am not sure that that was the name of the ranch that the cowboy gave, but it was a ranch that the Colonel did remember. He looked sharply at the cowboy for an instant and then shouted a response, naming the man and the ranch where they had met, nearly thirty years before. The Colonel's quick response, and his accurate and immediate placing of the man who had greeted him, brought a wild whoop from all the cowboys of the show that greatly pleased the Colonel. —*O. K. Davis*

Many times I observed that Roosevelt was noisy, but he never was loud. He often was rough, but he never was coarse. He was cruel sometimes as truth is cruel, but he was never brutal. —*Henry J. Allen*

Theodore Roosevelt's personality was an unsurpassed combination of the unterrified fighter of what he believed to be the worst, and the tender-hearted lover of what he believed to be the best in mankind. Whether he loved or hated, talked or read, worked or played, he did it with zest and eagerness. —*Lawrence F. Abbott*

I was asked to go over and tell the Young Men's Christian Association on the West Side what the "battle with the slum" meant to my city. And I did, and when I had told them the story I showed them a picture of Theodore Roosevelt as the man who had done more hard and honest fighting for those who cannot fight for themselves, or do not know how, than any other man anywhere. —*Jacob Riis*

On his own ranch he experienced the very hardest part of the work. On one occasion he was for thirty-six hours in the saddle, dismounting only to change horses or to eat. —*Carleton Case*

And has he then no faults, this hero of mine? Yes, he has, and I am glad of it, for I want a live man for a friend, not a dead saint—they are the only ones, I notice, who have no faults. He talks, they say, and I hope he will keep on, for he has that to say which the world needs to hear and cannot hear too long or too often.... I know he cannot dance, for I have seen a letter from a lady who reminded him of how he "trod strenuously" on her toes in the old dancing-school days when the world was young. And I have heard him sing—that he cannot do. The children think it perfectly lovely, but he would never pass for an artist. —*Jacob Riis*

There is no subject in which he does not seem to be interested, from baseball and balloons to the ethics of nations. He asked me where Ty Cobb had ended in the batting record and showed an intimate knowledge of the contention between the New York and the Chicago teams. —*Archie Butt*

Theodore, if there is one thing more than another for which I admire you, it is your original discovery of the Ten Commandments. —*Thomas Brackett Reed*

My own mental picture of him is perfectly clear and convincing. As I see him, he followed, from the day I first knew him to the end of his life, a thoroughly consistent course. His chief characteristics were vision, courage, decision, instant readiness for action, the simplest honesty and the most wholesome sanity. His mental engine ran at a higher speed than that of any other man I have ever known. His foresight was uncanny. His sympathy was so quick, his emotion so intensely human, that he penetrated the feelings of others often as if by magic. His sense of humor was a keen and never-failing delight. And he was as clean-minded as a girl.

These are the causes of his popularity. They are the essential qualifications of leadership and the unfailing sources of political strength. To me it is a cause of never-ending wonderment that men who aspire to political influence and power do not see and follow in Theodore Roosevelt's path. —*O. K. Davis*

Mr. Roosevelt never used tobacco in any form. He was not embarrassed by the fact and never excused it. When offered cigars, he frankly told the donors that he did not smoke. —*Christian Reisner*

Theodore Roosevelt was not a god. He made many mistakes. He compromised when he had to compromise. But if he was looking the other way when a bad man passed the gate he turned his head not in cowardice or connivance, but in inadvertence. His intention was good; his performance much better than fair, though of course, far from angelic. —*Jacob Riis*

Ted Junior and I became well acquainted after our experience in the Bull Moose campaign, and in the years before he went abroad in the First World War. Once he remarked quite casually *à propos* of some mention of his father: "The trouble with Father is, when he goes to a wedding he thinks he is the bride, and when he goes to a funeral he is the corpse." —*Samuel McCune Lindsay* [unpublished manuscript]

We walked from the Navy Department under the shade of the young trees that lined the streets that Summer day to the Army and Navy Club, had lunch, talked and talked, and still kept talking. He shattered the foundations of my political ideals. As they crumbled then and there, politically, I put his heel on my neck and I became his man.

I had never known such a man as he, and never shall again. —*William Allen White*

He is doubtless the most vital man on the continent, if not on the planet, to-day. He is many-sided, and every side throbs with his tremendous life and energy; the pressure is equal all around. His interests are as keen in natural history as in economics, in literature as in statecraft, in the young poet as in the old soldier, in preserving peace as in preparing for war. And he can turn all his great power into the new channel on the instant. His interest in the whole of life, and in the whole life of the nation, never flags for a moment. His activity is tireless. All the relaxation he needs or craves is a change of work. He is like the farmer's fields, that only need a rotation of crops. I once heard him say that all he cared about being President was just "the big work." —*John Burroughs*

As he started to leave the stand a man came running toward him, waving his right hand, and shouting out something that was unintelligible to any of those who heard it. It seemed a question, but might have been almost anything, even a curse.

Two or three men started toward this man, but the Colonel reached him first. With his left hand the Colonel caught the right wrist of the other and swung his arm quickly and sharply across in front of his own face, so that the man was partly turned around and did not directly face the Colonel. At the same time his right hand was rendered wholly useless for any attack, if he had wanted to make one.

"Now, what is it you want?" said the Colonel. It was only a simple question, after all, that the man had wanted to ask, and he had hurried because he saw the Colonel preparing to leave.

But it served to illustrate the Colonel's quickness and readiness to act on his own behalf in case of emergency. The man laughed at the way he had been handled, and admitted that he had been careless in his approach. And that ended the matter. —*O. K. Davis*

The President's carriage was run into by a trolley outside Pittsfield, Mass., September 3, 1902, and a Secret Service man in the carriage was killed. According to a newspaper clipping, "The car was filled with people, said [an aide], who were on their way to the country club to give the President a farewell cheer as he left the town. The President was thrown out and landed on his knees. I helped him to rise and gently squeezed his chest to see if any ribs were broken. He resented the action and asked to be left alone. Then he walked over to the motorman who had run him down and told him that if the collision was an accident it was excusable, but that if it were due to carelessness it was damnable." —*Carleton Case*

We began discussing the many struggles he had had…the battles on behalf of his public policies. "Oh, yes," he said, "people talk much of my battles in life! I had to battle in my early years for health and went West to win; I had to battle for my first modest place in public life, and for each successive place; and I know what a battle on the

32

battlefield means. The hardest battle I have had to fight, however, is one that no one knows about. It was a battle to control my own temper. That battle I never won until recent years. I now have won that fight and I consider it about the hardest struggle—it certainly was the longest—of my career." —*Henry L. Stoddard*

We had been summoned to the White House, my wife and I. I say "summoned" on purpose, because we had carefully avoided Washington; it was enough for us to know that he was there. But he would not have it, and wrote threateningly that he would send a posse if we didn't come. So we went. I do not think I ever saw a prouder woman than my wife when the President took her in to dinner. I heard her ask him if her smile reached from ear to ear because she felt like it. And I was proud and glad, for so it seemed to me that she had at last come to her rights, and I where there was nothing more to wish for. But withal I felt a bit unhappy. I had thought to do him the highest honor I could by wearing the cross King Christian gave me [*Riis was a Danish immigrant*], but it turned out that among the dozen diplomats and other guests no one wore any decoration save myself, and I didn't like it. The President saw, I think, that I was troubled, and divined the reason in the way he has. He slipped up behind me, at the first chance, and said in my ear: "I am so much honored and touched by your putting it on for me." So he knew, and it was all right. The others might stare. —*Jacob Riis*

[*Henry Adams was a descendant of two presidents; historian, author, and essayist; and a leading light of Washington's intellectual life between the 1870s and his death in 1918. His house on Lafayette Square, across from the White House, was close to his friend John Hay. Beginning in the 1880s, Theodore Roosevelt was a member of Adams's intellectual circle. In his autobiography* The Education of Henry Adams, *he employed the affectation of referring to himself in the third person.*]

Whatever one's preferences in politics might be, one's house was bound to the Republican interest when sandwiched between Senator Cameron, John Hay, and Cabot Lodge, with Theodore Roosevelt equally at home in them all; and [British diplomat] Cecil Spring-Rice to unite them by impartial variety. The relation was daily, and the alliance undisturbed by power or patronage, since Mr. [Benjamin] Harrison, in those respects, showed little more taste than Mr. [Grover] Cleveland for the society and interests of this particular band of followers, whose relations with the White House were some-times comic, but never intimate. —*Henry Adams*

At that time, I was in the habit of seeing the President two or three times a week, for private talks, some of which had been rather extended. I had found that the evening hour, when he signed the day's mail, was by far the best time to see him. He would come back to the Executive offices directly from his exercise, clear up his desk, and then go over to "the big house" to dress for dinner. He had an amazing facility for carrying on conversation while he was going over the mail. He would glance over a letter, make an addition or alteration with his pen, and sign his name at the same time that he was keeping up a steady fire of talk about whatever subject happened to be under discussion.

The evening when I presented to him [*The New York Times* Editor Carr] Van Anda's question as to his greatest achievement, instantly the President replied; "The Panama Canal, of course…. I shall always feel that this was the greatest single accomplishment with which I have had anything to do. It is the greatest fact in my career. Don't you think so?"…

"No, Mr. President," I replied. "I do not."

I can see to-day the expression of puzzled surprise that came over his face as he looked up at me and laid down the pen.

"Well, if the Canal isn't, what is?" he demanded.

"I have always thought that the greatest thing about you," I said, "and the thing that will live longest, and have most influence, is the example you have set to youth.

"I mean this. As a boy you were a weakling, physically inferior. You determined to overcome that weakness. By your own will you kept yourself everlastingly at it, with all kinds of exercise and work, until you have built that weakling boy into the great burly man that you are today, capable of more endurance, by far, than the average man, and of keeping up, in fact, with the exceptional man.

"That is one thing. There is another as great, and no doubt many persons will think it even greater. As a boy you fixed upon yourself the habit of application and of work. You have kept that up, until I sometimes think it has got a little the best of you, because you never seem able now to take it easy at all….

"I think these two habits of self-reliance and hard work constitute an example to youth of far-reaching and long-continuing influence that will outweigh, in the judgment of history, any single fact accomplishment in your career, such as the Panama Canal." The President got up from his desk and came around to the side on which I was sitting. I had been facing him directly across the desk.

"Now, O. K.," he said, "you have got me to talking, and you have got to listen to a lecture."

But instead of a lecture he proceeded to give me his own analysis of himself. "I am just an ordinary man," he began, "without any special ability in any direction. In most things I am just about the average; in some of them a little under, rather than over. I am only an ordinary walker. I can't run. I am not a good swimmer, although I am a strong one. I probably ride better than I do anything else, but I am certainly not a remarkably good rider. I am not a good shot. My eyesight is not strong, and I have to get close to my game in order to make any shot at all. I never could be a good boxer, although I like to box and do keep at it, whenever I can. My eyesight prevents me from ever being a good tennis player, even if otherwise I could qualify.

"So you see that from the physical point of view I am just an ordinary, or perhaps a little less than ordinary, man. Now, take the things that I have done in public life or in private life either, for that matter. I am not a brilliant writer. I have written a great deal, but I always have to work and slave over everything I write. The things that I have done, in one office or another, are all, with the possible exception of the Panama Canal, just such things as any ordinary man could have done. There is nothing brilliant or outstanding in my record, except, perhaps, this one thing. Whatever I think it is right for me to do, I do. I do the things that I believe ought to be done. And when I make up my mind to do a thing, I act.

"Having made a decision, I do not permit myself, as a rule, to reconsider it. That doesn't mean that I think my decisions are always right. I know they are not. I know that, of course, I make mistakes. But I also know that to permit yourself to be constantly reconsidering a decision you have once made, especially if you happen to be in public office where you are called upon to make a great number of decisions, is to develop yourself into a man of no decision. That promotes delay and piles up work and trouble.

"I believe that in the long run less damage is done through the mistakes resulting from sticking to decisions once made than would occur from getting into the habit of constantly worrying whether you had decided rightly or wrongly, and changing your mind all the time.

No man can get ahead on two or more courses. You have to go one way at a time to get anywhere....

"It was just that which made me act as I did in the Panama case, and that is just why we are going to have that Canal so soon. When we get there will never again be the necessity for sending a fleet on such a cruise as that the battleships are making now. That Canal will be a great factor in our national defense, and a great means of promotion of our commerce. After all, I think it is the greatest thing I have ever done." —O. K. Davis

[In his capacity as Civil Service Commissioner, and subsequently, Theodore Roosevelt locked horns with a "boss" of Pennsylvania politics, Senator Matthew S. Quay. A mutual sympathy developed when TR learned of Quay's ancestry, part Native-American.]

After Roosevelt assumed the presidency Senator Quay called on him and said, "Most men who claim to be reformers are hypocrites, but I deem you sincere." That formed a basis for teamwork, and often afterward Quay aided the president. Speaking to Senator Beveridge afterward, he said: "I confess that I have a personal liking for Quay. He stands for nearly everything I am against, but he is straightforward about it and never tries to fool me." When death approached he sent for Mr. Roosevelt and asked him to look after the Delaware Indians whose blood ran in his veins. At his demise the President sent Mrs. Quay a telegram:

"Accept my profound sympathy, official and personal. Throughout my term as President Senator Quay has been my staunch and loyal friend. I had hoped to the last that he would, by his sheer courage, pull through his illness. Again accept my sympathy. Theodore Roosevelt." —*Hermann Hagedorn*

Industrialist Mark Hanna was a mentor of William McKinley, eventually rising to become senator from Ohio and Chairman of the Republican National Committee. Through the years he was chary of support for Roosevelt, whom he called "that damned cowboy."

When Senator Hanna was taken ill the President was under his heaviest burden of duties, but he slipped away nevertheless to make a call on the sick man. The Senator was deeply moved and wrote a letter of warm appreciation for the personal call from so busy a man. He assured him that such attention "were drops of kindness that are good for a fellow," for they "touch a tender spot." —*Christian Reisner*

He was a friend, conceived of as a friend in a passionate and personal way as no other statesman in American history except Lincoln. He had learned of Him who said that if one did not love his brother whom "he hath seen, how can he love God whom he hath not seen?" —*Dr. Frank Crane*

Theodore Roosevelt was a giant; an overgrown personality. He was one of those sports that, appearing once or twice in a century or in an age, work tremendous havoc or harmony, and disappear apparently without spiritual progeny. Greatness, generally speaking, is an unusual quantity of a usual quality grafted upon a common man.

The thing which the gods gave Roosevelt in excess was energy. He was gargantuan in his capacity for work. It was one of those utterly unthinkable coincidences, coincidences so rare, so unbelievable that they almost force one to believe in the minute Divine direction of human affairs; that a man of Roosevelt's enormous energy should come to the Presidency of exactly that country which at exactly that time was going through a transitional period—critical, dangerous, and but for him terrible—between an old rural, individual order and a new highly socialized industrial order. —*William Allen White*

He unites great austerity with great good nature. He unites great sensibility with great force and will power. He loves solitude, and he loves to be in the thick of the fight. His love of nature is only equaled by his love of the ways and marts of men. —*John Burroughs*

Knowing him as he really is, you cannot help trusting him. I would have everybody feel that way toward him who does not do so already; for we are facing much too serious times, you and he and all of us, to be honestly at odds where we should pull together. —*Jacob Riis*

Service under Theodore Roosevelt in any capacity was extremely stimulating and delightful, but it was also exacting. Roosevelt's abounding vitality and the vigor and enjoyment with which he both worked and played kept his colleagues and subordinates always at concert pitch. He was not a taskmaster in any sense of the word, and there is constant allusion in Captain Butt's letters to his characteristic consideration for his associate. —*Lawrence F. Abbott*

One night Mr. [Richard Watson] Gilder [Editor of *The Century Magazine*] called at my house on Capitol Hill, Washington. "What do you think of Theodore Roosevelt?" he asked.

"He is a man of letters in love with life," I answered.

Mr. Gilder laughed. "He is more than that; he is about to make an epoch." —*Maurice Francis Egan*

The boyishness of Roosevelt was so conspicuous a trait that no one ever thought of him as other than a young man to the very day of his death. He had a number of grandchildren, yet he seemed at sixty a young man, like his sons. His youthfulness was not related to juvenility or immaturity. He had left those qualities behind him and had shown rare manliness while very young. His literary work had been surprisingly mature, so that the books he wrote in his twenties held their own—without apologies for the novice hand—on the shelf with the writings of his later years. —*Ferdinand Inglehart*

He sent for me to scold me about a book I'd written after a fledgling experience in the Indiana legislature. So far as I could learn, nobody else had read the book; but he had, and he was indignant because it displayed a damaging view of politics and politicians. "It's a destructive book," he said with his accustomed vigor. "It's a book that will help people to say, 'Why should I take the trouble to vote?...Leave it to the swine.' If it's left to the swine, how long do you think it'll be before only swine come to the meal?"

Who else, being President of the United States, would have time to straighten out the mind and exorcise the gloomy mood of a young man turned pessimist because of a brief and minor experience in "practical politics"?

The scolding was only one of the thousands of manifestations of the Colonel's great kindness to young people who were "trying to write." He always found time for that. —*Booth Tarkington*

He was not averse to expressing his affection for his friends. President [Nicholas Murray] Butler [of Columbia University] told me that, in private, he was exuberant in his manifestations. After saying of Mr. Riis that, next to his father, he was the "best man I have ever known," he added, "I learned to love him like a brother." —*Christian Reisner*

Theodore Roosevelt had a breadth of human sympathy as wide as the world, limited by neither creed nor race. He was equally at ease in the Sorbonne or addressing a group of men in a mining town. —*Henry Cabot Lodge*

I will always remember the workman who approached me one day and said to me: "I want to shake hands with you. You are the sister of my best friend. I have never met Colonel Roosevelt but he is nevertheless my best friend. I knew that if ever I wanted to write to him for advice he would answer." —*Corinne Roosevelt Robinson*

While Mr. Roosevelt was uniformly courteous and unassuming, there was a dignity in his intercourse which prevented familiarity by any except lifelong friends. While on campaigns he was pleased by the shout "Teddy," yet no one ever thus addressed him personally. Though he called a great many intimate friends by their first names, yet only when they had known him all their lives and were practically of the same age did they call him "Theodore." —*William Draper Lewis*

He seldom gave way to the "blues," but he nevertheless had to battle them. He had times of depression, usually caused by the fact that things did not come along as fast as he had a right to expect.... —*William Loeb*

He greatly needed to have men show that they had confidence in him. —*Henry Stoddard*

Mr. Roosevelt, sometimes I feel a little melancholy because it is so hard to persuade people to accept equal justice. —*"Bill" Sewall*

Because of what the President considered a brutal attack on another senator he withdrew a [White House] dinner invitation to Senator ["Pitchfork Ben"] Tillman [a virulent racist, opponent of anti-lynching legislation] and they became avowed enemies. Knowing this and desiring to defeat the bill forbidding railroad rebates, the Standpat Republicans so arranged matters that the advocacy of the bill would be in Tillman's hands. But enmity did not spoil "team work" and the bill was passed, the President remarking, "I was delighted to go with him or with anyone so long as he was traveling my way—and no longer." —*Christian Reisner*

President Roosevelt wrote Ethel an interesting account of a "rescue." Sloan, the secret service man, and he were en route to church when he saw two dogs chasing a kitten. He drove the dogs off with his cane while Sloan captured the "kitty." Then the President inquired from the smiling spectators if the cat belonged to them, but not finding an owner, he went down the block with the kitten in his arms until he saw "a very nice colored woman with a little girl looking out the window of a small house" and gave her the kitten. Then, straightening his clothes and brushing his silk hat, he went on to church in a better frame to "worship." —*Christian Reisner*

There never was a cleaner Christian in thought and in deed than Colonel Roosevelt. He not only was clean himself but he insisted on those about him being clean. For example, TR was not the man to tell or tolerate the telling in his presence of any risqué stories. There was that about him which made men careless in such matters as careful of their speech as they would be in the presence of a group of little girls. —*John J. Leary*

Our weekly [*The Outlook* magazine] staff luncheon was to occur at the National Arts Club, and two ambassadors from South American countries and other distinguished guests were invited. When we arrived, Mr. Roosevelt had found on the street a little lad who could not talk English, and who was crying bitterly because he was lost. His father, a Hungarian miner, and his mother were to take a boat home the next day and he wandered out of the hotel and didn't know its name or location. Mr. Roosevelt took the boy's hand, quieted him, got his confidence so he was willing to go with him to the police station, where Mr. Roosevelt secured the cooperation of the police and found the parents. Thirty minutes later he showed up at the luncheon without any excuse. That was mercy. —*Dr. Lyman Abbott*

During the tour of European capitals in 1910, Kaiser Wilhelm said to Colonel Roosevelt: "Call upon me at two o'clock; I have just forty-five minutes to give you."

"I will be there at two, your Majesty, but unfortunately, your Majesty, I have but twenty minutes to give you." —*Christian Reisner*

I once saw him come down the main stairway to greet a distinguished archbishop who was to be a luncheon guest. A small dog had arrived that morning from Oyster Bay and had not yet seen the head of the family. The joy of the little animal was so overwhelming as his master came down the stairs that, forgetting everything, the President was on the floor with the dog while the Archbishop stood at attention eight or ten feet away. But Mr. Roosevelt was himself again as President in fifteen seconds, and the Archbishop enjoyed and perfectly understood the boyishness of the nation's head; for the Archbishop, though an old man, had a boyish heart and knew the President well as a man whose sense of propriety was never really at fault.

I remember on another occasion a conversation with the most experienced of the White House ushers. This man had been attached to the White House staff through a number of administrations. He was waiting for the President to come down to breakfast, and with a sweeping remark that was complimentary about former incumbents of the White House, he went on to say:

"But there was never any man here like this man. He begins earlier; works harder; sees more people, and puts in longer hours than anybody who has ever been President. Yet he is never tired, no matter how late he works; and he always comes down the stairs in the morning looking *as fresh as the dew on the roses*! And he steps up to me and says, 'Well…how is everything about the place? If anything is going wrong just let me know and we will have it straightened out at once.'" At that moment the President came down the stairs with a firm tread, a clear eye, and a radiant smile, justifying everything that the admiring usher had said. —*Albert Shaw*

"Guess Who?"

Sometimes fantastical,
Often bombastical,
Always dynamic and never scholastical,
Slightly uproarious,
Bracing as Boreas,
Living each day with a zest that is glorious,
Bane of the highbrows and folk hypercritical,
Subject of many a plutocrat's curse,
Buried in state by his foemen political
Only to climb up and pilot the hearse!

There is an air to him,
There's such a flare to him,
There's such a rare, debonair do-and-dare to him!
Bulldog tenacity,
Mixed with vivacity,
Tempered with humor and sense and sagacity;
What if his speeches are crowded with platitudes,
Somehow he's built on the popular plan,

41

Actions and manner and sayings and attitudes,
All of them prove him a Regular Man!

Quite undistressable,
Most irrepressible,
Open and frank—yet a problem unguessable,
   Terse, though didactical,
   Learned, but practical,
Strong for preparedness, moral and tactical,
Vivid and vital and vervy and vigorous,
   Simply and humanly "playing the game,"
Preaching and living a life that is rigorous,
   —Give you three guesses to call him by name!

—Berton Braley, 1916

He well knew his popularity would pass from him, and in fact would shortly begin to wane.... "I know whereof I speak. I have been, and am, like a swimmer swimming in a deep sea on strong waves, and I have been swimming on the broad high crest of a wave, and I have had a good time and thoroughly enjoyed it. But after the crest of every wave comes a trough, and the depth of the trough is equal to the height of the crest, and soon, gentlemen, I must swim down into that trough. But, gentlemen, when I am down in the depths of that trough I shall still go on swimming!" *—Dr. Alexander Lambert*

Almost every day there were luncheon guests forming an agreeable group, quite dominated but always drawn out by the President's wonderful brilliancy, humor, and variety as a conversationalist. At these luncheon parties were to be found visiting statesmen, soldiers, scholars, literary personages, explorers, reformers, ecclesiastics and notable people from all parts of our own country and from Europe, South America, Asia and Africa. The President was so widely read and so active-minded that he derived healthy stimulus from meeting all these people, and was the better fitted for two hours more of afternoon work by reason of his personal contacts. *—Albert Shaw*

I was simply one of the million who saw him the day he arrived in New York on his return from that African journey, June 18, 1910. Why, a man must have had the soul of a wooden Indian if he could not have been moved by the sight of the crowds at the Battery... The "Rough Riders" were there; and they sure did give him some uproarious welcome. Col. Roosevelt had his arms around their necks; he slapped them on their backs; they hugged him—hand-shaking with that delegation was too tame entirely.

I was swept into a bunch of people that got headed his way and much to my surprise and delight the next minute I found my hand in his and heard myself saying: "Welcome, welcome back home!" And I heard him say, "Thank you! Isn't this great?" I was amazed at my own voice, and none the less at hearing him phrase his reply as he did; but knowing Theodore Roosevelt as we do now, how else could he have held the heart of America as he does if he had not first taken the hand of everybody in his wonderfully simple, human, friendly way.

That day in New York is a matter of history. I mention it as my greatest personal recollection of him because it actually was the deepest. From the Battery clear up to Forty-Third Street the Roosevelt section of the procession was just one constant center for the cheering thousands along the way—but there is no capacity in language that will adequately express the experiences of that triumphant march. —*Robert A. Alberts*

Once in a while we meet men to whom the Lord gave wondrous brains. Their heads are in the clouds. There is a surcharge of electricity, and the lightnings gather. They are men of action. They are restless and full of individual thought. They become leaders and as such with their militant minds they beget enemies as well as strong admirers. But after they leave us, their sterling qualities, their courage, their failures and their successes lead the public mind to adore them and show their appreciation by pilgrimages to the place of their burial. Such a man was Roosevelt. In the history of the United States there are but few men, big and forceful, like himself. And yet these men who thunder away, in their private life are mild, peaceful and devoted and congenial in their homes. They are as their children are, sweet and lovable. —*Gordon K. Dickinson, MD*

From college days, Theodore Roosevelt was my idol. During the succeeding years, especially after he became president, he taught me more politics in the Aristotelian sense than all the specialists in my college courses. He also taught me much of the art of living. —*Samuel McCune Lindsay*

Although in common with a great many Americans, I had always been an ardent admirer and follower of Roosevelt, and that was the

first opportunity I had ever had to meet and come in close contact with him. And needless to say I endeavored to make the most of it. What impressed me most about Roosevelt was his personal magnetism and the warmth of his nature. He was intensely human and possessed a personality as pleasing as a summer zephyr. Although he was not what one would term an orator, he was nevertheless a most entertaining and instructive and enthusiastic public speaker. He could elicit shrieks of laughter with his keen shafts of humor, particularly when he pitched his voice in that famous falsetto key which he was accustomed to use when ridiculing an opponent. He could awaken the conscience and stir the sluggish souls of his hearers with his earnest, plain spoken, easily understood words and phrases, delivered forcefully and at times with a sledge-hammer effect into which he seemed to throw all the energy and feeling of his wonderful nature. And with clenched fists, tightly closed jaws, half shut eyes and that militant poise of head, he could fairly "burn up" an opponent's position, policy or argument, with withering sarcasm. When he scored some of his most telling points, particularly when speaking on Americanism, you would almost feel constrained in your elation to rush up and hug him, so magnetic was the force of his personality.
—*James W. McCarthy*

[At Sagamore Hill] he was showing me his curios and treasures, and exhibited a gold ring of marvelous Oriental workmanship, which was given him by a visiting Chinese prince. The ring bore a curious intaglio inscription which was a rebus or pictured jest in the syllables of Roosevelt's name.

I admired it greatly, and handed it back to him, when Mrs. Roosevelt said: "Perhaps you didn't hear aright. Mr. Roosevelt is giving you the ring."

Overcome with embarrassment and pleasure both, I explained that I was slightly deaf, but was delighted to accept the ring. Whereupon the donor of the gift said, with a beaming smile: "That's all right—I shall remember."

And he did, never again speaking to me without using the clear, low tone that only the hard of hearing appreciate at its full value.
—*Carolyn Wells*

We were leaving the convention hall for a bite of lunch and were walking over to the trolley car, when crowds of people appeared and commenced to talk about wanting to get a look at Theodore Roosevelt. My father was interested, too, for he had never seen him closely; as we turned, I saw him very close behind us with a small group of men. We stopped, and when they came abreast of us, to my very great surprise, he looked up, stepped toward me, took me by the hand and called me by name and inquired for our mutual friend, Arthur Hecox. And by that I knew that the only time he had ever seen me in his life [was two years previous], and yet he remembered, with that marvelous gift he had, not only my face but even the incident and circumstances under which he had me cataloged. Surely I shall cherish my personal reminiscence of Mr. Roosevelt and my sense of reverence for his great life as long as I have memory. —*John S. Watson*

Though his language is forcible, it is never "strong" in the usual sense of that word as applied to language.... He is himself what he called Admiral Mahan, "a Christian gentleman," but, as Disraeli wrote of someone, "his Christianity is muscular."

I talked to him on many subjects which had he been a profane man would have elicited profanity, but he was not betrayed....

Quite the most awful word I have ever heard him apply to any man was the word "Skunk-k-k," applied by him in a moment of great irritation....

He doesn't need to swear, because he can say "Pacifist" or the name of some condemned individual in tones which must make the recording angel shudder. The only Roosevelt "dam" is the one they named for him in Arizona. —*Christian Reisner*

Mr. Roosevelt was greatly concerned over the custom of treating divorce so lightly in America. He insisted that it was becoming so common that morals might get down to the plane of the barnyard if we were not guarded. He did not understand how society at large could permit it. He said, "But perhaps I have the morals of a green grocer, they are so old fashioned." —*Dr. Alexander Lambert*

Recently Colonel Roosevelt said to me: "You remember the walk we had from the church to the White House, a dozen years ago, when I turned my heart inside out to you, and told you I believed God had raised me up to lead the nation in its desperate fight for its life against the illegal despotism of combined wealth in collusion with corrupt municipal, state, and federal office holders, and that my daily

prayer was that God would spare my life long enough to see that menace to the republic removed? He did spare me, and I thank Him."
—*Ferdinand Iglehart*

W. L. Marsh, the station agent of the Long Island Railroad at Oyster Bay, for many years handled Colonel Roosevelt's private and official telegrams and business of every kind connected with the local station. He told a number of incidents illustrating the admirable traits of the Colonel's character. This was one of them: "Once in the presence of quite a large delegation of big men in national and state affairs I saw him place his hand on the shoulder of a poor, good, honest fellow-citizen and say, 'By George, this man is my friend! Gentlemen, I love to lean on just such men.'" Was there ever a truer illustration of one of the greatest elements of Theodore Roosevelt's success, his absolute faith in the common people and his firm reliance upon them in his public undertakings? —*Ferdinand Iglehart*

A famous London doctor, accustomed, as many doctors are, to give to his patients of his own [electrical current] vitality [a scientific theory of the day], declared that Roosevelt was the only person he had ever treated who reversed the current, so to speak, giving off vitality instead of absorbing it. —*Joseph Bucklin Bishop*

Rev. Geo. W. Roesch, a former minister of Oyster Bay and a warm personal friend of Mr. Roosevelt, said that the Colonel told him that during the previous year, with the help of secretaries, he had answered twenty-five thousand letters, twenty-five hundred of which were invitations to speak in public. This story illustrates Mr. Roosevelt's prodigious capacity for work. History does not furnish his superior. As a tireless worker he wrought more years with more correct methods, with deeper intensity and with larger meaning than any other man of our time. The incident also shows how immensely popular he was and how the people craved his personal presence and service...

Funny, but a most compact and accurate assessment was the estimate of the Texas ranchman who had heard [TR] speak, and talked with him for a moment. Later, to a group of approving cattlemen, he gravely summed up his impression—"Most any sort of man," he said, "can be President of the United States. But that man could be elected Marshal in any town in Texas!" —*Herbert Knox Smith*

About seventeen years before the famous African hunting trip the Colonel was having some repairs made at Sagamore Hill. The work done by one of the mechanics was not progressing in the manner he intended and he drew attention to the work. The response was short and sharp, "I take my orders from the boss." Roosevelt, therefore, saw the contractor and the work was soon changed. On his return from Africa, seventeen years later, citizens of Long Island and New York City attended the mighty hunter's reception at Sagamore Hill. On the long reception line among others, was the before-mentioned mechanic. He shook hands with the Colonel, received a few appropriate words, and passed on. He had gone, however, but a few steps, when Roosevelt reached after him, pulled him back and demanded with his hearty chuckle, "Say, do you still take your orders from the boss?" This anecdote reveals that never-failing memory, and also that kindly forgiving spirit, that were cardinal Roosevelt traits. —*Rev. George W. Roesch*

In his charming essay on Recreation, Lord Edward Grey has noted the fact that Theodore Roosevelt was a man to whom adventures happened naturally. It is also true that every reminiscence of him is a recollection of something striking. You did not merely see him or pay your respects to him. He always came upon you like a sunrise or a cloud-burst. He left you warmed or nearly drowned. —*George Wharton Pepper*

The words and ways of the time are gone for him. He spoke them and he trod them. But what was timeless in him was what we loved in him. —*William Hard*

Personally, I think I saw into the secret spirit of his nature.... I believe the basic passion of his soul was spiritual. His annual messages to Congress were more than political essays. Sham he loathed. He dreaded with the emotion of a nightmare America becoming rich without also becoming great. Always there was in his talks, both in public and private, the forcefulness of the man eager for progress— progress that was based on human improvement and was always toward God. —*Commander Evangeline Booth*

The Colonel sat in a Pullman car talking to two or three friends. All the passengers, and the conductor as well, were listening to every word he said and were making no attempt to conceal the fact. All attention was focused upon him and he held that attention throughout the journey. I have often thought since then that car was the world in microcosm. Wherever he went everybody wanted to see him and hear him. Whether you agreed with him or not, he was always absorbingly interesting.

And if you wanted to dislike him, you had to keep away from him altogether. —*George Wharton Pepper*

During his term as president the citizens of Oyster Bay gave [Roosevelt] a reception as he went to Washington, and when he came back. These were usually held at the depot. I shall never forget the one we gave him as he went to Washington for the last time during his term. He was very fond of music and our male chorus led the singing. He addressed us in tender words and then we sang, "God Be with You Till We Meet Again." Tears filled his eyes. I have been with him often, but I never saw him cry before. The tears that filled his eyes fell down in big drops on his cheeks, and the whole audience was melted with emotion. It certainly seemed that God was there and would be with him till we met him again. —*Rev. Warren I. Bowman*

While Mr. Roosevelt had a profound and workable creed, he seldom talked about or detailed it. Yet he lived a very definite one. Theories interested him very little; he demanded practice. He agreed with James: "I will show you my faith by my works." Nevertheless, he emphasized the necessity of faith and worship. —*Christian Reisner*

His strengths were no more open to the world than his weaknesses. He had no hypocrisies; his sincerity in his friendships was as real and as apparent as his dislikes. —*Mary Roberts Rinehart*

While Colonel Roosevelt had no end of self-confidence, he was singularly free of egotism. —*Edward Bok*

E. F. Cheshire, the cashier of the Oyster Bay bank, was a warm friend of Mr. Roosevelt. He said the Colonel often came into their bank, where he had his account, and that he invariably removed his hat on entering the door; the reason he did so was that two of the bookkeepers were women and he removed his hat out of deference for them. Though often apparently rough, he was one of the politest of gentlemen. —*Ferdinand Iglehart*

[Theodore Roosevelt, a Harvard graduate, attended the Commencement in 1902. When he was a house guest of the University President:]

He hastily threw his coat and waistcoat on the bed, and drew from his hip pocket a good-sized pistol, which he laid on the dressing-table. President McKinley had been assassinated the previous September. When I asked if he habitually carried a revolver he replied, "Yes, when I am going into public places. I should have some chance of shooting the assassin before he could shoot me, if he were near me."
—*Charles W. Eliot*

His walk was never a strut. —*Joseph S. Auerbach*

He had come back, not long before, from one of his hunting trips, and it was said that fever was still troubling him. The people wish to know if this is true, and one of the men on the sidewalk, a reporter probably, steps forward and asks him a question.

He stops for a moment, and turns toward the man. Not much thought of sickness is left in the mind of anyone there! His face is clear, his cheeks ruddy—the face of a man who lives outdoors; and his eyes, light-blue in color, look straight at the questioner. One of his eyes, it had been said, was dimmed or blinded by a blow while boxing, years before, when he was President. But no one can see anything the matter with the eyes; they twinkle in a smile, and as his face puckers up, and his white teeth show for an instant under his light-brown moustache, the group of people all smile, too.

His face is so familiar to them—it is as if they were looking at somebody they knew as well as their own brothers. The newspaper cartoonists had shown it to them for years. No one else smiled like that; no one else spoke so vigorously.

"Never felt better in my life!" he answers, bending toward the man.

"But thank you for asking!" and there is a pleasant and friendly note in his voice, which perhaps surprises some of those who, though they had heard much of his emphatic speech, knew but little of his gentleness. He waves his hand, steps into the automobile, and is gone.
—*Edmund Lester Pearson*

The historian of the future who delves through [old] newspaper files…will conclude that the most important news of the period was Mr. Theodore Roosevelt, President, politician, statesman, sociologist, reformer, defender of the faithful, exposer of shams, protagonist, antagonist, hunter, diplomat, apostle of Peace, wielder of the Big

Stick, and founder…of the Ananias Club [the virtual place where TR consigned liars and purveyors of "fake news"; all of which] have made him an inexhaustible Golconda of inspiration for the cartoonist….

Mr. Roosevelt has been a cornucopia of suggestions for the cartoonists and newspaper makers. —*John T. McCutcheon*

As I stood by the open grave, I did not think of Roosevelt the soldier, the orator, the author, the naturalist, the explorer, the statesman, the leader of men, or the former President of the greatest of republics. I could think of him only as a friend and brother in whom elements were so mixed. —*Henry A. Wise Wood*

Roosevelt declined the offer of a Colonel's commission and asked to be made Lieutenant-Colonel, with Leonard Wood, of the regular Army as his Colonel.

When you hear or read that Roosevelt was a conceited man, always pushing himself forward, it may be well to ask if that is the way a conceited man would have acted. —*William Hard*

What was the greatest contribution which Theodore Roosevelt made to the life of his generation? This, as it seems to me, that in the eyes of America and the world, he defined anew in terms of personality, the ideal of America. The world had need of such a representation as he set forth of our national character and ideals. —*Rev. William E. Barton*

"I have kept the promise that I made to myself when I was 21. That promise was to live my life to the hilt until I was 60, and I have kept that promise." These words Theodore Roosevelt said to his sister a few days before he died. And this, indeed, he did. —*Will Hays*

[Julian Street visited Roosevelt, wracked with painful ailments, and when his children were in Europe during the Great War, in TR's last year. Christian Reisner recorded Street's impressions.]

"I never even heard him mention death until the last year before his demise." He concluded that his reference to it must have come from "a premonition that the end was perhaps nearer than those about him supposed."

He described Mr. Roosevelt as he lay in the hospital a few days after his operation, reading a book when he remarked, "Lying here, I have often thought how glad I would be to go now if by doing so I could only bring the boys back safe to Mrs. Roosevelt."

After Colonel Roosevelt's return from South America I took him to task for his having heedlessly squandered his health on an adventure. "See here..." he burst out, "I never grouch about the price I pay for what I do!" —*Henry A. Wise Wood*

[When Theodore Roosevelt died,] relatives were summoned, and the sad news was sent out to the world with special cables to the boys in Europe. That Monday afternoon three aeroplanes flew over the home on Sagamore Hill and each dropped a wreath of laurel close to the elm tree. They were in memory of the father and also of the son [Quentin, who was killed in aerial combat], their comrade and hero.

At noon on Wednesday a brief funeral service was held in the trophy room at Sagamore Hill, attended by the family and a few most intimate friends, and then the body was taken to Christ's Episcopal Church in Oyster Bay. It was possibly the simplest funeral service ever held for a distinguished man. There was no firing of guns, beating of drums, blowing of bugles or bands of any kind; there were no honorary pallbearers nor distinguished ushers. —*Ferdinand Iglehart*

"Great-Heart"

["The Interpreter then called for a man-servant of his, one Great-Heart." —Bunyan's *Pilgrim's Progress*]

Concerning brave Captains,
*   Our age hath made known*
For all men to honour,
*   One standeth alone,*
Of whom, o'er both oceans
*   Both Peoples may say:*
"Our realm is diminished
*   With Great-Heart away."*

In purpose unsparing,
*   In action no less,*
The labours he praised
*   He would seek and profess*
Through travail and battle,
*   At hazard and pain....*
And our world is none the braver
*   Since Great-Heart was ta'en!*

Plain speech with plain folk,
    And plain words for false things,
Plain faith in plain dealing
    'Twixt neighbours or kings
He used and he followed,
    However it sped....
Oh, our world is none more honest
    Now Great-Heart is dead!

The heat of his spirit
    Struck warm through all lands;
For he loved such as showed
    'Emselves men of their hands;
In love, as in hate,
    Paying home to the last....
But our world is none the kinder
    Now Great-Heart hath passed!

Hard-schooled by long power,
    Yet most humble of mind
Where aught that he was
    Might advantage mankind.
Leal servant, loved master,
    Rare comrade, sure guide....
Oh, our world is none the safer
    Now Great-Heart hath died!

Let those who would handle
    Make sure they can wield
His far-reaching sword
    And his close-guarding shield:
For those who must journey
    Henceforward alone
Have need of stout convoy
    Now Great-Heart is gone.

—Rudyard Kipling, 1919

Roosevelt was asked, "What did you expect to be or dream of being when you were a boy?" And TR replied, quoting Scripture: "I do not recollect that I dreamed at all or planned at all. I simply obeyed the injunction, 'Whatever thy hand findeth to do, do with all thy might,' and so I took up what came along as it came. Since then I have gone on Lincoln's motto, 'Do the best; if not, then the best possible.'" —*William Roscoe Thayer*

"I cannot comprehend Roosevelt. He is so complex," a friend once remarked to me. "Back down just a minute," I replied. "You're all wrong. Roosevelt's chief trait is his simplicity. To understand him you must accept him as a very simple and primitive man." Some time afterward my friend came to me and admitted that I was right. Because other men evolve for themselves circuitous routes to their own objectives, they are not prepared for straightforwardness in a man of such great accomplishment. Roosevelt always came out in the open and then went directly to the point. He never dallied in marshes and jungles off the main trail. The result was that very few things made trouble for him. —*Carl Akeley*

To have known Roosevelt is to have known the greatest man of his time; and though I first met him only three and a half years before his death, I came to know him very well, and I should be assuming a false attitude were I to attempt concealment of my pride in the friendship that he gave me. —*Julian Street*

He is dead now and all the world is seeing what I saw forty years ago, and saying about him what I said when we lived under the same roof in the Dakota days. I knew him well, for I saw him under all conditions. He was always the same staunch gentleman, always a defender of right as he saw it, and he saw right himself.... There have been many great men in the history of the world, but they have almost always had some bad defects. Theodore Roosevelt's defects were not great—and such as they were, time will only soften them. —*Bill Sewall*

He was just like the rest of us, except that there was so much more of him. —*Gifford Pinchot*

CHAPTER II

Theodore Roosevelt: President and Politician

The public servant's remarkable use of tactics and strategies, persuasion, and pressure to achieve myriad goals

"Ted Heads"—devotees; historians; collectors; general admirers of Theodore Roosevelt—often are asked about the origin of their attraction and interest. Among the references to his exploits and accomplishments, a common element is esteem for his integrity.

Not lost in the occasional haze of American history is TR's enduring reputation as a reformer; as an incorruptible advocate; as a fighter for his principles; as a man who fought the system—seemingly any system—when he saw the need.

Theodore Roosevelt's political maxims, as with other quotations, often are misattributed to him, especially on the Internet. It is a testament to his fame and America's residual affection for him that there is a desire to associate almost any positive sentiment to him. TR himself was always careful to credit the sources of his colorful slogans and phrases.

TR's iconic "Speak softly and carry a big stick," which served as a life-lesson as well as a boon to political cartoonists, he cited as a West African proverb he had heard. "Do what you can, with what you have, where you are," which is attributed to Theodore Roosevelt via uncountable bits in web posts, was not originally said by him. He credited the rural Virginian "Squire Bill" Widener.

Yet the many colorful and concise slogans and phrases that TR did use reveal a politician's instinct for what later generations would call sound bites and marketing. "My hat is in the ring"; "the Bully Pulpit"; "the lunatic fringe"; "hyphenated Americans"; "I took Panama and let Congress debate me"; "Don't flinch, don't foul, and hit the line hard!"; and many more. Valuable tools of a master politician.

These days it is almost axiomatic that politicians commit compromises. By Roosevelt's code, he often charted the most effective ways to achieve his ends, which was less compromise than being practical. "Keep your eyes on the stars," he said, "but keep your feet on the ground." Even speaking softly is not a compromise or even a subterfuge but a tactical method of achieving one's goals; many people forget that the second half of that aphorism is "… and you will go far."

One of TR's watchwords was actively shared after his death, on memorial plaques and medals: "Aggressive fighting for the right is the noblest sport the world affords."

In the larger context—that is, beyond partisan and electoral activity—Roosevelt was a politician in the best sense. His "rules of engagement" were universal. When he addressed his children's disputes or lectured schoolboy sports teams, he applied the same standards and concepts—often the same words—as he did when maneuvering a bill through Congress, settling a major labor dispute, or negotiating the cessation of a bloody foreign war.

Books have been written (and remain needed to be written) on the multitude of machinations, especially early in his second presidential term, to achieve his policy goals. A more accomplished and resourceful politician has never served in the White House; nor one more successful. The record of Theodore Roosevelt's management—with few exceptions, successful management—of all these matters, is significant testimony to his skills as a politician.

One of history's persistent stereotypes is of Roosevelt the Egomaniac. But TR frequently worked behind the scenes. He often let others, even political rivals, take credit that could have been his. He flattered, he cajoled, he "traded" as his conscience would allow, with senators and congressmen, with industrial tycoons, and with foreign powers. In Roosevelt, a masterful politician added modesty to his arsenal of policy stratagems. Only years later were his fingerprints discovered on the settlement of foreign crises and the passage of domestic reforms.

Roosevelt loved the spotlight, but he also relished the adoption of "My Policies" by whoever could see them through. Overseeing both modes left a record of reform and success in many offices and activities.

* * *

A school-teacher in Syracuse asked a little girl in class to name the head of the government.

"Mr. Roosevelt," she replied.

"That is right, but what is his official title?"

"Teddy!" was the instant response, made with great assurance.
—*George William Douglas*

Theodore Roosevelt's political creed was indeed, from the very beginning, a distinctively human one. He liked men of all sorts and conditions of life so long as they were really men. He was not a "hail fellow well met" of the shoulder-slapping variety. No man knew better than he how to command respect and how to preserve his own dignity. But when he formed a friendship—and no man of our time has had wider, deeper, or more varied friendships—his personal relations with his friends were natural, simple, and confident. For him, a fundamentally good quality in a man covered, like charity, a multitude of sins, which would have repelled a more austere and exacting judge. At the same time his own standards were extraordinarily high and consistent.

Yet he was often accused of associating and working with political publicans and sinners —by men whom it is perhaps not unfair to call political Pharisees. This apparent anomaly was clearly seen to be no anomaly at all by those who understood his own doctrine of political association. —*Lawrence F. Abbott*

When the gentlemen who had been accustomed to run the lower house of the Legislature [New York State Assembly; Roosevelt's first elective office at age twenty-two], no matter which party was in power, found that they could not control Mr. Roosevelt, that he could be neither bought nor bullied, they resorted to the desperate expedient of hiring a thug to administer physical chastisement as a rebuke for his temerity in opposing their will. The mere fact showed the caliber of the men who had been in almost absolute control of legislation in the State—and the need of men like Roosevelt in public life.

One night, in the lobby of the old Delavan House in Albany, since burned, the thug and his expected victim met. There the legislators were accustomed to congregate every evening and much of the "inside" business of the session was transacted. Mr. Roosevelt started to leave the hotel at 10 o'clock on the night in question, after spending some time chatting with fellow-members. As he passed a door leading to the buffet, a noisy group emerged, as if by signal. Among them was a pugilist known as "Stubby" Collins, and this fellow proceeded to jostle Mr. Roosevelt with some force. Instantly, the latter, who was alone, realized the nature and animus of the act. He paused, on guard, and Stubby struck at him, demanding with a show of indignation what he meant by running into him that way.

Stubby's blow did not land on the young legislator. His employers had not told him that Mr. Roosevelt had been one of the best boxers at Harvard, and enjoyed a fight. But he had been paid to "beat up" the young man and went ahead to earn his fee.

With great coolness Mr. Roosevelt awaited the attack which he knew was coming. He took up a position where he could see not only the thug, but all the group accompanying him, and in the background certain others whom he suspected of being the real principals. As he stood waiting, Stubby made his rush.

The fight lasted less than a minute, for the thug had more than met his match. He had the surprise of his life. As his friends picked him up from the floor, a badly beaten man, Stubby gazed in astonishment at the smiling Roosevelt and realized that he had much to learn about boxing and "beating up."

As the thug was removed for repairs, Mr. Roosevelt walked across the lobby and pleasantly informed the astounded promoters of the affair that he understood their connection with it and was greatly obliged to them. He said he had not enjoyed anything so much for a year.

Respect for his personality was thenceforth among the mingled feelings with which he was regarded by the inner circles of legislation at Albany, and his influence grew apace. —*Carleton Case*

When the average man left his club for the caucus or convention, the legislature or Congress, he would accept things as they were and thank God he was not as other men. Roosevelt balked. He fought for things as they should be and can be. He spent his life trying to do much that the common man had dreamed should be done. — *William Allen White*

Not only was he our first president in the 20th century. He was the first of our leaders to live in the 20th century, which is something quite different. He saw that the United States was a developing power. The power that would burden us with responsibilities...and he was not afraid of power. —*Major General Frank Ross McCoy*

I went down to the police headquarters to see Commissioner Roosevelt. I said to him, "Mr. Roosevelt, you do not know me; I never met you; I saw you once. It was at the National Republican Convention in Chicago which named James G. Blaine for the Presidency and John A. Logan for the vice-presidency [1884]. You were in the New York delegation, in the group with George William Curtis, who was working for the nomination of Senator Edmunds for the presidency. You had on a little straw hat and were not so fleshy as you are now. You were young and had not been long out of Harvard, but you were one of the notables of the convention and you were pointed out to me as such. I did not speak to you, nor have I seen you since that day. I have come down this morning to introduce myself to you, and to congratulate you on your courage in determining to close the Sunday saloons. The city has waited for twenty-five years for the coming of such a man. It ought not to be counted a heroic thing for a man to keep his oath solemnly made and to earn his salary by the discharge of his official duty, but the moral sense of the community is so low through the polluting influence of the liquor dealers, and their collusion with corrupt officials, that a man is counted a hero who dares keep his oath to enforce the law or earn his salary by so doing. I will stand by you till the last hour in the day; you are in a fight for the people and for God, and I belong in it and am proud to have such a leader. Our church will stand by you, too. In my sermon yesterday morning I asked all good people to sustain you in this crusade." — *Ferdinand Iglehart*

I think it was in February, 1893, that we spent a week in Washington. We dined one night with the Roosevelts. I made some pleasant allusion to his future in public life. He looked at me, seriously and almost sadly. (Roosevelt was then Civil Service Commissioner.) Then he said: "My future? How can I have a future in public life? Don't you know as Civil Service Commissioner I have made an enemy of every professional politician in the United States? I can't have any political prospects." —*Brander Matthews*

A very prominent Republican Congressman was in my office one day after he had made a bitter attack in the House upon Civil Service reform, repeating many of the cheap current charges and criticisms upon the work of the Commission, and particularly singling out Mr. Roosevelt for sarcastic comment. While he was talking with me the Commissioner came in. They did not speak to each other, and I was tactless enough to introduce them; when almost immediately the fireworks began, and in a minute or two the lie passed. I got between the two, and the Congressman at once left the room. Mr. Roosevelt apologized to me, and said he realized that any man who struck another in the President's house could not remain his appointee, and he had determined if blows were exchanged at once to write out his resignation.

The sequel to this story, as related, is that some years afterward, in the same room, President McKinley and the Congressman were having a friendly chat. Mr. Roosevelt entered and, seeing who was present, sat down in a corner chair, awaiting his departure. The Congressman, without apparent change in manner, but in a voice distinctly heard, said: "McKinley, you remember a fellow named Roosevelt, who was Harrison's Civil Service Commissioner. He was the most impracticable man ever. I notice you have, as Assistant Secretary of the Navy, a person with the same name, but it can't be the same man, for your man is about the most efficient officer I have ever known."

Mr. Roosevelt sprang to his feet, walked across the room, extending his hand to his old-time enemy, saying, "Put it there; it's all right, hereafter." They shook hands heartily, and from that day remained the best of friends. It was Roosevelt 's way." —*Colonel E. W. Halford*

One lesson in the "square deal" was taught by Mr. Roosevelt, while President of the New York Police Commission, when a notorious foreign agitator [Hermann Ahlwardt] came to New York. This person, who was widely known as a "Jew baiter"...was to open a campaign in the United States. His first speech was to be delivered in New York, and his friends came to Mr. Roosevelt with an appeal for police protection. "He shall have all the police protection he wants," the Commissioner assured the delegation.

Then he sent for a police inspector and said: "Select thirty good, trusty, intelligent Jewish members of the force, men whose faces most clearly show their race, and order them to report to me in a body." When thirty chosen representatives of the chosen people stood before him, a broad smile of satisfaction spread over his face, for he had never seen a more Hebraic assemblage in his life.

"Now," he said to these policemen, "I am going to assign you men to the most honorable service you have ever done, the protection of an enemy, and the defense of religious liberty and free speech in the chief city of the United States. You all know who and what Dr. Ahlwardt is. I am going to put you in charge of the hall where he lectures and hold you responsible for perfect order throughout the evening. I have no more sympathy with Jew-baiting than you have. But this is a country where your people are free to think and speak as they choose in religious matters, as long as they do not interfere with the peace and comfort of their neighbors, and Dr. Ahlwardt is entitled to the same privilege...

When the Jew-baiters came to the hall, looking for a mob of Jews, they could hardly believe their eyes, for they saw the place guarded at every approach and the interior lined by those uniformed Jewish protectors. The agitator and his followers walked between rows of stern, solemn Jewish policemen, standing mute and stiff as statues. The Jews, moreover, who came bent on disturbing the meeting, were restrained by the mere presence of their brethren, who stood before them charged with the duty of keeping the peace.... The meeting failed utterly from lack of opposition, and the great national movement against the Jews was ruined, at the outset. —*Carleton Case*

I noticed the singular politeness as well as dignity of a policeman at Fifth Avenue, at a shopping street. "Would you like to be promoted?" I said one day. He answered, "There isn't a ghost of a chance of my being promoted. I am a poor man and have no money to buy any promotion or any 'pull' of any kind. I guess I will have to stick on this job."

"I understand that under the Roosevelt administration [of the New York City Police Department] money is not needed for promotion, and that the offer of it would be a reason for putting a man to the rear," I said to him. "I happen to be a friend of Commissioner Roosevelt, and if you would like to change your beat I will talk with the Commissioner about you. You come up to our parsonage at any time you indicate and I will find out something about your individual history." —Ferdinand Iglehart

[When Theodore Roosevelt was elected governor of New York State, he assured "machine" Republicans who were opposed to reform that he would "consult" the GOP boss Thomas Collier Platt on all appointments.]

Roosevelt's critics failed to see that a man brave enough to say squarely to Platt's enemies that he would consult Platt, would make that consultation honorable. Platt found this out. At these consultations Platt suggested the names of several unfit men for high offices. Roosevelt refused to appoint them. Platt vainly pleaded, blustered, threatened. Roosevelt, courteously, yet finally and with emphasis, told Platt to name honest men or none. Platt named honest men. They were appointed. So Roosevelt "consulted Mr. Platt." —William Allen White

[TR and former president Grover Cleveland at McKinley's burial:]

An incident of the White House shows what kind of regard grew up between them as they came to know one another. It was the day President McKinley was buried. President Roosevelt had come in alone. Among the mourners he saw Mr. Cleveland. Now, the etiquette of the White House, which is in its way as rigid as that of any court in Europe, requires that the President shall be sought out; he is not to go to anyone. But Mr. Roosevelt waved it all aside with one impulsive gesture as he went straight to Mr. Cleveland and took his hand. An official who stood next to them, and who told me, heard him say: "It will always be a source of pride and pleasure to me to have served under President Cleveland." Mr. Cleveland shook hands, mute with emotion. —Jacob Riis

Suddenly he was called down the mountain one dark night, when McKinley died, to take the oath of office as President of the United States. When he appeared in Buffalo he wore his black slouch hat and a business suit with trousers all bagged and wrinkled from a tedious journey; a day's beard on his face, youth in his eyes, high visions glowing in his countenance, and justice crying in his heart. He stood in the Milburn House parlor as he took the oath of office among the frock-coated, high-hatted dignitaries of the day; a sort of political stepchild, to be taken into the fortress of a privileged plutocracy and tolerated there for a brief season and maybe smothered in its gloomy dungeon, "And so Childe Roland to the dark tower came." —*William Allen White*

PUNCH, OR THE LONDON CHARIVARI.—September 25, 1901.

"THE ROUGH RIDER."

WITH MR. PUNCH'S BEST WISHES TO PRESIDENT ROOSEVELT.

As President, Mr. Roosevelt was a great news-maker and a great news-giver. At the same time he was a stickler for the exact proprieties in handling news that came from him. When he gave his confidence to a correspondent, he gave it completely, and trusted to the correspondent's judgment and sense of propriety as to the use that was made of it. I have had many confidential talks with him, and doubt if there were half a dozen times when he uttered any word of caution as to the use to be made of what he had said.

The standing White House rule, that the President is never quoted, was, of course, enforced strictly. Any violation of that terminated a correspondent's usefulness to his paper, so far as the White House was concerned....

It was all or nothing with him. He either talked [to reporters] with entire frankness and freedom, about anything and everything, or he didn't talk at all. —*O. K. Davis*

It matters less that Theodore Roosevelt is President, but it matters a good deal that the things prevail which he represents in the nation's life. It never mattered more than at this present day of ours—right now. —*Jacob Riis*, writing about the 1904 presidential campaign

At the White House one day, and in a confidential chat with the President, I told him one of my sons was going as a missionary to Japan. He instantly said with deep feeling, "Oh, I am so glad. I am so proud of that boy and I feel so proud for you. God bless him and bless you." He said, "I have told you so many times that I consider the Christian ministry as the highest calling in the world, most intimately related to the most exalted life and service here and destiny beyond, and I consider it my greatest joy and glory that, occupying a most exalted position in the nation, I am enabled, simply and sincerely, to preach the practical moralities of the Bible to my fellow-countrymen and to hold up Christ as the hope and Savior of the world. I believe down deep in my soul, as you know, my friend, that I have preached the same gospel that you and your boy are called to preach." —*Ferdinand Iglehart*

The President sent for his stenographer and dictated a brief message he proposes to send to the Senate next week. It was a curious sight. I have often seen it, and it never ceases to surprise me. He storms up and down the room, dictating in a loud and oratorical tone, often stopping, recasting a sentence, striking out and filling in, hospitable to every suggestion, not in the least disturbed by interruption, holding on stoutly to his purpose, and producing finally, out of these most unpromising conditions, a clear and logical statement, which he could not improve with solitude and leisure at his command. —*John Hay*

[It is recalled that, just as Secretary of State John Hay had been a friend of TR's father—Hay's successor Elihu Root had a lifelong association with Roosevelt. He had been one of a small but influential group of men who endorsed the twenty-two-year-old Roosevelt for his first campaign to the New York State Assembly.]

Elihu Root, then Secretary of War, called attention to the dominating will of the President in the spring of 1903 at a dinner in his honor. Mr. Root was talking about the Manchurian question and the possible effect of Russian control of the territory on the course of the United States in maintaining its rights in the East.

"We must never forget, gentlemen," said he, "that the War Department is only an emergency bureau, and that the controlling portfolio in the present administration is held by the Secretary of Peace, Theodore Roosevelt." —*George William Douglas*

Perhaps the most famous of Roosevelt's epigrammatic sayings is, "Speak softly and carry a big stick." The public, with its instinctive preference for the dramatic over the significant, promptly seized upon the "big stick" half of the aphorism and ignored the other half. But a study of the various acts of Roosevelt when he was President readily shows that in his mind the "big stick" was purely subordinate. It was merely the *ultima ratio*, the possession of which would enable a nation to "speak softly" and walk safely along the road of peace and justice and fair play.

The secret of Roosevelt's success in foreign affairs is to be found in another of his favorite sayings: "Nine-tenths of wisdom is to be wise in time." He has himself declared that his whole foreign policy "was based on the exercise of intelligent foresight and of decisive action sufficiently far in advance of any likely crisis to make it improbable that we would run into serious trouble." —*Harold Howland*

Contrary to the opinion held at one time by men, [Theodore Roosevelt] was a true friend to business. He appreciated the place of finance in the scheme of things. He had true regard for the tested lessons of sound economics. —*Otto H. Kahn*

It is not because President Roosevelt is antagonistic to capital, or a partner in that hatred of wealth which is so odious and so threatening, that certain financial interests, expert in the manipulation of the markets, are scheming to prevent his election to a second term. They know very well that he is no enemy to capital. They know that by birthright, by education and by long political training he is a supporter of sound money, an advocate of a protective tariff, a firm upholder of the rights of property. They know that he is the last man in the world to lead in an assault on capital lawfully applied to the development of the commercial enterprises of the country. They have no fear that he will be led by ambition or impulse into paths of Socialism....

What, then, is the reason why these financial interests are scheming to defeat him? The answer is plain.

They cannot control him.

All efforts to control him through his ambition have failed. Any attempt to control him by grosser forms of bribery would, of course, be useless. Effort to move him by sophistical arguments framed by clever corporation lawyers into departure from the paths of duty and law have not succeeded.

He is a friend of capital. He is a friend of labor. But he is no slave of either. —*Wall Street News*, newspaper editorial, 1904

It was characteristic of Theodore Roosevelt that he disregarded red tape. He brought to the problems of the White House a realism that had never previously pervaded the executive offices. It was because he was vitally interested in realities that he captured the imagination of the American people and became their great Evangelist in a demand that the government serve the people.

It is entirely in keeping with the general character of the man that he should be the first President to use in an official message to Congress the term "organized labor." —*Samuel Gompers*

Theodore Roosevelt was not a radical man. He believed in law and order. He believed in the right of property. He had sound economic views, but injustice aroused him and led him into denunciation that often was mistaken for a radicalism that he really did not entertain. His radicalism, such as he had, took the form of undervaluing the necessity for orderly procedure and of seeking a shortcut to the reform of evil. He did not fully realize the ultimate results of such shortcuts. —*William Howard Taft*

[On the presidential yacht Mayflower, hosting Russians and Japanese envoys as TR mediated an end to the destructive Russo-Japanese War:]

A characteristic incident happened at the first meeting of the Russo-Japanese conference in this country.... Roosevelt told me that he was somewhat puzzled what to do about the delicate question of precedence. "If I took in Count Witte," he said, "the Japanese would be offended; on the other hand, if I took in Baron Komura it would displease the Russians, so when luncheon was announced I simply said, 'Gentlemen, shall we go into luncheon?'; and we all walked in together, pell-mell. I dare say both Russians and Japanese were somewhat astounded at this informality, but they probably put it down to my American inexperience in social matters!" —*Lawrence F. Abbott*

His ambition? Yes, he has that. Is it to be President? He would like to sit in the White House, elected by the people [versus succeeding upon a president's death], for no man I ever met has so real and deep a belief in the ultimate righteousness of the people, in their wish to do the thing that is right, if it can be shown them.

But it is not that. If I know anything of the man, I know this: that he would fight in the ranks to the end of life for the things worth fighting for, rather than reach out a hand to grasp the Presidency, if it were to be had as the price of one of the principles upon which his life has been shaped in the sight of us all.

He might, indeed, quarrel with the party...for he would as little surrender his conscience to a multitude of men as to one, and he has said that he does not number Party loyalty with the Ten Commandments, firmly as he holds to it to get things done. Party allegiance is not a compelling force with him; he is the compelling force. —*Jacob Riis*, regarding the 1904 re-election campaign

"He's Good Enough For Me!"

COPYRIGHT, 1904, BY THE MAIL AND EXPRESS CO.

From the N. Y. Evening Mail

Naturally when the President declared so emphatically that he would not consider the nomination in 1908 for himself, I wanted to know whom he preferred, and I asked him, directly. His reply was just as direct.

"I would rather see Elihu Root in the White House than any other man now possible," he said. "I have told several men recently that I would walk on my hands and knees from the White House to the Capitol to see Root made President. But I know it cannot be done. He couldn't be elected. There is too much opposition to him on account of his corporation connections.

"But the people don't know Root. I do. I knew him when I was Governor of New York, and I have known him here, very intimately, during the years he has been in my Cabinet. The very thing on account of which there is so much objection to him would make him an ideal President. He is a great lawyer. He has always given all that he had to his clients. He has great intelligence, wonderful industry, and complete fidelity to his clients.

"What the people do not understand about him is that if he were President they would be his clients. He would be serving the nation with absolute singleness of purpose, and with all that intelligence, industry, and fidelity.... But it can't be done." —O. K. Davis

Imagine [him] at the desk sometimes, on the divan sometimes, sometimes in a chair in the farthest corner of the Cabinet room, more often on his feet—it may be anywhere within the four walls—the muscular, massive figure of Mr. Roosevelt. You know his features— the close-clipped brachycephalous head, close-clipped mustache, *pince nez* [glasses], square and terribly rigid jaw.

Hair and moustache indeterminate in color; eyes a clear blue; cheeks and neck ruddy. He is in a frock-coat, a low collar with a four-in-hand, a light waistcoat, and grey striped trousers—not that you would ever notice all that unless you pulled yourself away from his face and looked with deliberate purpose. Remember that he is almost constantly in action, speaking earnestly and with great animation; that he gestures freely, and that his whole face is always in play. For he talks with his whole being—mouth, eyes, forehead, cheeks, and neck all taking their mobile parts. The President is in the pink of condition today.... Look at him as he stands and you will see that he is rigid as a soldier on parade. His chin is in, his chest out. The line from the back of his head falls straight as a plumb-line to his heels. Never for a moment, while he is on his feet, does that line so much as waver, that neck unbend. It is a pillar of steel. Remember that steel pillar. Remember it when he laughs, as he will do a hundred times a day—heartily, freely, like an irresponsible school-boy on a lark, his face flushing ruddier, his eyes nearly closed, his utterance choked with mirth, and speech abandoned or become a weird falsetto. For the President is a joker, and (what many jokers are not) a humorist. He is always looking for fun—and always finding it. He likes it rather more than he does a fight—but that's fun too. You have to remember, then, two things to see the picture: a room filled with constant good humor, breaking literally every five minutes into a roar of laughter—and a neck of steel.

Not that the President always stands at attention. He doubles up when he laughs, sometimes. Sometimes—though only when a visitor whom he knows well is alone with him—he puts his foot on a chair. When he sits, however, he is very much at ease—half the time with one leg curled up on the divan or maybe on the Cabinet table top. And, curiously, when the President sits on one foot, his visitor is likely to do the same, even if, like Mr. Justice Harlan or Mr. J. J. Hill, he has to take hold of the foot and pull it up.

Remember that Mr. Roosevelt never speaks a word in the ordinary conversational tone. His face energized from the base of the neck to the roots of the hair, his arms usually gesticulating, his words bursting forth like projectiles, his whole being radiating force. He does not speak fast, always pausing before an emphatic word, and letting it out with the spring of accumulated energy behind it. The President doesn't allow his witticisms to pass without enjoying them. He always stops—indeed, he has to stop till the convulsion of merriment is over and he can regain his voice.

The President enters into a subject which arouses him. He bursts out against his detractors. His arms begin to pump. His finger rises in the air. He beats one palm with the other fist. "They have no conception of what I'm driving at, absolutely *none*. It *passes belief*—the capacity of the human mind to resist intelligence. Some people *won't* learn, *won't* think, *won't* know. The amount of—stupid *perversity* that lingers in the heads of some men is a miracle."

The President's good-humor and candor have not been sufficiently appreciated. It is good to have a President with a laugh like Mr. Roosevelt's. That laugh is working a good deal too; hardly does half an hour, seldom do five minutes go by without a joyful cachinnation from the Presidential throat.... The fun engulfs his whole face; his eyes close, and speech expires in a silent gasp of joy.

He is, first of all, a physical marvel. He radiates energy as the sun radiates light and heat.... It is not merely remarkable, it is a simple miracle, that this man can keep up day after day—it is a sufficient miracle that he can exhibit for one day—the power which emanates from him like energy from a dynamo.... He radiates from morning until night, and he is nevertheless always radiant.

Never does the President appear to meet a personality than which he is not the stronger; an idea to which he is a stranger; a situation which disconcerts him. He is always master. He takes what he pleases, gives what he likes, and does his will upon all alike. Mr. Roosevelt never tires; the flow of his power does not fluctuate. There is never weariness on his brow nor, apparently, languor in his heart…. The President ends the day as fresh as he began it. He is a man of really phenomenal physical power, a fountain of perennial energy, a dynamic marvel.

The President is able to concentrate his entire attention on the subject in hand, whether it be for an hour or for thirty seconds, and then instantly to transfer it, still entirely concentrated, to another subject…. He flies from an affair of state to a hunting reminiscence; from that to an abstract ethical question; then to a literary or a historical subject; he settles a point in an army reorganization plan; the next second he is talking earnestly to a visitor on the Lake Superior whitefish, the taste of its flesh and the articulation of its skeleton as compared with the shad; in another second or two he is urging the necessity of arming for the preservation of peace, and quoting Erasmus; then he takes up the case of a suspected violation of the Sherman law, and is at the heart of it in a minute; then he listens to the tale of a Southern politician and gives him rapid instruction; turns to the intricacies of the Venezuela imbroglio, with the mass of details of a long story which everybody else has forgotten at his finger tips; stops a moment to tell a naval aide the depth and capacity of the harbor of Auckland; is instantly intent on the matter of his great and good friend of the Caribbean; takes up a few candidacies for appointments, one by one; recalls with great gusto the story of an adventure on horseback; greets a delegation; discusses with a Cabinet secretary a recommendation he is thinking of sending to Congress. All this within half an hour. Each subject gets full attention when it is up; there is never any hurrying away from it, but there is no loitering over it. —*William Bayard Hale*

I was one of those who wanted Mr. Roosevelt to take another term, and one afternoon, when I had an opportunity to talk with him alone, I brought the matter up. It seemed to me that there was no longer any real difference of principle between the Republican and Democratic Parties. The essential difference was mostly one of partisanship. The real cleavage of the voters was along the line between what, for [convenience's] sake, may be called liberal and conservative. The Democrats had clearly swung away from their original constitutional principles, and the Republicans were not much better.

To my surprise the President discussed the matter most freely. He began with a reference to the effort that was going on to get him to renew or disavow his 1904 statement [against running for another term in 1908]. It disgusted him that the people generally, and the newspapers particularly, did not at once see and explain his position.

"They want me to keep repeating myself," he exclaimed, "and they don't see that it would make people think I didn't believe myself. If what I say isn't worth believing when I say it, what additional value would it have from being repeated?" —*O. K. Davis*

[The very first National Governors' Conference was convened by President Roosevelt to address conservation. The perennial Democrat presidential candidate William Jennings Bryan had also been invited. TR chatted privately with Bryan:]

"When you see me quoted in the press as welcoming the rest I will have after March the 3rd [when Roosevelt would retire from the presidency] take no stock in it, for I will confess to you confidentially that I like my job. The burdens of this great nation I have borne up under for the past seven years will not be laid aside with relief, as all presidents have heretofore said, but will be laid aside with a good deal of regret; for I have enjoyed every moment of this so-called arduous and exacting task."

This is really his feeling on the subject. He bounds in and out like a schoolboy, and except when he is very angry always seems to be in a good humor. —*Archie Butt*

At the White House one day President Roosevelt came into his room, greeted me cordially, as was his custom, and then slipped over to another gentleman and greeted him. He brought that gentleman over to where I was, and said, "Dr. Iglehart, permit me to introduce to you Father ———, who has been doing very important work among the Indians and has come to talk with me about it." And then, placing himself between us, he said, "Here's the great Catholic church with its millions represented by this Catholic priest, on one side of me; and here on the other is the great Methodist church, with its millions represented by my old friend; and I am only a poor little Dutch Reform layman between the two."

THE MOST INTERESTING AMERICAN

The twinkle in his eye evidenced the fun that was always bubbling over within him. I replied, "No, Mr. President, you are not the poor little Dutch Reform layman between them. You are the great head of the nation and a Christian with a universal heart. You are large enough to belong to all the churches and all of us claim you as such, and we have reason to believe that you consider that all of us belong to you."

He warmed up instantly and answered, "My friend, you are quite right…. The Protestant minister, the Catholic priest and the Jewish rabbi, and the millions that they represent, have vied with each other in sustaining me, and my arm has been as strong as the millions that they represent, in smiting evil and in building up the right. You can see how correct you were in saying that I belong to all of you and that all of you belong to me." —*Ferdinand Iglehart*

I know of no instance when I had to wait to see him for more than a few minutes. I accepted him as a friend with brain, sympathy, and willingness to serve, and he believed in me and at times accepted my advice and acted upon it. Our relations were of the cordial and confidential character. Frequently he talked very bad Holland Dutch to me. —*Samuel Gompers*

I once heard Attorney General Knox say to Mr. Roosevelt: "You are the most difficult man to state a proposition to I have ever met. Before I am half through stating it, you have grasped it all, and have rendered your decision before you know what my conclusions are." —*Leslie M. Shaw*

I was in the Senate during the whole of his Presidency and saw him nearly every day. It was a delight to visit the Executive Office or to meet him in the closer associations of the White House. He was the most outspoken of public men. As I was entering his room one morning a Senator was coming out. This Senator had made some request of the President which had angered him. Theodore shouted to me so the Senator could hear him, and everybody else: "Do you know that man?" I answered, "Yes, he is a colleague of mine in the Senate."

"But," the President shouted, "he is a crook." —*Chauncey Depew*

By chance it happened that Adams was obliged to take the place of his brother Brooks at the Diplomatic Reception immediately after his return home, and the part of proxy included his supping at the President's table, with Secretary Root on one side, the President opposite, and Miss Chamberlain between them. Naturally the President talked and the guests listened; which seemed, to one who had just escaped from the European conspiracy of silence, like drawing a free breath after stifling.

Roosevelt, as everyone knew, was always an amusing talker, and had the reputation of being indiscreet beyond any other man of great importance in the world, except the Kaiser Wilhelm and Mr. Joseph Chamberlain, the father of his guest at table; and this evening he spared none. With the usual abuse of the *quos ego* common to vigorous statesmen, he said all that he thought about Russians and Japanese, as well as about Boers and British, without restraint, in full hearing of twenty people, to the entire satisfaction of his listener; and concluded by declaring that war was imminent; that it ought to be stopped; that it could be stopped: "I could do it myself; I could stop it tomorrow!" and he went on to explain his reasons for restraint.
—*Henry Adams, as was his style in his autobiography, referring to himself in the third person*

Very many people, powerful elements in the community, regarded him at one time as a dangerous radical, bent upon overthrowing all the safeguards of society, and planning to tear out the foundations of ordered liberty. As a matter of fact, what Theodore Roosevelt was trying to do was to strengthen American society and American Government by demonstrating to the American people that he was aiming at a larger economic equality and a more generous industrial opportunity for all men; and that any combination of capital or of business which threatened the control of the government by the people who made it, was to be curbed and resisted, just as he would have resisted an enemy who tried to take possession of the city of Washington. —*Henry Cabot Lodge*

Mr. Roosevelt's speech might be described as a characterized speech, in that he expressed himself in emphatic language and accompanied his words with gestures equally emphatic. His manner indicated that he was enjoying the fight, and the more vehement the denunciation, the more vigorous the applause. —*William Jennings Bryan*, who attended the 1912 Republican Convention in the role of newspaper reporter

Roosevelt is prompt and energetic, but he takes infinite pains to get at the facts before he acts. In all the crises in which he has been accused of undue haste, his action has been the result of long meditation and well-reasoned conviction. If he thinks rapidly, that is no fault; he thinks thoroughly, and that is the essential. —*John Hay*

Between extremes are the words of a man who was not a jurist, but whose intuitions and perceptions were deep and brilliant—the words of President Roosevelt [in his message of December 8, 1908, to Congress].... He was not positing an ideal. He was not fixing a goal. He was measuring the powers and the endurance of those by whom the race is to be run. —*Benjamin N. Cardozo*

[A few days before TR left office] he was at his desk going over a mass of papers and scarcely noticed my entrance. But after a few moments he paused, pushed the papers away from him, and leaned back in his chair with his head lowered as one lost in a reverie. After a minute or two he seemed to notice me. He got up and walked around his desk to where I stood. He paused and turned about slowly, taking in the whole room. Then he put his hand on my shoulder and said:

"Well, James, we've had a lot of fun here together, haven't we?" —*James Amos*

[*The New York Times reporter and subsequent Roosevelt aide O. K. Davis asked—not for the first time—whether President Roosevelt could be induced to break his pledge and run for re-election in 1908:*]

"Colonel, how about the White House again for yourself?"

"I don't care that for it," he replied instantly, with a little gesture that was characteristic of him, snapping his thumb and forefinger together with a motion as if tossing something very light over his right shoulder.

"... I've been there for seven and a half years. I've had all the work and all the fun, all the honor and all the glory of it, and I wouldn't give that [repeating his gesture] for any more of it.

"I am the only man in the United States who can speak of the presidency without the thrill that always comes to the man who has never been in the White House. To go to the White House again simply for the sake of being President doesn't interest me in the least. There are so many things that I haven't yet done and that I want so much to do. I want to take some time now, in the next few years, to do some of those things. I have done something in geography and

74

something in ornithology, and something in other lines. I want to put myself in a position where I can be rightfully recognized as a scientist in one or two of these lines.

"Most men in this country think of the presidency as the supreme thing, and that is natural and all right. But I've had that, and another term could not add anything to what I have had there. Of course, if there were a big job of work to be done, which the people of the country wanted me to handle, that would be a different thing. But then it would be going back in order to do a particular thing, and one that I had not done before. It would not be going back simply for the sake of being President again." —*O. K. Davis*

"Missing"

I lay down my fresh morning paper,
I drop it at once from my hand;
No thrilling account of his caper
    Appears there to stir up the land,
There's nothing on roses or rabies,
    There's nothing on taxes or teeth,
There's nothing on ballots or babies,
    No sword is a-clank in its sheath—
It makes me feel terribly solemn;
No longer he fills the first column.

I used to get up every morning
    And read while my breakfast grew cold
A blending of promise and warning,
    A mixture of praising and scold;
I used to call out to my neighbor:
    "Well, here he is at it again"—
Alas, he has beaten his sabre
    Into a contributing pen.
It makes me tremendously solemn
To miss him now in that first column.

He hasn't gone up with the flyers,
    He hasn't whizzed out on the train,
He hasn't named four or five liars,
    He simply is not raising Cain!
Why, hang it! it doesn't seem proper

A paper like this to peruse!
There's nothing comes out of the hopper
*   Except the day's run of the news.*
I stand here with countenance solemn
And ask why he left the first column.

So sudden it was—in a minute
*   That column relinquished his name.*
One day he was certainly in it,
*   Next morning it wasn't the same.*
It interferes some with my eating;
*   There's nothing but items to read—*
No speaking, or parting, or greeting,
*   No frazzles, or challenge to heed.*
By gracious! I've felt mighty solemn
Since he fell out of the first column!

—Jefferson Toombs, 1909

[Subsequent to heeding appeals from many Republicans based on the view that President Taft had betrayed Roosevelt policies and winning the majority of primary contests is the setting for this account by one of the supporters of a Third-Party candidacy in 1912. In a conclave that also included publisher Frank Munsey and financier/philanthropist George W. Perkins, on the decision to run in 1912; Roosevelt's conversation with Edwin Van Valkenburg, Editor of the Philadelphia North American:]

[Roosevelt] turned toward me and said: "Van, this ends my public career. I had hoped I might serve the public for a long while. But duty calls and I must enter this fight as a soldier goes into battle

and there risks his life. I am no better, and must be willing to 'die' for my country."

Suddenly he turned toward the door and said, "Let me bring Edith in," and soon he came back hand in hand with Mrs. Roosevelt, like the lovers they were, and asked her to tell me about the decision. She recounted the incidents and added, "Though we know the outcome is defeat, I am *serenely* happy; and whatever comes now, it is all right."

It was holy ground on which we stood. Mr. Roosevelt accepted the call as God-sent and without question went forward in the way as he found it marked out, step by step. —*Edwin Van Valkenburg*

Mr. Roosevelt read character and so picked his associates. He usually forgave his adversaries, but Mr. [Henry] Stoddard [publisher of the New York *Mail*] told me of a nationally known writer who had published a widely circulated article making serious charges against Mr. Roosevelt. Later [in 1916] he wanted to apologize and renew friendship, but Mr. Roosevelt was unwilling, saying: "He has known me eight or ten years in an intimate way. If when he thus knew me he could make such charges, he proves himself to have a character I dare not trust in the future." —*Christian Reisner*

[TR believed that he should deliver the most important address of his career before the breakaway Bull Moose Party convention began deliberations. His aide O. K. Davis, and others, advised that the speech would be buried and lost in the press among subsequent convention activities. Roosevelt relented.]

"This speech is to be delivered at the convention, on Tuesday afternoon, after the nomination has been made."

Colonel Roosevelt looked up at me with a grin, and pounded the desk in front of him with his doubled-up fist.

"It is not!" he declared, with regulation Rooseveltian emphasis. "This speech will be delivered by me just as soon as I reach Chicago. I shall go to the hotel from the train, walk out on the balcony, just where I spoke at the Republican Convention, and deliver this speech."

"I am sorry to hear you say that Colonel," I replied, "for it is our unanimous judgment at headquarters that it should be delivered in the convention, after the nomination." The Colonel swung around so that he faced the desk and pounded it with both fists. "And it is my unanimous judgment that it will not!" he exclaimed, accenting every word with a resounding thump of the desk.

[His secretary], who had been taking dictation of some notes as the Colonel worked over the proofs, sat beside him open-mouthed. Apparently he had never seen anyone venture to differ with the Colonel before, much less take on a real and vigorous controversy with him. —*O. K. Davis*

[Regarding an offer from the Taft forces to Roosevelt, at the boiling-point of the contentious Republican convention of 1912, to compromise on Governor Herbert Hadley of Missouri:]

"You surely surprised me, that night," I said.

"Why?" he asked.

"Because," I replied, "in all my experience and acquaintance with you, you had 'played the game.' You had described yourself as a 'practical' man, and I went down to you that night, thinking only of the chance to win that fight, which had been so hard and bitter. I was thinking of the practical politics of the proposition, and of you as a practical politician who would play the game at that time."

"Yes," he said, "I am a practical politician, and I have played the game. But that was something very different. There was a question of simple honesty involved in that fight at Chicago, the principle of right and wrong [about the "stolen" nomination]. It had gone far beyond a mere question of expediency or political shrewdness. It was a question of fundamental morality."

He went on to talk about that incident and all its bearings for some time, and out of that talk I got a new impression of Colonel Roosevelt. It took me back to the many months he had spent in Africa, the first period in many years of his busy, active life when he had the experience of detachment from contact with his fellows and their affairs. Then, for the first time since he had quit his North Dakota ranch, he had had opportunity for quiet reflection, and had had the advantage of perspective, which distance and solitude only could give him, on his country and his own relation to it. It was in that period of comparative solitude in Africa, when even his own son did not share his tent, that Colonel Roosevelt had the time for that introspection and reflection which were the real reasons why he refused to "play the game" that June night in Chicago.

The Roosevelt who came back from Africa was the same physical being who went there, but in other and greater respects he was permanently changed. The experiences of his camp life, followed by his contact with the crowned heads and courts of Europe, as well as with the plain people there, had developed and enlarged him. He came home with a passion for service that outweighed other considerations, and made that of 'self' the least and last of all. —*O. K. Davis*

He would have been entirely useless if he had not been a politician. Not even the most altruistic statesman could swim above the currents of the whirlpool of political life in a republic, without taking into account the value of opportune compromises. But Theodore Roosevelt, in my experience, never compromised for a base motive. —*Maurice Francis Egan*

On a trip to Boston with Mr. Roosevelt on the day after his decision to be a candidate for the nomination in 1912, he said "he was a very sad man" because duty compelled his candidacy. On receiving enthusiastic assurances of success he replied, "It may be possible, but we must be prepared to lose—it is our duty to make the fight." —*George H. Payne*

[Roosevelt, after the Bull Moose campaign defeat in 1912, felt a strong obligation to lower-ballot candidates and citizens who had worked for the cause, often sacrificially:]
He felt that he was losing his influence with the American people [during the lonely and doomed 1914 Progressive campaign appearances], just at the very time when he most wanted it. For he had in mind an attempt to rouse them to an active sense of their duty in Europe, and he was more eager and keen about it than he had ever been about anything where he himself was concerned or would benefit.

It was the first time I had seen the Colonel in that mood, and it made a lasting impression on me.... The longer that response was delayed, the bluer the Colonel became, and the more certain that he had lost his following among the people.

We were getting near to New York City one night when the Colonel leaned over and whacked me on the knee with his hand.

"Well, O. K.," he said, "I've got only a few hours more of this campaign, and then I shall be through. I'll be out of politics then for good and all, and I'll be a free man. I shall have paid every political obligation that I owe to anybody anywhere. I have done a great deal of foolish and useless work this fall, but, after all, it has been worthwhile from one point of view. It has paid all my debts. Hereafter no man can claim anything from me in politics. Not a single obligation is left. I have done everything, this fall, that everybody has wanted.

This election makes me an absolutely free man. Thereafter I am going to say and do just what I damned please."

That was one of the very few times I ever heard Colonel Roosevelt use the big D, and the emphasis with which he uttered it showed how thoroughly he meant it. —*O. K. Davis*

Long before he became President he saw that America had reached the point where a transition from an outworn to a modern economic and social order was indispensable. To effect this transition was the great work of his life, and it is the accomplishment of that fundamental advance that makes his career epochal.

He became President of the United States just after one of the most serious developments in American history. This development was the disappearance of free land. Until that point of time which marks the beginning of what always will be called the "Roosevelt Period," anybody could get a farm and a home of his own by the simple process of taking up substantially free land and living upon it. This process indeed had been going on since before the Revolution. —*Albert J. Beveridge*

Race, creed, color, were not determining factors with him. He took a man for what he was.... With clearness of vision, energy, unfaltering faith, he labored through his entire career to transform politics from a corrupt traffic to a public service. With a very passion for justice and equality before the law he sought with voice and pen, with every resource at his command, to obtain for men everywhere their constitutional guarantee of life, liberty, and the pursuit of happiness. —*Franklin Delano Roosevelt*

His life, when he is on his own continent, is one damn caller after another!

Sagamore Hill was overrun with little governors, [political confidants], and South American explorers one sunny afternoon, while I waited to see TR in a side room that was full of wild animals he had known.

After greeting me, his next remark [anent drawing Roosevelt's portrait] was, "My full face is better than the side!"

As a matter of fact it is no such thing. Bows on, his face is strangely like a nice blond Japanese war-mask. His profile seems to belong to a different man. His super-dreadnaught head might have been done by Rodin.

I asked him if his hair was sunburnt [this was shortly after Roosevelt's harrowing expedition in Brazil] and he said: "No, it always was the color of old rope!"

I expected to see him looking played out, but on the contrary he was tanned, vigorous, and full of the usual pep.

He excused himself during the short sitting to say a few thousand things to some other callers who were leaving. When he booms "Good bye," his inflection makes the word sound something like, "Good-boy!"

[At another sitting] he posed for me, and when he looked at the drawing, said, "That's very good of you!" I was puzzled how to take that. —*James Montgomery Flagg*, cartoonist and illustrator, assigned by *Harper's Weekly* to draw TR's portrait for its "Roosevelt Number" in 1914

CHAPTER III

Theodore Roosevelt: Outdoorsman and Disciple of the Strenuous Life

Shakespeare wrote, "All the world's a stage, And all the men and women merely players." Typically, TR had his own spin on accepted wisdom. To him, not merely the whole world, but every aspect, every corner, were his chosen stages.

Almost forgotten in Roosevelt's consequential "New Nationalism" speech in Osawatomie, Kansas, in 1910 was his paean to hardy life in the outdoors: "There is a delight in the hardy life of the open. There are no words that can tell the hidden spirit of the wilderness that can reveal its mystery, its melancholy, and its charm."

But the "Strenuous Life" meant more than many Americans thought—and think—TR intended. The miracle of his "rebuilt" body in the face of childhood ailments, his incessant activities, and the obsessive physicality are well known. Yet his book *The Strenuous Life* is not an exercise manual, but rather a collection of articles and speeches on the moral engagement of a virtuous citizenry.

Roosevelt's virtually constant physical activities—the challenges he set himself, and overcame, in many realms—logically go hand-in-hand

83

with his love of the outdoors. And the outdoors of God and God's nature logically grew from his first loves: nature studies and natural history. They can be considered as related facets in the gem that is TR.

"Outdoorsman" is a Rooseveltian term as broad as the landscape of the American West itself, and to continue the analogy, as varied as the detailed, changing, compelling Badlands of the Dakotas that he adopted—or that adopted him—as a second home. Not the least were the challenges to the body and soul of life in the wilderness.

The Outdoors to Theodore Roosevelt were more than stages for hunting trips. His passionate cause was the outdoors and its freedoms, and he served that cause magnificently. As a young boy—and without cease—he discovered, identified, and preserved species for others to appreciate in various museums, through books, and as a speaker.

America's virgin wilderness; the heritage of native Americans whose lives and dignity Roosevelt respected and worked to preserve; and of course among his iconic achievements, the eternal preservation of federally protected lands and the conservation of natural resources—these were vital components of Theodore Roosevelt's vision before, during, and after his presidency.

Roosevelt's father was a co-founder of the American Museum of Natural History (AMNH) in New York City, so TR inherited a love of natural history, the scientific aspects; and—not in the least—nature itself, in the raw. Through the decades, Roosevelt assisted the museum in many ways, most notably collecting hundreds of specimens in Africa, many of which appeared on display and in dioramas. (In his mature years, both the Smithsonian and the American Museum of Natural History sponsored and benefited from his work.) The Theodore Roosevelt Rotunda at the AMNH was dedicated to his memory, and the museum provided a home for a magnificent equestrian statue of TR, until it acceded to a passing burst of political frenzy in 2020 as demanded by New York City and various pressure groups; the statue was removed with the collusion of some of TR's descendants, at night and replaced with a pagan-flavored and vaguely sexual sculpture of a woman. Through the years—not only in Africa, but also Brazil—Roosevelt collected more than specimens, he discovered and postulated genetic relations of previously unknown species and theorized about intercontinental migrations and protective coloration—more "interesting" credentials.

Such were his habits and inclinations: love of the outdoors for hunting, for study, for the national economy. "Conservation" had precise meaning—to manage development where it was deemed a possibility; not to ban visitors and enjoyment; and to act as a sort of antidote to urban life. TR envisioned national parks as geographic pressure-valves for the growing American classes who would need psychic relief in the wonders of God's nature. "We cannot improve upon it," he said of the Grand Canyon; and was fiercely devoted to preventing desecration.

Roosevelt never lost interest in the outdoors, personally or as an advocate. He was a founder of the Boone and Crockett Club, still in existence as a major voice for hunters and the management of wilderness lands and wild game. His very first published work was a pamphlet produced with a friend when they were barely twenty years old: *The Summer Birds of the Adirondacks in Franklin County, N.Y.*

That the scion of an urban patrician family would find solace in the Maine woods or the Montana mountains or the Dakota Badlands is not unusual, but the extent to which Theodore Roosevelt identified with the outdoors is significant…and, to be sure, a key to understanding the man. He harbored an almost mystical love of the Outdoors.

He said in a speech to townspeople of Dickinson, Dakota Territory, before his decision to return East:

"Like all Americans, I like big things: big parades, big forests and mountains, big wheat fields, railroads—and herds of cattle too; big factories, steamboats and everything else. But we must keep steadily in mind that no people were ever yet benefited by riches if their property corrupted their virtue. It is more important that we should show ourselves honest, brave, truthful, and intelligent than that we should own all the railways and grain elevators in the world…I am myself at heart as much a westerner as an easterner."

And in a panegyric perhaps not as colorful a phrase as the "Strenuous Life," but as revelatory—almost a poetic confession—he further said of the Dakota outdoors: "I must say that here, in this country of hills and plateaus, the romance of my life began…. I had studied a lot about men and things before I saw you fellows, but it was only when I came out here that I began to know anything or to measure men right."

* * *

I go back in my mind and think of him as a little delicate boy in the nursery in the house on Twentieth Street when my brother Elliott and I, even younger but less delicate children, were always asking for a story. And Theodore Roosevelt in those days, delicate as he was, breathing terribly with that curse of asthma that was on him, never refused the story to the two younger ones in the nursery....

And then later when grown more powerful, more powerful because of his determination to make his own body, which he accomplished by sheer, absolute determination and will-power, I remember the lovely long days at Oyster Bay when we were all children together, the days in the boats, the little tiny boats. He never wanted a big boat; he wanted a little boat that was always nearly swamped in the Sound in the big waves. He didn't want to sail, he wanted to row; he wanted that hard manual labor. He wanted to have a bigger wave than the boat could quite get over; he wanted to have a big neck of land that he pulled the boat over himself. He was always a person who wanted an obstacle to overcome, and he always wanted to go over and through and never around. And that attitude was characteristic from his early boyhood. —*Corinne Roosevelt Robinson*

Just before entering Harvard, Roosevelt, on the advice of two of his cousins, took a step which had a lasting influence on his life. They sent him down in Maine to their old guide, Bill Sewall of Island Falls. With this born woodsman he learned to know and love the wilderness. There he developed tastes which later led him out into the wild West, to be a ranchman, a hunter, and finally the organizer of the Rough Riders, things which have done so much to shape his fortunes. Besides, he made a lifelong friend of Bill Sewall, as true a one as he could count among all his friendships. —*Hermann Hagedorn*

The next fall [young TR's tutor and some Roosevelt relatives] came again to Maine and brought a thin, pale youngster with bad eyes and a weak heart. That was Theodore Roosevelt.

They had come by way of Lake Mattawamkeag, and it was about dark when they got there. Arthur Cutler took me off to one side. He said: "I want you to take that young fellow, Theodore, I brought down, under your special care. Be careful of him, see that he don't take too hard jaunts and does not do too much. He is not very strong and he has got a great deal of ambition and grit, and if you should take such a tramp as you are in the habit of taking sometimes, and take him with you, you never would know that anything ailed him. If you should ask him if he was having a good time he would tell you he was having a very good time; and even if he was tired he would not tell you so. The first thing you knew he would be down, because he would go until he fell."

I took him and I found that that was his disposition right away, but he wasn't such a weakling as Cutler tried to make out. We traveled twenty-five miles afoot one day on that first visit of his, which I maintain was a good fair walk for any common man. We hitched well, somehow or other, from the start. He was different from anybody that I had ever met; especially, he was fair-minded. He and I agreed in our ideas of fair play and right and wrong. Besides, he was always good-natured and full of fun. I do not think I ever remember him being "out of sorts." He did not feel well sometimes, but he never would admit it.

I could see not a single thing that wasn't fine in Theodore, no qualities that I didn't like. Some folks said that he was head-strong and aggressive, but I never found him so except when necessary; and I've always thought being headstrong and aggressive, on occasion, was a pretty good thing. He wasn't a bit cocky as far as I could see, though others thought so. I will say that he was not remarkably cautious about expressing his opinion. —*Bill Sewall*

Theodore was about eighteen when he first came to Maine. He had an idea that he was going to be a naturalist and used to carry with him a little bottle of arsenic and go around picking up bugs. He didn't shoot any big game, just ducks and partridges. We did a bit of trout-fishing. Theodore was never very fond of that. Somehow, he didn't like to sit still so long.

That fall I had engaged another guide, so that the party would be little better provided for. Wilmot Dow was his name. [In a few years Dow was also hired to be a Roosevelt ranch hand in the Badlands, with Sewall.] He was a nephew of mine, a better guide than I was, better hunter, better fisherman, and the best shot of any man in the country. He took care of the rest of the party himself mostly. I was with Theodore all of the time. At the end of the week I told Dow that I had got a different fellow to guide from what I had ever seen before. I had never seen anybody that was like him, and I have held that opinion ever since. —*Bill Sewall*

Island Falls was then beyond the railway and on the very edge of the immense wild lands of the Pine Tree State. In that village the pale, stoop-shouldered young gentleman from New York made himself at home, and one of the villagers has declared: "Everyone in the Falls liked him, for he was as plain as a spruce board and as square as a brick." He lived like a son in the simple home of the backwoodsman and tramped and camped with Bill as a chum.

The experience was an object lesson in democracy, which was not lost on [Roosevelt's] youthful imagination. —*Bill Sewall*

I went down to New York that spring to see him and to talk things over [about Roosevelt's offer to Bill Sewall and Wilmot Dow to join him in the Badlands]. He said he would guarantee us a share of anything made in the cattle business, and if anything was lost, he said he would lose it and pay our wages. He asked me what I thought of the proposition. I told him that I thought it was very one-sided, but if he thought he could stand it, I thought we could. Whatever happened, he said, we should not lose by it. That was all the bargain there was and all the bargain we needed from him. We knew that we were just as safe as if we had had a contract. —*Bill Sewall*

While he was away on this hunting-trip we heard that a man who was known as a trouble-maker and who worked on the ranch of a Frenchman named de Mores, a marquis who laid claim to the large piece of country on which our ranch was situated, had threatened to shoot Roosevelt. I told Theodore about it when he came back.

He said, "Is that so?"

Then he saddled his horse and rode straight to where the man lived. Theodore found him in his shack and told him that he had heard that a man had said he wanted to shoot him, and, said Theodore, he wanted to know why.

The man was flabbergasted, I guess, by Roosevelt's directness. He denied that he had ever said anything like it. He had been misquoted, he said.

The affair passed off very pleasantly and Roosevelt and he were good friends after that. —*Bill Sewall*

During his two years in the West as a ranchman, Mr. Roosevelt lived the life of the hardiest plainsman. On round-ups he endured all the hardships of his men. He spent much of his time hunting, and killed specimens of all the game to be found on the plains and in the mountains. He was particularly fond of bear hunting, which requires a nerve as steady and an aim as sure as the pursuit of any game in the United States.

But Roosevelt was never a "dead shot." He always talked and wrote in a most dispassionate way about his "misses." —*Carleton Case*

Theodore Roosevelt was filled with the spirit of the pioneer. It bodied itself forth in every aspect of his manifold activities. In whatever he did he pushed out by choice from the cities into an open space where he could look about him clearly and in final analysis take counsel with himself alone.

All his life was punctuated by these adventures, great and small. The Dakota experience, the Africa experience, and the South America experience were, I believe, the episodes of the most complete satisfaction to him. And, in spite of the wider general significance of South America and Africa, I venture to guess that when all was balanced, Dakota gave him the most. There he most fully blended with the actual, everyday, workaday life of the men busily engaged not in exploration merely, but in the actual making of a new country. —*Stewart Edward White*

Theodore invested over $50,000 to stock our claim, in cattle and horses—about one hundred head of the latter—and he lost most of it, but came back physically strong enough to be anything he wanted to be from President of the United States down. He went to Dakota a frail young man suffering from asthma and stomach trouble. When he got back into the world again he was as husky as almost any man I have ever seen who wasn't dependent on his arms for his livelihood. He weighed one hundred and fifty pounds, and was clear bone, muscle, and grit. That was what the ranch did for him physically. What it did for him financially was a different story. I do not believe Theodore Roosevelt ever made a dollar out of his cattle or ever saw again more than a small part of his original investment. —*Bill Sewall*

In making or breaking camp he was as handy as a pocket in a shirt and seemed to know just what to do. On the first night out, when we were twenty-five or thirty miles from a settlement, we went into camp on the open prairie, with our saddle-blankets over us, our horses picketed and the picket ropes tied about the horns of our saddles, which we used for pillows.

In the middle of the night there was a rush, our pillows were swept from under our heads and our horses went tearing off over the prairie, frightened by wolves. Away they tore, and we heard the saddles thumping over the ground after them. Mr. Roosevelt was up and off in a minute. Together we chased those frightened horses over the prairie until they slackened speed and we caught up with them. The night was dark and there was little to guide us on our return. Mr. Roosevelt's bump of locality was good, and he led the way back to camp straight as a die. —*Joseph A. Ferris*

Say, this fellow worked for his troopers [the Rough Rider regiment] like a cider-press. He tried to feed them. He helped build latrines. He cursed the quartermasters and the—"dogs"—on the transports to get quinine and grub for them. Let him be a politician if he likes. He was a gentleman down there. —*Stephen Crane*

He loved mountains and mountain lions and days of hardships, and a night camp under a tree. Above all, he loved the spirit of freedom. —*Albert Bushnell Hart*

His contests President Roosevelt held not only with his boys and other members of his family, but with Cabinet officers and foreign diplomats. Capitals of Europe were sometimes highly entertained by accounts of their representatives following the President who had invited them for afternoon walks, across fences, ditches, and through mud, ankle deep. Pouring rain never prevented the President from taking his walks with members of the foreign embassies, and he was always delighted with credit given him for inaugurating the strenuous life in Washington. The outdoor life lived in Washington was but a repetition of that enjoyed at Sagamore Hill, typical haven of domestic bliss and always a scene of rational pleasures. Whether the Colonel was in or out of office, his delightful country home was always his favorite abode. —*Hermann Hagedorn*

Friday he asked me to play lawn tennis. Secretary Garfield, Captain McCoy, the President, and I made the foursome. We played seven sets and came out about even, Mr. Garfield playing the best game, I next, and McCoy and the President about evenly matched, I should say. I wore my *jai alai* shoes, which the President greatly admired. I have several extra pairs and offered him one pair, but when we went to examine his feet we found the shoes several sizes too large for him.

I have not got a large foot myself and wear only a seven, but his foot is absurdly small, he wears a number four or five. —*Archie Butt*

ONE OF MR. ROOSEVELT'S QUIET DAYS

He devotes a few moments to San Domingo	He hands Mr. Castro a few	He jumps on the U. S. Senate
He dashes off an essay about the race question	He lands on the Standard Oil Co.	He attends a banquet in New York
He superintends the preparations for Inauguration Day	He passes a hot message to the Senate	He pauses for a moment to make plans for a hunting trip

Mr. Roosevelt was devoted to his horses; he was a splendid rider—sat to the saddle perfectly—had easy control of his horse and enjoyed riding, as a sport and exercise, amazingly. It was his custom to go riding about every morning at ten o'clock and the madam rode with him. He never seemed so happy as when he was with Mrs. Roosevelt, and never happier than when they went out together on these morning rides which lasted usually a couple of hours. While at Washington, the President did a large amount of cross-country riding; in fact, he went regularly in the mornings. The landowners had given him the right of way to cross their fields and woods at will, and so he started out and jumped the fences and the little streams

91

and galloped over every obstacle. He had three fine jumpers down there, their names were Bleistein, Rusty and Ordgy. Bliestein was one of the finest jumpers in America. He had as much fun in getting over the high fences as the rider did—and that was a good deal. —*Ferdinand Iglehart*

One morning when we was starting out, Roosevelt's horse took a notion to buck a little, and threw Roosevelt three times. The last time, Roosevelt struck on his hand and throwed his thumb out of joint.

"You better change horses with me, Mr. Roosevelt," says I.

"No, Billy, by Godfrey," says he, pulling his thumb back into joint and showing his teeth as big as gravestones. "I've started out to teach this critter who is master," says he, "and I'm not a man to throw up a big job." —*Billy Hofer*, from a clipping in Edith Roosevelt's scrapbook

While I was dressing, I received a message from the White House saying that the President wanted to see me at one o'clock—so, as usual when such requests come, you wipe the slate clean and begin all over again.

It seems that the President had ordered his fine horse Roswell and had been told that it was out of commission, that it had been kicked. This was enough to put anyone in a fury, and had it happened to my horse I would have been in a fury and damned everyone connected with the stables. So from eleven to one I was somewhat nervous, as you may imagine, for I expected to see his Excellency in a real towering Napoleonic rage. On my arrival in Washington he had asked me to take charge of the stables, which, being in my line, I was glad to do. So I really felt responsible for the horses.

When I reached the White House, the President had just returned from the Lutheran or whatever church he attends and was in the barber's chair. He asked me to come in and to excuse the informality. Instead of being angry as I expected and as I should have been, he asked most gently how Roswell was kicked and said he was interested as he had no other animal to ride except an old plug of the orderly. I told him I had crawled the collar of every one at the stables and that I did not think anything like it would happen again.

"Well, I am glad you crawled their collars," he said....

He really was most polite, and I, who have been accustomed to see our military people fly off their heads for much less than this, was charmed at the simplicity of the President's kick. —*Archie Butt*

I was in Washington August 18, 1904, being then on the editorial staff of the *New York Tribune*. A boyhood chum of mine—I do not care to mention his name, as he is still in the Government service—met me and asked if I knew the President and could get him an interview.

I replied I knew William Loeb, the President's secretary, who told me to bring my friend to the White House. We went. There was a line of more than 100 people waiting. I sent my card in to Mr. Loeb, who came out in a few minutes and beckoned us to come in.

In his private office the President hurried to greet us and said to my friend—who was amateur boxing and wrestling champion of the District of Columbia: "You are the finest looking man in boxing togs I ever saw. Now tell me—how did you knock out [your opponent] that night I saw you at the club?"

"Why, Mr. President, it was a punch like this," he replied. He illustrated it in the air.

"Show it to me! Show it to me! Hit me on the chin as you hit him."

My friend did it, but softly. "No, no; that won't do. Hit me hard. Hit me the way you hit him."

My friend did it. He gave the President an awful punch in the jaw. "That's it, that's it. I've got it now," exclaimed the President delightedly. "Now let me try it on you."

He did. He hit my friend and sent him reeling.

"I've sure got it," the President said. "I'm going to try it tomorrow on Lodge and Garfield. Won't they squirm?" And the President laughed like a boy.

I said to him: "Mr. President, you've got the strongest back I ever saw."

"Yes, it is quite strong," he replied, immensely pleased.

Then I told him our errand. "Yes, I know all about you," he said to my friend. "No man in the service is more entitled to promotion than you. You shall have it tomorrow." We had been there an hour, talking and scuffling. I was scared for fear some Secret Service man might see us from the window.

I learned afterward that among the waiting crowd were a member of the firm of J. P. Morgan & Co.; General Boynton; one of the managers of the Associated Press; and several politicians of national fame, who wished to see the President about his campaign. —*Robert J. Mooney*

Colonel Roosevelt was a bit amazed and somewhat puzzled by the prominence given an incident one Monday morning after he had talked with a group of reporters at Jack Cooper's health farm, near Stamford, Connecticut, where he had gone to take off some surplus weight....

My notebook tells me that his story as to how he lost the use of the left eye was led up to by a question of the Colonel's as to a rumor about his being in poor health then going the rounds. "What do they say I have?" he inquired.

"Arteriosclerosis."

"Just what is that?"

"A hardening of the walls of the arteries—a loss of elasticity in the blood vessels."

"Well, on that definition they are right. I have had arteriosclerosis for a long time. Ever since I was about forty, I have had to cut out violent exercises one after the other until now there is nothing left except what a grandfather might expect....

"I used to like to box, but I had to stop when I hurt my left eye in the White House. You know it is blind; a loss, but not nearly as bad as if it were the right one. It happened this way: I was boxing with a naval officer, a husky chap and a cousin of Mrs. Roosevelt. He countered a hot one on the side of the head—right over the eye. One of the hardening arteries ruptured. Then the eye gradually began to film over. Soon all the sight was gone. That's how I lost it.

"So far as I know the officer never learned the result of his blow. To have told him would have only caused him to feel badly."
—*John J. Leary*

I propose to describe Theodore Roosevelt, the fighter, untrammeled by legal restriction, the lover of fistic encounter, as I know him; the man of brawn and muscle, with a genuine fighting spirit and the courage of two ordinary men to sustain its promise. I intend further to describe his methods of attack and defense, and to note the analogy between the spirit he exhibits in boxing and that which has urged him on in those political encounters which have made him famous.

A succession of glove-fights with him, covering a period of more than ten years, in which we have met as man to man, where it was give and take, with no restrictions, gives me the right to speak authoritatively, and I wish to say here that, whether or not he was champion of his class in college, about which there has been some discussion in the press, it is admitted that he was an able fighting man then, ready to take his medicine and try again.

I can say that he is the same man now, a man who asks no favors, cool in a fight, determined, aggressive, consumed with the purpose to overcome resistance, to win; a glutton for punishment, as the ring phrase goes. It is no exaggeration when I say that, in some mix-ups with him, I have been compelled to resort to all the arts and devices that have come to me from years of serious fighting, often to slug right and left to save myself....

I have a vivid recollection of my first fistic encounter with Theodore Roosevelt. The Governor left me in the old billiard-room of the Executive Mansion at Albany, which he had fitted up as a gymnasium for his boys, in order that they might begin their physical education under his eye.

He then went downstairs to don his boxing clothes.

In a few minutes he returned.

It was the Governor of the State of New York who had left me. It was a fighting man who entered the room. He wore a sleeveless flannel shirt, his khaki Rough Rider uniform trousers and light canvas shoes without heels. First, I was struck by the expression of his eyes, which are large, light blue, placed well apart, aggressive, fearless, persistent. He is about 5 feet 8 inches in height, but his great breadth of shoulders and bulk of body make him seem shorter. His arms are short, but heavy and well-muscled. His head is that of the typical fighter. It is broad and symmetrical, poised on a powerful neck. A plumb-line could be dropped from the back of his head to his waist. That formation shows not only the fighting spirit, but the physical vigor to sustain it. His short, thick body, with its high, arched chest, is sturdily set on unusually strong, sinewy legs.

I noticed he wore no belt, and told him he had better put one on. He borrowed one from my brother Jerry. After pulling on his gloves he stepped forward onto the mat.

Most men, on coming to box for the first time with a champion, present or retired, show some trepidation. There was none of that here. After we shook hands I studied him carefully. Then I led a left jab, following it up with a faint-hearted right that landed like a love-tap high up on his cheek. He dropped his hands and stopped.

"Look here, Mike," he said indignantly, "that is not fair."

I was afraid I had done something wrong. "What's the matter, Governor?" I asked.

"You are not hitting me," he said, shaking his head. "I'd like you to hit out."

"All right, Governor," I said, thinking to myself, This man has a pretty good opinion of himself.

We started in again, and I sent in a hard right to the body as he rushed in, and then tried a swinging left for the jaw. He stepped inside and drove his right to my ear. It jarred me down to the heels. I realized from that moment that the Governor was no ordinary amateur. If I took chances with him I was endangering my reputation.

From that day, I have taken no chances with Theodore Roosevelt with the gloves. I've hit him many times as hard as ever I hit a fighter in the ring, without stopping him, and thousands know how hard I can hit. I want to say, now, that I never saw him wince or show even by an involuntary sign that he was discomfited in spirit, no matter how severe the bodily pain. On the contrary, it met with only that characteristic turning of the head a bit to the side, a grim smile and a determined setting of the bulldog jaw, followed by another rush.

Roosevelt is a strong, tough man; hard to hurt, and harder to stop. —*Mike Donovan*

"The only game that I can't play," said the President, "is baseball. I must wear glasses, and I think I am afraid of only one thing—a baseball coming at me in the dark." —*Maurice Francis Egan*

[When Theodore Roosevelt and his dwindling party of explorers virtually were lost in the Brazilian wilderness, and almost out of provisions, TR developed a 105-degree fever. When not delirious, and with a serious leg wound, he considered suicide to lighten the party's load.]

I don't think any of us would have come out [from the Brazilian wilderness] had the Colonel not been with us. And yet the Colonel almost stayed there. There were a good many days, a good many mornings, when I looked at Colonel Roosevelt and said to myself, he won't be with us tonight; and I would say the same thing in the evening, he can't possibly live until morning. I can't speak of the others, but I know as far as Kermit and myself were concerned, the fact that the Colonel was with us gave us energy to do things we couldn't possibly have done otherwise....

Colonel Roosevelt called Kermit and me to him and said—he was unable to walk—he turned first to me and said, "Cherrie, I want you and Kermit to go ahead. We have reached the point where some of us must stop. I feel I am only a burden to the party." He was prepared to make the great sacrifice. It isn't necessary for me to say that both Kermit and I immediately said and did everything that was in our power—there wasn't a moment from that time forward that either Kermit or myself didn't watch the Colonel, to prevent him from carrying out what he felt was a necessity, that is, that he must relieve the party of what he considered a burden to the party. Thank God he came through.

During the night when we camped at the foot of the canyon, Kermit was on his watch, I could have reached the Colonel from my hammock. I had been dozing off, and was awakened with the murmur of voices, the Colonel and Kermit talking. The first thing I heard was the Colonel saying to Kermit, "Did Cherrie have a good dinner tonight?" As a matter of fact we hadn't had very much of anything. Kermit said, "Yes, father, Cherrie had a fine dinner."

"That is good," said the Colonel, and there the conversation dropped. —*George Cherrie*

Colonel Roosevelt told me about his serious illness in South America, and related one phase of it which I should not mention here if it were not for the fact that it has been referred to, and inexactly. It had to do with the Colonel's thought, at a time when his illness seemed likely to be fatal, of hastening the end by voluntary means. [In some accounts] the reason why the Colonel did not commit suicide was that he found he was likely to recover, and that all the party could get out. But the Colonel told it to me in quite a different way.

"I have always made it a practice on such trips," he said, "to take a bottle of morphine with me. Because one never knows what is going to happen, and I did not mean to be caught by some accident where I should have to die a lingering death. I always meant that, if at any time death became inevitable, I would have it over with at once, without going through a long-drawn-out agony from which death was the only relief.

"I have had a very full life, and am not at all afraid to die. As far as I, personally, am concerned, it would have meant nothing much, beyond the separation from my family, for that sickness in the jungle to terminate fatally. And when I found myself so ill that I was a drag on the party, and it began to look as if we could not all get out alive, I began to think it might be better for me to take my morphine and end it. I could not stand the thought that my illness was likely to keep Kermit in that jungle, too. His life was all before him. He was coming out to be married, and I could not endure the idea that because of my failure to keep up he might not make it, when without me he could.

"Then the other side of it came to me, and I saw that if I did end it, that would only make it more sure that Kermit would not get out. For I knew he would not abandon me, but would insist on bringing my body out, too. That, of course, would have been impossible. I knew his determination. So there was only one thing for me to do, and that was to come out myself. It was a hard fight, but I made it."

Colonel Roosevelt told me that quite naturally, and, I believe, without any thought whatsoever of self-exploitation. I know he was often accused of bragging about himself and his deeds, but in all I ever had to do with him there was never anything of that apparent. —O. K. Davis

Theodore Roosevelt in Popular Culture

James Earle Fraser, a pupil of Augustus Saint-Gaudens, designed iconic works like the Indian Head / Buffalo nickel, and End of the Trail, symbolizing the plight of Native Americans, of whom he was an early and ardent advocate. He designed the Theodore Roosevelt equestrian statue that stood at the entrance to American Museum of Natural History until it was removed for alleged racial insensitivity. The Roosevelt plaque was one of several bronzes he produced in honor of TR after the latter's death. For years many of them hung in school rooms, public buildings, and homes.

Cover Boy

Over the course of his career and beyond, between the early 1880s into the 1920s, Theodore Roosevelt appeared on hundreds of magazine covers—political journals; cartoon and commentary weeklies; children's magazines; literary journals; Christian magazines; academic and specialty publications; general-interest weeklies.

This issue of The Outlook, *the weekly Christian magazine of news and commentary, of which Theodore Roosevelt was Contributing Editor, appeared shortly after he was shot in the chest while campaigning for President, and shortly before the election. The words are from his March 1912 speech at Carnegie Hall in which he addressed his willingness to sacrifice himself for great causes.*

Toys and Games

TR inspired toymakers and doll manu-
facturers. His iconic, smiling teeth held
a harmonica in one; his famous pince
nez spectacles were used in a rolling-ball
game. The eternally beloved Teddy Bears
he inspired were not only plush toys and
dolls, but storybooks, and images on
toys, ceramics, and postcards.

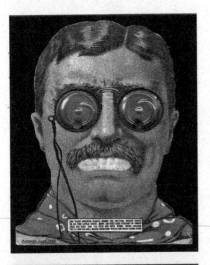

One of the original teddy bears atop
another of the many children's toys and
games inspired by TR. After a casual
newspaper cartoon referred to Roosevelt
sparing a bear while hunting, the public's
interest and sympathy grew to a sensa-
tion. A small toy shop in Brooklyn and
a major doll maker in Germany were
among many who manufactured the
beloved stuffed companions of generations of children.

"PROTECT AND PRESERVE THE REMAINING FORESTS UPON PUBLIC LANDS FROM DEVASTATION AND DESTRUCTION, WHICH HAVE BEEN THE FATE OF THOSE IN FOREST SECTIONS OF THE COUNTRY."

CHAPTER IV

Theodore Roosevelt: Conservationist

Throughout his life, TR had a passionate love affair with nature.
He revered the outdoors as God's handiwork, and "conservation
of natural resources" to him specifically meant managing the
environment, as a steward.

The previous chapter gathered the spiritual and physical connections Theodore Roosevelt had with nature, his devotion to natural history as one who communed with the outdoors and had scholarly interest in flora and fauna. With his heart, he loved the natural world; with his head and hands, he worked to preserve the environment. Many people commented on his passion, guile, and administrative prowess as he fulfilled his visions.

Beholding the beauty and expanse of Yosemite National Park; the grandeur of the Grand Canyon; the mysteries of Mesa Verde; the ancient discoveries in the Petrified Forest; the untamed denizens of birds and vegetation on Pelican Island; and at dozens of similar protected locations, many people are moved to consider these places as virtual holy grounds. It seems especially pertinent in this growing country, an industrialized society where "development" and exploitation subsume much...and are too often equated. Visitors may be moved to thank God for the wonders

He created. And they should silently thank Theodore Roosevelt, who did more than any other American to identify, protect, and preserve these lands and their species.

As a young boy, he had established an amateur's "Roosevelt Museum" in the family's New York City brownstone. He dutifully provided the museum with everything from detailed drawings to stuffed mice and birds. At Harvard, he gave serious consideration to declaring Natural History as his major course of study.

The protection of forests, waterways, wetlands, canyons, ancient lands, deserts, and mountains—as well as uncountable species of birds and animals—was more than the conceit of a vacationer or hunter, however. Hand in hand with protection was a type of preservation—"conservation"—that allowed for the sensible management of natural resources. Regulatory disciples of Roosevelt subsequently staffed agencies including the Forestry Service, the Bureau of Reclamation, the Fish and Wildlife Service, and the National Park Service. A balance largely has been maintained since Roosevelt's era between natural beauty and discreet use of rich resources. There has been a constant tug-of-war over logical priorities and choice, and there always will be, something that Roosevelt anticipated.

Statistics—cold numbers—help us appreciate the significance of Roosevelt's role in conservation. During his presidency, Theodore Roosevelt set aside 230 million acres under federal protection. Mathematically, that averages to eighty-four thousand acres a day during his term in office. Among these protected areas are 150 national forests, fifty-one federal bird reservations, four national game preserves, five national parks, eighteen national monuments, and twenty-four reclamation projects.

Roosevelt's chief lieutenants in his conservation work were Interior Secretary James R. Garfield and Chief Forester Gifford Pinchot. They were allies who subscribed to TR's precise choice of words: "Conservation of Natural Resources." While Roosevelt valued the heritage of open ranges, and even its opportunities for hunting as well as recreation, he understood the inevitability and importance of civilization's demands, such as farms and fences and the responsible management of water resources and old-forest underbrush.

Roosevelt likewise advocated the development of forestry lands, coal fields, and waterways; a growing nation required these things. He balanced exploitation with management: conservation, re-growth, and reclamation. More than replanting trees, he foresaw a national policy that would divert or dam rivers, reclaim land, and irrigate deserts. When Congress balked at further designations of parks, sanctuaries, and waterways, Roosevelt simply proclaimed them to be national monuments, over which he had authority to designate.

It was by this method that the Grand Canyon was preserved as it had always been, and as we know it today. The natural "wonder of the world," now a UNESCO World Heritage site, he managed to designate as a game preserve in 1906—whatever it took!—and a national monument in 1908. Only in 1919, three years after the National Park Service was formally established, did it become a National Park.

If average citizens and nature lovers (not to mention millions of animals and birds in their natural habitats) owe Theodore Roosevelt eternal gratitude, so do numerous families, farms, and towns, especially in the Southwest. Deserts bloomed and dry land became arable because of conservation. As managed development was an important component of conservation—even today, leases and lumber rights are granted on federal lands—the diversions of waterways, above and below ground, have changed the landscape of America.

There are more National Park Service units dedicated to Roosevelt's life and memory than to any other American. Fit and proper for the Conservation President.

"It is…vandalism wantonly to destroy or to permit the destruction of what is beautiful in nature, whether it be a cliff, a forest, or a species of mammal or bird. Here in the United States, we turn our rivers and streams into sewers and dumping-grounds, we pollute the air, we destroy forests, and exterminate fishes, birds, and mammals—not to speak of vulgarizing charming landscapes with hideous advertisements. But at last it looks as if our people were awakening." —*Theodore Roosevelt*

* * *

He was a very near-sighted boy and it was not until his fourteenth birthday that his father's gift of a pair of spectacles literally opened to him a new world of direct observation. At this time the veteran John G. Bell, a companion of Audubon, gave him his first lessons in preparing skins and in mounting birds. Thus...was prepared the little collection of the birds of Long Island now in the American Museum of Natural History collections. —*Dr. Henry Fairfield Osborn*

Once when we were walking Indian-file down a steep wood trail headed away from Sagamore Hill, he turned suddenly and said: "What book of mine do you like best?" And I answered without hesitation, for it had been running through my mind that very instant: "The foreword of your *Book-Lover's Holidays In the Open.*"

Then I quoted, as I often have in lectures: "The grandest scenery of the world is his to look at if he chooses; and he can witness the strange ways of tribes who have survived into an alien age from an immemorial past, tribes whose priests dance in honor of the serpent and worship the spirit of the wolf and the bear. Far and wide, all the continents are open to him as they never were to any of his forefathers; the Nile and the Paraguay are easy of access, and the border-land between savagery and civilization; and the veil of the past has been lifted so that he can dimly see how, in time immeasurably remote, his ancestors—no less remote—led furtive lives among uncouth and terrible beasts, whose kind has perished utterly from the face of the earth." —*William Beebe*

The President's nature-love is deep and abiding. Not every bird student succeeds in making the birds a part of his life. Not till you have long and sympathetic intercourse with them, in fact, not till you have loved them for their own sake, do they enter into and become a part of your life. —*John Burroughs*

[Many people are] not aware that Colonel Roosevelt's first love was natural history and not politics, and that it was only an untoward combination of circumstances that prevented him from embracing the career of a naturalist. —*John Augustine Zahm, CSC*, who provided the inspiration for Roosevelt's decision to explore the River of Doubt

Theodore Roosevelt lived during the period of ultra-microscopic specialization in the study of animate nature...The keenness of his observation, coupled with his intimate first-hand knowledge of nature, enabled him to recognize the necessity for field work and convinced him of the absolute need of museum specimens for exact studies of animals and plants.

" WHOA ! "

If his major interests had not been diverted into the time-consuming field of politics he would have been one of America's foremost naturalists. —*C. Hart Merriam*

The children had found a bird's nest on the ground, in the grass, a few yards below the front of the house. There were young birds in it, and as the President had seen the grasshopper sparrow about there, he concluded the nest belonged to it. We went down to investigate it, and found the young gone and two addled eggs in the nest. When the President saw those eggs, he said: "That is not the nest of the grasshopper sparrow, after all; those are the eggs of the song sparrow, though the nest is more like that of the vesper sparrow. The eggs of the grasshopper sparrow are much lighter in color—almost white, with brown specks." For my part, I had quite forgotten for the moment how the eggs of the little sparrow looked or differed in color from those of the song sparrow. But the President has so little to remember that he forgets none of these minor things! His bird-lore and wood-lore seem as fresh as if just learned. —*John Burroughs*

For his own sake he undoubtedly regretted the passing of the frontier, missed its presence in our national life, never forgot its haunting spell. The hold which it had upon him showed in the special feeling and cordiality with which he always welcomed the friends whom it had brought him, and also in his frequent returns to what was left of it when he took holidays in his middle years.

The Dakota chapter may be said to mark the close of his youth. Not spiritually; in that sense he was boy perpetual; it flashed out in him to the end. Not illness, not grief, neither fatigue nor chagrin could penetrate to this central place in him, although they could and did draw lines on his face, weaken his body, and at times darken the blazing cheerfulness of his mood and mind. —*Owen Wister*

Born observers are about as rare as born poets. Plenty of men can see straight and report straight what they see; but the men who see what others miss, who see quickly and surely, who have the detective eye, like Sherlock Holmes, who "get the drop," so to speak, on every object, who see minutely and who see whole, are rare indeed.

President Roosevelt comes as near fulfilling this ideal as any man I have known. His mind moves with wonderful celerity, and yet as an observer he is very cautious, jumps to no hasty conclusions. —*John Burroughs*

As a naturalist and lover of animals, his intimate knowledge was a surprise to all of those who were thrown in close contact with him. Time after time have I seen this illustrated, and never more strikingly than at my home at Pass Christian, where we found twenty-seven different varieties of bird nests in the yard, among which was that of a crested flycatcher. This bird had already hatched and with its young was in the yard. The Colonel asked whether I had ever made a careful examination of the nest of this bird, as he had never failed to find a snake skin in the hollow which they invariably select for their nest. My reply was, "No, but let's look at this one and see what's in it," and to his great delight when I pulled out the straws and feather[s], there were two snake skins.

When he made his trip around the various bird islands, men who were naturalists and who had known bird life for years were amazed at his intimate knowledge, not only of every species of birds which we found, but as to their nests, their habits, and even the number of eggs they laid.

He was a splendid woodsman, had an excellent knowledge of direction and was at his best in camp. There was not a single trip on which he did not endear himself to everyone, and his thoroughly democratic manner made these trips a pleasure to him and a delight to those who had the privilege of being a member of the party. —*John M. Parker*

He had just returned from England where Sir Edward Grey, the noted naturalist, had taken him on a long journey to a deep forest, where they had counted over forty different species of birds and heard at least two-thirds of them sing....

[Roosevelt recalled:] "On the evening of the first day I sat in my rocking-chair on the broad veranda, looking across the sound toward the glory of the sunset. The thickly grassed hillside sloped down in front of me to a belt of forest from which rose the golden, leisurely chiming of the wood thrushes, chanting their vespers; through the still air came the warble of vireo and tanager; and after nightfall we heard the flight song of an ovenbird from the same belt of timber. Overhead an oriole sang in the weeping elm, now and then breaking his song to scold like an overgrown wren. Song-sparrows and catbirds sang in the shrubbery; one robin had built its nest over the front and one over the back door, and there was a chippy's nest in the wisteria vine by the stoop. During the next twenty-four hours I saw and heard, either right around the house or while walking down to bathe, through the woods, forty-two birds." And then he gave the names of them. —*Ferdinand Iglehart*

The great spirit of Theodore Roosevelt, an inspiration to naturalists, bird-lovers, conservationists and sportsmen, today rests upon the nation like a mighty benediction. Men of the open loved him and the faces about his campfire, whether black or yellow, white or copper, bent their gaze upon him with that respect and affection which men of towering nobility have ever inspired.

He was a scientific collector of birds in his youth and in manhood sought the fiercest animals of the jungle and brought his trophies to museums where the public might look upon them, and learn. As President he established the principle of government bird-reservations and created thirty-eight of these national wild-life sanctuaries. He awoke the nation to the need of saving its forests and other natural resources.

He taught and practiced clean, straight sportsmanship with a power that has caused thousands of men afield to walk in straighter paths. He discussed questions understandingly with our greatest technical naturalists and at the same time was president of the Long Island Bird Club that feeds the wild birds in winter and teaches little children to love them.

The man or woman who is wedded to the open knows these facts and many others. It is because of this knowledge and of a desire to give some tangible expression of esteem in which his memory is held that the plan has been formed to erect at some appropriate spot a memorial that speaks of the wild birdlife in which Theodore Roosevelt was so deeply interested. —*The National Association of Audubon Societies*, 1919

CHAPTER V

The Importance of Family

"The life of the State rests and must ever rest upon the life of the family and the neighborhood."

The famously rugged and manly outdoorsman and hunter, cowboy and rancher, and amateur boxer and Police Commissioner of New York City frequently, in the latter role, roamed the streets of New York City's rougher districts at night. Always in the company of a newspaper reporter, their mission was to discover whether cops on the beat were truly on duty, or perhaps, as reported, malingering in saloons or soliciting bribes. Or were even more compromised.

Commissioner Roosevelt received a tip that members of criminal gangs were stalking him, certain they would catch him, and not the corrupt policemen, in embarrassing situations. His reporter friend, Jacob Riis, wrote that Roosevelt's first reaction was not anger but something between contempt and pity, almost drawing tears.

"What? And I, going home to my babies?" he asked, almost surprised that any other scenario was possible.

The anecdote is very revealing of Roosevelt—not only as a man without guile, but displaying the family man's tenderness, above and beyond probity and duty. He worked hard; he played hard; he required that his children follow his examples. Yet he was tender toward his wife and children, and all children, with an almost feminine regard, it was said, when affectionate care was appropriate. Into their adult years, the Roosevelt children invariably kissed their father good-night every evening.

TR did not live a double life which many prominent figures do even innocently. Occasionally a sort of public/private dichotomy naturally attends celebrities or busy professionals. With little pretense of saintliness, Roosevelt seemed to feel uncomfortable if temptations were upon him. What he called the "elemental values" were both private and public—integrity, honesty, justice, understanding, tenderness, and sympathy. Wisdom flows from such standards to the husband and father. When disciplining his children he demanded "the truth—first!" and then extenuating circumstances or explanations would follow. These generally are not the ways of the world, but it simply was the case with Theodore Roosevelt in the home, or on the world stage.

The Roosevelt family into which Theodore was born in 1858 were patricians. They were wealthy and prominent New Yorkers, but their ancestors first arrived on American shores around 1640, as ordinary as many of their fellow immigrants. Their bloodline was Holland Dutch (the Netherlands) and they planted themselves in New Amsterdam, almost literally where they disembarked. "Roosevelt" means "field of roses," and was spelled in various ways before "Roosevelt" became standard in their third American generation. It was pronounced by Theodore, as I was told by his daughter Alice, "ROSE-v'lt." TR himself wrote to a correspondent that the middle vowel "a" also could be pronounced. (It is surprising today that after almost one-fifth of the twentieth century having a Roosevelt in the presidency, in addition to so many other family distinctions, that otherwise informed Americans still pronounce it "Ruce-a-velt.")

TR's forebears were like thousands of other immigrants to the American continent: soon fairly comfortable, very industrious, and extremely determined. Unlike many others, they had not fled religious oppression nor racial discrimination in the Netherlands. They simply wanted to experience opportunity in the beautiful, abundant, welcoming New World. Claes Maartenszen van Rosevelt, the head of the family, possessed a pioneer spirit—a spirit that would be inherited by his descendant Theodore Roosevelt, who would be born in the very same Manhattan, at 28 East 20th Street, two centuries after the family's arrival in America.

The Roosevelts involved themselves in many businesses, first farming (Claes bought a fifty acre farm in what is now Midtown Manhattan, where the Empire State Building stands today), and ultimately the importation of glass. Later they spread their activities to banking and real-estate investment. The Roosevelts became a very wealthy family, though they never reached the heights of the famous Astor and Vanderbilt fortunes. Nevertheless they were "in society" with these families, and the Morgans and Whitneys. The Roosevelts were also famously generous, involved in many philanthropic endeavors and charities.

The father of President Roosevelt, as well as his son, were all named Theodore; and none bore middle names. This has caused confusion, if not outright consternation, among amateur historians and dedicated scholars. In custom, if not in law, "Junior" and "Senior" are used to indicate direct lineage and exact names (II and III indicate same names of members of different generations or, say, uncles or cousins). Complicating the Theodore Roosevelts under consideration is the fact that the world has welcomed TR IV and TR V as they have called themselves (or taken the nicknames pronounced TR Four and TR Five).

Within the family, formally and informally, the presidential Roosevelt's father was nicknamed Thee. The subject of this book was nicknamed Teedie as a child, and as noted preferred Theodore as an adult; his own son was called Ted within the family and among friends. Thee was among the founders of hospitals and orphan homes, the Museum of Natural History, and the Metropolitan Museum of Art. He was so identified with charitable work that a friend once said that when he saw Roosevelt walking toward him in the street, he spoke first and said, "All right, how much this time, Theodore?" while reaching for his checkbook.

Thee Roosevelt was remembered by his son TR as "the best man I ever knew." His marriage to "Mittie" Bulloch was the talk of Manhattan, as well as antebellum Georgia, where they married. Her family home, Bulloch Hall, which still stands in Roswell, is generally assumed to be the model for Tara in *Gone with the Wind*; and Mittie herself was said by friends of author Margaret Mitchell to be the inspiration for Melanie (certainly not Scarlett). After moving to New York City, Mrs. Theodore Roosevelt was widely regarded as a porcelain-skinned beauty, fragile yet determined, the essence of charm, an eccentric but gracious hostess and member of Society.

There were four Roosevelt children: Anna, the eldest, nicknamed Bamie (a diminutive of "Bambina," little girl) or Bye; Theodore ("Teedie," as noted, when he was a youngster); Elliott (father of Eleanor Roosevelt, who would later marry her distant cousin Franklin from another branch of the family); and Corinne ("Conie"). As in many families, the children had distinct, but also strong, personality traits. Bamie suffered through her life with a spinal malformation, requiring a brace or wheelchair. Many people assayed her sagacity and wisdom and declared that if women had been allowed to run for president, she would have been the first Roosevelt in the White House. Corinne was of a literary bent and became a prominent poet.

Teedie as a boy suffered from chronic *cholera morbus* and frequent, severe attacks of asthma. He often was carried in his father's arms at night when the boy scarcely could breathe or was driven in the family's sleigh through cold, crisp winter nights to inhale fresh air. The father built a gymnasium in half of a floor in the family's brownstone so that Teedie could "build his body as well as his mind."

Elliott, generally regarded as the most social and good-looking—Theodore the most intellectual—of the siblings, was close to Teedie and a frequent companion on hunting trips as they matured. But as Elliott aged, he exhibited symptoms that a few scattered Roosevelts have exhibited through the years and on far-flung branches of the family tree: indolence and alcoholism. He was more than a heartache of the family and an embarrassment in their "position." He had married well, the beautiful and dreamy Anna Hall, yet he mistreated her, drank to excess, and had illicit affairs. He died, practically a suicide, in the 1890s. With the fragile Anna dead too, their only child—Anna Eleanor—was frequently, but not exclusively, in Theodore's household. Eventually, after marrying a distant cousin, Franklin, she became a prominent First Lady of the United States.

The Roosevelt children practically worshiped their father and adored their mother. Theirs was an exceptionally happy childhood affected only by the two health-related factors. Mittie and her sisters (who lived in the Roosevelts' home) had relatives who were prominent in the Confederacy and for that reason, presumably, Theodore Senior did not serve in uniform. But after meeting with President Lincoln, he headed an Allotment

Bureau, traveling to soldiers' encampments, arranging for men to send portions of their military pay to families at home.

After a home education for the frail young Roosevelt, he was accepted by Harvard College. His father at this time was drawn into politics— actually a civil-service, not a political, position—nominated by President Hayes as Collector of the Port of New York. He was specifically charged with "cleaning the Augean stables" of the famously corrupt center of brib- ery and favoritism. New York's martinet of a senator, Republican Roscoe Conkling, generally disdained reformers, and took offense at not being consulted on the appointment. Also, a reformed Port of New York would threaten Conkling's elaborate apparatus of corruption and kickbacks. So he opposed the elder Roosevelt's nomination in the Senate.

Hayes was uncharacteristically adamant, so Conkling rallied fellow corruptibles and resorted to smearing Roosevelt's reputation. The con- troversy was grueling, the worst of gutter politics, and on a national scale. Ultimately, Roosevelt was not confirmed. A few weeks later he died, yet in his forties, of intestinal cancer that might have been exacerbated by the humiliating trial.

TR was at Harvard at the time, not aware of the severity of the politi- cal rhubarb; and unable to be at his father's side as he rapidly slipped away from an aggressive cancer. He was devastated. He afterward wrote in his diary, "Nothing but my faith in the Lord Jesus Christ could have carried me through this, my terrible time of trial and sorrow."

He also had met a beautiful seventeen-year-old, Alice Hathaway Lee, a society blue-blood of Chestnut Hill. Roosevelt immediately fell in love, pointed to her across the room and told a friend that she would be his wife someday. Some day was not immediately coming, but Alice relented and they married on his birthday, two years later, in 1880. Their honeymoon was in Europe. A doctor had warned the still-fragile Roos- evelt not to attempt any strenuous activity…so, naturally, he climbed the Matterhorn.

Roosevelt the new family man and his bride Alice established them- selves in Manhattan. He worked on his massive history, *The Naval War of 1812*, and surprised not a few family members and people in his social set by deciding to run for the New York State Assembly. Politics, even Republican politics of the era, especially of the relatively local variety much less the national turmoil such as his father endured, was not regarded as a profession for respectable men. He was elected, and re-elected, and was assessed almost immediately as a rising star, nominated for Speaker and chosen as Minority Leader.

In February 1884, Roosevelt received a telegram on the Assembly floor that Alice was delivering their child. His train raced through a snowstorm to Manhattan and he was met at the door with the news that "Alice is dying. Mother is dying too." Alice delivered a daughter but died of Bright's disease in Theodore's arms. Only hours earlier, his mother, downstairs, had died of typhoid fever, unrelated. "There is a curse on this house," he murmured.

The double funeral was attended by hordes of New Yorkers—Roosevelt in the front pew, almost insensate. Subsequently, he returned to his work at the Assembly in voluminous fury; he attended the Republican National Convention, a leader of the New York delegation. Despite his young age, twenty-six, he was a major figure, advocating reforms and successfully managing the election of a Black Mississippian, John Lynch, as temporary Convention Chair. Then, he faced his future.

Roosevelt previously had visited hunting grounds in the Dakota Territory, and he decided to change course and become a rancher. He persuaded guides he had met in Maine to be his managers, and he purchased large herds of Texas Longhorns. He claimed two tracts of land near the small town of Medora, and built cabins. Bamie had offered to rear "Baby Alice" back in New York. History's verdict can never be rendered, but despite his dreams of a new career, it can be assumed that Roosevelt, even subconsciously, was determined to lick his wounds, commune with nature, and build his body. He joined his cowboys on round-ups and sometimes rode the Badlands ranges for forty hours at a time. And he restored his equilibrium.

Circumstances dictated some of his next courses. Two years after Alice's death, he encountered his childhood sweetheart, Edith Carow, on a visit to New York. Unknown to her friends Bamie and Corinne, a romance blossomed. They married, in London, in 1886, and they moved into the estate that previously had been started in Oyster Bay, Long Island.

In short order, Theodore Roosevelt became quite the family man. "Baby Alice" soon was joined by another Theodore, Kermit, Ethel, Archie, and Quentin. The children of TR and Edith could be obstreperous—to the delight of reporters and cartoonists—but the chaos ultimately was managed. There were many stories: once, when Archie was sick in bed, his siblings secreted his pony Algonquin up on the White House elevator to his bedroom. Another time Quentin, the youngest of the children, was cornered by a nosy reporter seeking news about the president. The boy replied, "I see him occasionally, but I know nothing of his family life."

TR seldom missed his afternoon romps with the children. Every year at Sagamore Hill he would play Santa Claus for the village children, and he hosted fireworks and picnics on the Fourth of July. Roosevelt frequently took his children, their cousins, and village friends on camping trips, which invariably included impromptu ghost stories around campfires, told with great theatrics by the President of the United States.

Of course, all this was assisted by the fact that TR himself was still a child in many ways. Edith frequently said so, with a sigh. "You must remember," said Cecil Spring-Rice, the British diplomat who was best man at TR's second wedding, "the President is about six." When Roosevelt was fifty-four and planned a trip into the Brazilian Wilderness—where he charted a major, previously unknown river and almost died in the process—he dismissed warnings, saying it was his "last chance to be a boy."

TR's children all were gifted and interesting in their own rights, but Alice was famously independent and was America's sweetheart in her early White House years. She was beautiful and rebellious; she smoked, rode in automobiles to parties, and fell into fountains while galivanting with friends. TR once said while president, "I can run the country, or I can control Alice. I cannot possibly do both."

At the other end of the spectrum of siblings was Quentin, whose group of friends included Charlie Taft, son of the Secretary of War, and boys from the local public school Quentin attended. They dubbed themselves the White House Gang. In a solemn ceremony, they once voted the President of the United States an honorary member. It was the least they could do for a President who once, riding in a carriage through Washington, spotted the boys and made wild and silly faces for all to see.

The Roosevelt boys—even Ethel and her husband—volunteered to fight in World War I. Ted and Archie were seriously wounded; they and Kermit were decorated. Quentin, a pioneer aviator, was killed in a dogfight over the German lines. The eldest, Theodore, was the mover behind the establishment of the American Legion after the war. In World War

II, he rejoined the Army, and as a Brigadier General, landed on D-Day at Normandy. He was the oldest soldier and the only general on the beaches, and, with his son Quentin in the assault force too, they were the only father-and-son military members in the historic engagement.

After Gen. Roosevelt's honors were bestowed, adding to his Great War medals, he became the most decorated soldier in US Army history at the time. And when TR's Medal of Honor from the Spanish-American War was belatedly awarded, the two Theodores became the first father-and-son recipients of that honor.

Already gravely ill when he directed landing troops at Normandy, Gen. Roosevelt died of a heart attack only weeks later. His pallbearers included the generals George S. Patton and Omar Bradley. It is hard to imagine that the Family Man Roosevelt could have been any prouder of his "babies."

In Theodore Roosevelt's *Autobiography*, rather hastily written in the aftermath of the unsuccessful Bull Moose campaign (and therefore having the strong flavor of a campaign document), the standout chapter, different in tone from the rest of the book, was his proud celebration of family life, his family, and their activities. It is clear, as he maintained, that no accomplishment in life is, or should be, as satisfying as that of a husband and father who is justly proud of his family.

* * *

I wonder whether birds and children and home did not have a deeper interest for Roosevelt than soldiering or pioneering or statesmanship? After all is said and done, should not the final estimate be that he was, not a literary man, not a political man, not a military man, but a homely man? —*Lawrence F. Abbott*

"To Theodore Roosevelt" (Christmas Eve, 1902)

Son of a sire whose heart beat ever true
    To God, to country and the fireside love
    To which returning, like a homing dove,
From each high duty done, he gladly flew.
Complete, yet touched by genius through and through,
    The lofty qualities that made him great,
    Loved in his home and priceless to the state.
By heaven's grace are garnered up in you.

Be yours—we pray—the dauntless heart of youth,
The eye to see the humor of the game—
The scorn of lies, the large Batavian mirth;
And—past the happy, fruitful years of fame,
Of sport and work and battle for the truth,
A home not all unlike your home on earth.

—*John Hay*, 1902

We were always up for breakfast together. Half-past eight was the regular breakfast time, though sometimes it was as early as quarter-past seven if some [guest] had to take the first train to town. Father was always in particular good spirits in the morning, and there was as much talk and fun when there was just the family together at breakfast or any other meal as when there were guests eager to talk with him or hear him talk. —*Alice Roosevelt Longworth*

The day begins at exactly 8:30 at the White House. The President himself pours the coffee at breakfast. It is one of his privileges, and he looks fine as host.... Oatmeal, eggs and bacon, coffee and rolls—one morning's menu. I don't think they would object to my telling, and I like to think that in thousands of homes all over our land they are sharing the President's breakfast, as it were. It brings us all so much nearer together, and that is where we belong.

From breakfast to luncheon the President is in his office, seeing the people who come from everywhere to shake hands, or with messages for the Chief Magistrate. Along in the afternoon the horses are brought up and the President goes riding with Mrs. Roosevelt or alone. —*Jacob Riis*

I noticed that he always took between five and seven lumps of sugar in his coffee, and I bethought me of the hummingbird which lives on sweets, and is one of the most strenuously active of vertebrates. —*Richard Henry Dana III*

[Theodore Roosevelt] used to say that a man who professes to love all other families as much as he loves his own is likely not only to be a failure as a husband and father but also to be an undesirable neighbor. "Keep your eye on such a man," he once remarked; "he is not only foolish, but he is liable to be dangerous. —*Lawrence F. Abbott*

Roosevelt had no patience with the communistic vagaries of the French revolutionary philosophers. While socially and economically he was much more democratic than Hamilton or even, I venture to think, than Washington, he liked them better and trusted them more than Jefferson because of Jefferson's flirtations with the unpractical and closet idealists of the First French Republic. —*Lawrence F. Abbott*

No matter how great the pressure of public duties, or how severe the strain that the trials and burdens of office placed upon the nerves and spirits of the President of a great nation, this devoted father and whole-hearted companion found time to send, every week, a long letter of delightful character to each of his absent children. —*Joseph Bucklin Bishop*

When they were little, the Roosevelt boys and girls went to the Cove School, which is the public school of the district, where the children of the gardener and the groom go, as well as those of their employers if they live there in the school season. Now, in Washington, the Roosevelts follow the same plan. The public school first, as far as it will carry the children to advantage, thereafter the further training for college. It is the thoroughly sound and sensible way in which they do all things in the Sagamore Hill family. So only can we get a grip on the real life we all have to live in a democracy of which, when all is said and done, the public school is the main prop. So, and in no other way, can we hold the school to account, and so do we fight from the very start the class spirit that is the arch enemy of the republic. —*Jacob Riis*

At Sagamore Hill he is the American gentleman in his country home. The place is three miles from the station, upon a height reached by a long, winding drive leading from the high road. The house, which has a lawn and trees about it, and has a view over Long Island Sound, is a very American-looking structure of red brick and gray painted wood. It is not at all an "imposing" residence, although that other word, "rambling," which is so much used in describing houses, may with justice be applied to it. It is a house which, from the outside, does not look nearly so spacious as it actually is.

Through the center of it runs a wide, dark hall, to the right of which, near the front door, is the library, or rather the room which Colonel Roosevelt uses as an office, for it is improper to refer to any especial room at Sagamore Hill as a library, since all are filled with books. This room is a small museum. There are animal skins upon the floor and mounted heads of animals upon the walls. Among the pictures on the walls are a portrait of Mrs. Roosevelt, one of Colonel Roosevelt's father, and others of Lincoln, Washington, and Daniel Boone. Also there is the bronze cougar, by Alexander Proctor, which was presented to the colonel by his famous "Tennis Cabinet," and a bronze cowboy, by Frederic Remington.

Even more like a museum than the library is the great living room which has been added of late years, at the end of the hall. It is a very large room two stories high, with a trilateral ceiling and wainscoting of wood in a pleasing shade of light brown, oiled but not polished. Large as this room is, and rich as it is in trophies and souvenirs of all sorts, its finest quality is its freedom from seeming imposing. It is not in any way magnificent or austere, yet it is a very handsome, dignified room, with the kind of handsomeness which does not smite the eye nor overpower the senses, but which, on the other hand, makes the stranger feel welcome and at ease, and tells him that he is in the home of a prosperous but simple and cultivated American family.
—*Julian Street*

[Eleanor Alexander, TR's daughter-in-law, wife of Ted], came to Sagamore for the summer, bringing her baby Grace. For the Colonel and his wife, having their first grandchild in the house for months on end was an experience that made a presidential candidacy seem so secondary as to be in the nature of an impertinent periodic interruption.

She had not been at Sagamore twenty-four hours before she recognized that nothing in her bringing-up had remotely prepared her for the furious activity into which she was plunged. "Something was going on every minute of the day," she wrote some fifteen years later. "The house was always full of people. They came by ones, by twos, and by tens. All day long, conferences were held in every room downstairs. The telephone never stopped ringing. A car full of newspapermen was always in the offing."

Her first day at Sagamore she panted for the night as the hart panteth for the water-brooks. Surely, after all this activity everyone would be glad to go to bed early. Nothing could have been farther from the reality. "The Roosevelt family enjoyed life far too much to be willing to waste time sleeping. Every night they stayed downstairs until midnight; then, talking at the tops of their voices, they trooped up the wide, uncarpeted oak staircase and went to their rooms. For a brief ten minutes all was still; and, just as I was dropping off to sleep for the second time, they remembered things they had forgotten to tell each other and rushed shouting through the halls. I used to go to bed with cotton in my ears, but it never did any good."

The first night she found consolation in the assurance that no one was likely to wake up before eight at the earliest. "That won't be so bad." Eight? By six, the younger ones were up, and by seven, "I was the only one who was not joyously beginning the day."

One morning, "a boiling hot day," she described it, her father-in-law at breakfast proposed a picnic. Everyone was enthusiastic, including Eleanor. She liked picnics—the cold chicken, the lemonade, the lettuce sandwiches and other delectables, wrapped in waxed paper. It would be pleasant on so blisteringly hot a day to have lunch outdoors in the cool shade of some big tree, not too far away, and easily reached.

She found shortly, however, that the Roosevelts had ideas about picnics which bore no relation to hers. The provisions were plentiful but consisted of a large basket of clams, another of thick ham sandwiches and a demijohn of water.

By ten o'clock a dozen friends and cousins had gathered at the house. Carrying the supplies, they walked the half-mile through the woods to the beach at a pace that seemed to Eleanor uncalled for, until the mosquitoes started operations. The mosquitoes in those woods were "as big as bats," she remembered.

On the beach were five rowboats, two of them more desirable than the rest, since, in the stern, they had comfortable back supports. Eleanor waited for someone to suggest that her place was in one of those, but no one spoke. Subsequently, she learned that she should have run ahead, leapt into one of the boats with back supports, and held it against all comers. At Sagamore picnics it was everyone for himself and the Devil take the hindmost. Eleanor finally found a place, squeezed between the basket of clams and the demijohn.

"Under the blazing sun, we rowed and rowed. There was not a vestige of breeze; the Sound was as calm as glass. By and by I began pointing out places where we might stop, but they were all declared quite unsuitable and far less attractive than the spot to which we were going. Some two hours later, we landed on a beach precisely like the one from which we had started, except that it was farther from home.

There was not the least shade. Because of the poison ivy we could not go near the trees."

A roaring fire raised the temperature to heights that no one dared measure. "When the clams were judged ready, my father-in-law selected one, opened it, sprinkled it with pepper and salt and handed it to me. It was very large and had a long neck." By a valiant effort she managed to get all of it in her mouth. "At first, although gritty with sand, it was delicious; but that soon wore off and it became like a piece of old rubber hose."

Eleanor looked around. Everybody else was consuming large quantities of the clams. How did they do it? The more she chewed, the larger the clam seemed to get. This was dreadful; this might go on forever. Surreptitiously, she slipped the clam under a log.

"You're not as persistent as Archie was when he was small," remarked her father-in-law, who had observed her desperate strata- gem. "The first time he ate a clam on a picnic, he chewed for a time, then ate three sandwiches, half a dozen cookies and an orange. About half an hour later he came to me and asked me what he should do with the poor little dead clam. It was still in his mouth!"

As the party was packing up to go home, a head wind sprang up. The two-hour row of the morning was a five-hour row back. "Faces and necks were burned to a crisp; hands were blistered. My father-in- law had a difficult time reaching shore at all as the boat in which he was rowing my mother-in-law began to leak badly. In spite of it all, everybody considered that the picnic had been a great and glorious success." —*Eleanor Alexander Roosevelt*, as per Hermann Hagedorn

The Chinese have a saying that the host is the servant of his guests as long as they remain in his household, and that was the spirit that guided the President and Mrs. Roosevelt while we were with them. Their consideration for our pleasure and comfort was exquisite. When Mrs. Turner and I were ready to retire at night, the President and Mrs. Roosevelt, the former with a lighted candle, always accompanied us to the door of our chamber and there bade us "Good Night." —*George Turner*

His respect for women was profound. He appreciated their position and influence in the world as few men do. He was clean of speech, and his life was clean and moral. He abhorred, above all, suggestive speech, loose living, and immorality. —*Leonard Wood*

One of his remarks I well remember: "The Salvation Army has won my highest admiration for its teaching of the love of home and the sacredness of family ties." I replied: "Your loyalty, Mr. Roosevelt, to the letter and the spirit of home life has made a very strong appeal to our ranks." —*Commander Evangeline Booth*

A man's general attitude toward his fellow beings can be pretty well determined if you can find out what he thinks of children and how he treats them. What Roosevelt thought of children and family life is expressed in this paragraph from his autobiography: "There are many kinds of success in life worth having. It is exceedingly interesting and attractive to be a successful businessman, or railroad man, or farmer, or a successful lawyer, or doctor, or a writer, or a president, or a ranchman, or the colonel of a fighting regiment, or to kill grizzly bears and lions. But for unflagging interest and enjoyment, a household of children, if things go reasonably well, certainly makes all other forms of success and achievement lose their importance by comparison." —*Lawrence F. Abbott*

Sexual crimes sickened Roosevelt. Rape he thought worse than murder. When raids were made on disorderly houses during his police commissioner days, the men were jailed along with the women. [He supported legislation] that provided corporal punishment for white slavers. —*Edward Wagenknecht*

"Hide and Seek" with Father was played [at Sagamore Hill] on gray rainy days, or at dusk; all that he had to do was go to the gun room or one of the other rooms on the third floor, and when we approached in our search he would moan or growl, whereat we would scuttle away downstairs again in a state of delighted terror. He used to say that it was the most restful game for him that he could possibly imagine. —*Alice Roosevelt Longworth*

Soon after the Roosevelts took up their residence at the White House a fawning society woman asked one of the younger boys if he did not dislike the "common boys" he met at the public schools. The boy looked at her in wonderment for a moment and then replied:

"My papa says there are only tall boys and short boys and good boys and bad boys, and that's all the kind of boys there are."
—*Carleton Case*

The great day is when he goes camping with the Sagamore Hill boys and their cousins whose summer homes are near, and who plan it for months ahead. A secluded spot alongshore is chosen, with good water and a nice sand beach handy, and the expedition sets out with due secrecy, the White House guardsmen being left behind to checkmate the reporters and the camera fiends. Mr. Roosevelt is sailing-master and chief of the jolly band. Along in the afternoon they reach their hiding-place; then bait and fishing-poles are got ready—for they are real campers-out, not make-believes, and though they have grub on board, fish they must. When they have caught enough, the boys bring wood and build a fire. The President rolls up his sleeves and turns cook.

"Um-m!" says Archie; "you oughter taste my father's beefsteak! He tumbles them all in together, —meat, onions, and potatoes, — but, um-m! it is good." I warrant it is, and that they eat their fill!
—*Jacob Riis*

[After supper the President told the young boys] stories of big game out West, of mountain lions and grizzly bears, while the little fellows watched the shadows around them. One night they heard a fox barking in the woods, which thrilled them through and through, and they discussed the chance of seeing him in the morning. And sure enough they saw him running along the shore while they and the President were in for their early swim. —*James Morgan*

I remember one day [when President Roosevelt and Leonard Wood led children on a romp through Washington's Rock Creek Park] one of my own youngsters running up to me and in great excitement saying: "The father of all the children has fallen into the water!" I rushed back to the edge of a deep pool in which Mr. Roosevelt was piloting the children by climbing along a fallen tree. During the process he had fallen in, to the great excitement and amusement of the youngsters. —*Leonard Wood*

It was the privilege of Mr. Roosevelt, when he was nearer home, to give the children at the Cove School their Christmas gifts, and the memory of those occasions is very lively in Oyster Bay. Mr. Roosevelt made a good Santa Claus, never better than when he was just home from the war, with San Juan Hill for a background. That time he nearly took the boys' breath away. Nowadays someone else has to take his place; the gifts come, as in the past, and the little "coves" are made happy.

[Now, as President, he] comes into their lives only twice or three times a year—at Christmas and when he comes home for his vacation; perhaps on the Fourth of July. Mrs. Roosevelt is part of it all the time, and a very lovely, because a loving, part of life in the little village. When I hear of her going about among its people, their friend and neighbor in the true sense, I think of her husband's father, the elder Theodore, who systematically took one day out of six for personal visitation among his poor friends; and how near they, both he and she, have come to the mark which the rest of us go all around and miss with such prodigious toil and trouble. Neighborliness—that covers the ground. It is all that is needed. —*Jacob Riis*

I dined with the Olivers last night and Ethel Roosevelt was there. She told me that her father had read a letter out to them all at the table that he had written to [Joel Chandler] Harris [*author of the Uncle Remus stories and influential editor of* The Atlanta Constitution] about the "Battle Hymn of the Republic..."

She said her father had also written a private note to Uncle Remus to publish his letter in his magazine if he thought it worth it. He discusses a lot of things with his children, so Mrs. R. says, mentioning only those things which he thinks will do them good or which he thinks they ought to know.

> *Mine eyes have seen the glory of the coming of the Lord;*
> *He is trampling out the vintage where the grapes of wrath*
>   *are stored;*
> *He hath loosed the awful lightning of His terrible swift sword:*
> *His truth is marching on.*

TR hoped that this officially would become America's National Anthem. —*Archie Butt*

Mr. Roosevelt took the keenest delight in acting as Kris Kringle each Christmas time at the Cove School. All through public life, Theodore Roosevelt never lost sight of School No. 10 at Oyster Bay where his two sons, Archibald Bulloch Roosevelt and Kermit Carow Roosevelt took the elementary steps of their education. Theodore, Jr., also learned his A B C's at Cove School. —*Albert Loren Cheney*

I was very hungry and enjoyed my dinner, being helped twice to nearly everything. We had soup, fish, fried chicken, and corn on the cob, and jelly. There was nothing to drink but water. The President asked me if I would have something, but as it was not the custom I declined....

I was much interested in meeting the family in this way and never saw less restraint than at the President's table. Every child has something to say, and when one makes a remark it is certain to bring forth a volley of denials or contemptuous rebuttals from the others. In fact, there was nothing studied or formal, and every member came in for a little fun before the dinner was over. Even the guests did not escape. —*Archie Butt*

[Theodore Roosevelt was famously bad at finances, sometimes concerning national economics, but even to family budgets and pocket change...which Edith usually parceled out to him. In a minor way, Sagamore Hill was a working farm, as this story illustrates.]

Questions of [TR's] own finances or private business never entered Mr. Roosevelt's mind. He simply signed the checks and Mrs. Roosevelt or his secretaries did the rest.

A shrewd local tradesman was seen coming from Sagamore Hill one day, seated on a big load of hay. A fellow townsman asked him if he had driven a sharp bargain with Mr. Roosevelt.

"Roosevelt, me eye!" replied the man, and added: "I bought this hay from Mrs. Roosevelt, and gave her more than the market value because she's a mighty fine woman!" —*Albert Loren Cheney*

When his children saw their father after a separation they would pat him on the shoulder as they passed him in the room, and he would detain them a moment to hold their hands.

"I must talk that over with Edith and Alice," was his frequent reply when some personal matter was up for his consideration. "They have such good judgment." —*Hermann Hagedorn*

At the last cabinet meeting under the Theodore Roosevelt regime, the children of the cabinet officers were invited, and I was there. I was not a small child; I was at prep school, about sixteen—but there were two very small children there. We all came in and were shown to our fathers' cabinet chairs, and we all sat in them, and TR sat at the head, in his chair.

And then he went and shook hands with each of us, and finally to the two small ones. There were American Beauty roses on the desk nearby outside the table—and he took one rose, and took each thorn off it before he gave it to the child so that the child, in getting the rose, would not be hurt by the thorns.

It seemed to me that that was typical of him—that strong man who was known for his strenuous life—his kindness and consideration for people. —*Roger Williams Straus*

He always ate a light breakfast and one of his favorite dishes was peaches and cream. This he liked in abundance. I have a plate at home in which Mr. Roosevelt used to have his peaches and cream served. It's a good, generous dish, about the size of an ordinary soup plate. And his idea of a dish of peaches and cream was this plate well piled up with the fruit. His lunch was always quite light. But at dinner he was always very hungry and he enjoyed that meal immensely.

After dinner he liked mints. There was always a dish of them on the table and Mr. Roosevelt would nibble at these when he was through eating. He was also fond of ginger snaps. When he played tennis—which he did almost every evening—he and his guests would always adjourn to the White House where ginger-snaps and orangeade would be served. —*James Amos*

It rained all the morning, but that did not prevent us from going in swimming and playing tennis. We started off with a good breakfast and everyone was keen for it. Peaches and cream, handed twice, and fried liver and bacon, and, strange as it may seem, hominy, served as we serve it in the South. Not big hominy but grits, as they call it in the North.

"Why, Mr. President," I exclaimed, "this is a Southern breakfast. I have never seen hominy served anywhere out of the South in this way before."

"What did I tell you, Edith? Yes, it is just the breakfast my mother always had, varied as to the meats, of course. I have the hardest time with most of my guests, who usually want to eat the hominy with sugar and cream, and some think it a fruit. We eat it just as you do in the South with salt and butter and nothing more."

The President has his own coffee pot and slop bowl and cream pitcher and sugar. I think it is a complete set in itself. Mrs. Roosevelt says that it is next to impossible to get his coffee to suit him, and as he is a great coffee drinker, she provided him with a service of his own, and if the coffee is not right he has no one to blame but himself. He drinks several cups at his breakfast and makes each one a matter of great formality. It is really interesting to see how much pleasure he gets out of it.

I note with some hesitancy to speak of it that the President is a good eater. You think me a large eater; well, I am small in comparison to him. But he has a tremendous body and really enjoys each mouthful. I never saw anyone with a more wholesome appetite, and then he complains of not losing flesh. I felt like asking him to-day: "How can you expect to?" He does not smoke, and the time when other men take to the weed he gets the papers and magazines and for about ten minutes is absorbed in them. —*Archie Butt*

The children came to his car to take him to church, and when the people had all been seated two little girls for whom there was no room stood by his pew. He took them in and shared his hymn-book with them, and the three sang together, they with their clear girlish voices, he with his deep bass. They were not afraid or embarrassed; he was just their big brother for the time. And there was the tenderness in his voice I love to hear as he told me of them.

"You should have seen their innocent little faces. They were so dainty and clean in their starched dresses, with their yellow braids straight down their backs. And they thanked me so sweetly for sharing the book with them that it was a hardship not to catch them up in one's arms and hug them then and there." —*Jacob Riis*

Colonel Roosevelt sat for two hours at the elbow of Justice Hoyt in Children's Court, New York, heard the cases, and acted as unofficial consulting Justice. Once, leaning over, he whispered to a youngster, "It's all right this time, sonny. You're all right. But remember, don't do it again, or he'll send you away! He'll send you away!" And again, after hearing how some other juvenile malefactor of little wealth had made full restitution to the pushcart man or somebody, the Roosevelt fist thumped the arm of the chair, with "That's a fine boy! That kind make first-rate citizens!" —*Newspaper clipping, 1917*

Their country place at Oyster Bay swarmed with all kinds of strange pets. A little girl out in Kansas threw a live badger on the platform of the President's car, and he brought the queer thing home for his children. They had a lot of fun with him in spite of his habit of biting their bare legs. First and last they had such playfellows as a lion, a hyena, a wild-cat, a coyote, two big parrots, five bears, an eagle, a barn owl, several snakes and lizards, a zebra which the Emperor of Abyssinia sent them, kangaroo-rats and flying squirrels, rabbits, and guinea-pigs.

Many of these animals and reptiles were thrust upon the family as gifts, and after a time were added to the public zoological collection in New York. The kangaroo-rats and flying squirrels slept in the pockets and blouses of the children, whence they sometimes made unexpected appearances at the breakfast and dinner tables or in school. —*Carleton Case*

At Oyster Bay he usually wears an olive-drab suit with knicker-bockers, and golf stockings, and though he is a most hospitable and

tactful host, one feels that when the guests have gone he will welcome the opportunity to go tramping off through the woods with Mrs. Roosevelt or to take her rowing in the skiff.

Without Mrs. Roosevelt the house at Sagamore Hill would be as imperfect as without the Colonel. She is a woman of the greatest charm and tact—precisely the kind of woman to be the wife of a public man, precisely the kind of woman who so seldom is. She makes everyone who comes to Sagamore Hill feel instantly at ease, and she has the gracious faculty for seeming to know about and be genuinely interested in the people whom she meets, instead of wishing them to know about and be interested in her. —*Julian Street*

It is easy to imagine the atmosphere in which his own children were brought up in the family homestead. Sagamore Hill, at Oyster Bay. They swam, rowed, went barefoot, or camped in the woods or on the beach of Long Island Sound. They learned to shoot—for there was a rifle-range at Sagamore Hill. They made pets of the various animals on the home farm in the summer, and they coasted and skated in the winter. In this bringing up of the children in the vigor of outdoor life Mrs. Roosevelt was an active partner. —*Lawrence F. Abbott*

Mr. Roosevelt had an experience with a dog while on a bear hunt in Colorado. A little black and tan in the hunting pack picked him as his favorite. Skip would run forty miles a day on the chase but liked best a front seat on the President's horse. At night he would sleep on the foot of his bed, and growl defiance at anybody and anything that came near.

"I grew attached to the friendly, bright littler fellow, and at the end of the hunt I brought him home as a playmate for the children." Some of Skip's new companions at Oyster Bay bore names far more imposing than his. There was a black bear with an uncertain temper whom the children had named Jonathan Edwards in honor of the famous divine, who was an ancestor of their mother. There were guinea-pigs who bore names in compliment to Bishop Doane of Albany; Father O'Grady, a neighboring priest; Dr. Johnson; Fighting Bob Evans; and Admiral Dewey.

A distinguished man, who was calling on the President, did not understand this custom, and therefore was bewildered to hear one of the children rush in and breathlessly report, "Oh, oh! Father O'Grady just had children!" —*Hermann Hagedorn*

Perhaps the most honored representative of the animal kingdom at Oyster Bay was Algonquin, a little calico pony from far-away Iceland, which Secretary Hitchcock gave to Archie. Skip, as well as Archie, delighted to ride Algonquin....

Once when Archie was sick in the White House...the stable boys were sure that if the invalid could have a visit from the pony, it would do him more good than medicine. They conspired together, secretly smuggled him into the basement and into the elevator, and thus carried him up to the sick-room, to the unbounded joy of the patient. —*Newspaper clipping*

A family point of view that I ignored was about smoking, though they never actually ordered me not to smoke. They began by requesting that I not smoke "under their roof." Whereat I smoked on the roof, up the chimney, out of doors, and in other houses. Then I was told not to smoke in their presence, and even that lapsed, and I puffed away when and where I pleased except in public.

Many years later at Sagamore Hill, Father once said, "Alice, perhaps I ought to have been firmer with you about smoking." I replied, "Father darling, it would have done no good." —*Alice Roosevelt Longworth*

In 1916–1917 [TR] wrote, and published anonymously in *The Ladies' Home Journal*, a department called "Men" in which he discussed such problems as how a father should behave the first time a young man came to call on his daughter. I know of no more cogent testimony to the sincerity of his interest in the family and its problems; and I can think of no other president who would have been capable of this. — *Edward Wagenknecht*

The President is a boy with his boys there. He puts off the cares of state and takes a hand in their games; and if they lagged before, they do not lag then.... The President himself teaches his boys how to shoot; he swims with them in the cove and goes with them on long horseback rides, starting sometimes before sunrise. On fine days, as often as he can get away, luncheon is packed in the row-boat and he takes the whole family rowing to some distant point on the shore, which even the Secret Service men have not discovered, and there they spend the day, the President pulling the oars going and coming. Or else he takes Mrs. Roosevelt alone on a little jaunt, and these two, over whose honeymoon the years have no dominion, have a day to themselves, from which he returns to wrestle with powers and principalities and postmasters with twice the grip he had before; for she is truly his helpmeet and as wise as she is gentle and good. —*Jacob Riis*

[While Roosevelt was in a conference with congressmen, a boy entered the office and called to his uncle, the President.]
"It's after four!"
"So it is," responded Mr. Roosevelt, looking at the clock. "Why didn't you call me sooner? One of you boys get my rifle."
Then he turned to his guests and added, "I must ask you to excuse me. We'll talk this out some other time. I promised the boys I'd go shooting with them after four o'clock, and I never keep boys waiting. It's a hard trial for a boy to wait."
Then he walked off down the lawn with a crowd of boys surrounding him, all talking at the same time. —*George William Douglas*

Thomas A. Robbins, a prominent businessman, recounted the visit of Mr. Roosevelt to his house for a formal breakfast with prominent men. While he was taking off his own overcoat Mr. Roosevelt rushed up three flights of stairs with the man's son and was soon stretched out on the floor with the lad before a miniature electric train and was saying, "That's right, Tommy, safety first." He had forgotten all about the waiting dignitaries downstairs. —*Newspaper clipping*

Edward Bok [Editor of *The Ladies' Home Journal*], in his autobiography, describes an experience when his "lad," who had nearly died with typhoid fever, was told that he could have for his Christmas present anything he requested. When told to think about it, he replied: "But I know already. I want to be taken down to Washington to see the President." The trip was finally arranged, and Mr. Roosevelt turned away from various groups of importunate callers during business hours to talk and visit in a familiar way with the lad. —*Christian Reisner*

When we drove back to the village that November day I caught him looking back once or twice toward the house in its bower of crimson shrubs, and I saw that his heart was there. You would not wonder if you knew it. I never go away from Sagamore Hill without a feeling that if I lived there I would never leave it, and that nothing would tempt me to exchange it for the White House, with all it stands for. But then I am ten years older than Theodore Roosevelt; though it isn't always the years that count. For I think if it came to a vote, the children would carry my proposition with a shout.

Not that Sagamore Hill has anything to suggest a palace. Quite the contrary: it is a very modest home for the President of the United States. On a breezy hilltop overlooking field and forest and Sound, with the Connecticut shore on the northern horizon, its situation is altogether taking. The house is comfortable, filled with reminders of the stirring life its owner has led in camp and on the hunting-trail, and with a broad piazza on the side that catches the cool winds of summer. It is homelike rather than imposing. It is the people themselves who put the stamp upon it—the life they live there together. —*Jacob Riis*

The Empress Dowager's emissary, a charming old Chinese mandarin, in yellow jacket and peacock feather, stood with his host on the piazza [of Sagamore Hill], looking over to the Connecticut shore, and appraised his surroundings with alert eyes. Finally, in the manner of one who has solved an interesting problem in quadratics, he remarked gravely that the President's home had an excellent *feng shui*, "a better *feng shui* indeed, than any other house I have seen in America, except Mount Vernon."

The President replied, in effect, "That's nice, but what, if you don't mind enlightening me, is a *feng shui*?"

Feng shui, the mandarin replied, signified the capacity of a house to be hospitable to the good spirits, resistant to the evil spirits. No one built a house in China, he explained, without careful thought for its *feng shui*. —*Hermann Hagedorn*

[*After TR was shot in the chest while campaigning in 1912, he was hospitalized in Chicago after delivering his planned speech.*]

A shoal of telegrams had come, and these had to be looked over. One, from Mrs. Roosevelt, had arrived just as we were pulling out, and after the Colonel had gone to sleep.... It was a wonderful message, showing that the woman who wrote it lived on the same plane with the man to whom she sent it.

"Don't you think you had better come to Sagamore right away?" she asked, and followed it with the argument that "you always rest so well here." —*O. K. Davis*

There were times when [Roosevelt] got pretty emotional about [sex and family matters], as when he declared that "artificially keeping families small" involves "pre-natal infanticide...and abortion, with its pandering to self-indulgence, its shirking of duties, and its enervation of character." —*Edward Wagenknecht*

On the way up to Peoria [campaigning in 1913, a year after the Bull Moose presidential campaign] we fell into conversation and began talking about the Centralia meeting. He had brought something into that speech about his favorite theme of the size of families. That afternoon he began to talk again on that subject.

"Well, Colonel," I said, "did it ever strike you that it isn't quite fair for you to bear down so heavily on that subject with such an audience?"

"What do you mean?" he demanded.

"Simply this. Never in your life have you had to give an instant's thought to the most important question that comes to every one of those people, every day. The thing that is right in front of them, morning, noon, and night, is the question of where and how their families are going to be housed, fed, and clothed. But, all your life, you have been so situated that that question has never given you one moment's anxiety."

"By George, O.K.," he replied, "that's so, and I never thought of it."

He was silent for some time after that, but then he came back to the discussion, saying that in future, when he referred to that subject, he should take into consideration the point I had raised. —*O. K. Davis*

Both Father and Mother were good disciplinarians as far as we were concerned. I am sorry to say that when the grandchildren arrived it was very different. To begin with, the ruling as to places was entirely voided. Father was allowed to have the grandchildren sit by him.

It was at this time that we, the older children, noticed this astonishing breakdown in moral fiber on the part of both Father and Mother. They let our children do things they never would have permitted us to do.

Our little Teddy [TR's grandson] was sitting one morning in a highchair by Father. Now Father was very fond of coffee and always had a special cup. It was so large it was more in the nature of a bathtub. Mother had given it to him for a present. This particular day Teddy, sitting in his highchair, a bib tied neatly around his neck, was watching with interest his grandfather's coffee being placed on the table. He had a salt spoon in his hand and a salt cellar nearby. Remarking in a sepulchral voice, "Put salt in Grandfather's soup," he dumped a whole spoonful into the coffee. If we had done that when we were little, the least we could have expected was banishment from the table. Was Teddy banished? He was not. Father merely remarked mildly, "Please don't, Teddy. That is not soup, it is coffee," and had another cup brought to the other side where it would be out of the little boy's reach. —*Ted Roosevelt*, son of TR

[During American participation in the Great War] he remarked to a friend that for the first time in his life he couldn't sleep. He had always been able to throw off any worries while he was President. "But now," he said, "I wake up in the middle of the night wondering if the boys are all right, and thinking how I could tell their mother if anything happened." —*Carleton Case*

Early the next morning a newspaper reporter [assigned to] Oyster Bay went out to Sagamore Hill to carry the sad news of Quentin's death. He rang the bell; the Colonel himself came to the door, and, going out on the porch together the awful news was broken. The Colonel walked the porch in silence for a while and then said to the visitor, "But—Mrs. Roosevelt! How am I going to break it to her?"

He then turned about and started into the house to perform one of the bravest acts of his life—to tell Mrs. Roosevelt that Quentin had been killed. And she, with a soul as brave as that of her husband, received the news with supreme heroism. They sent out this joint letter to the world which will be read centuries from now as a specimen of the highest heroism:

"Quentin's mother and I are very glad that he got to the front and had a chance to render some service to his country and to show the stuff that was in him before his fate befell him." —*Ferdinand Iglehart*

One recalls that Sunday morning before Quentin sailed, how he came to church for his last communion. We felt it would be the last, but we talked otherwise. Then came the letter from abroad in which was written, "I have just been to service in Notre Dame Cathedral. It was fine. But I would rather have been in Christ Church."

And then came the cable message, and early next morning, when so many would have stayed away, the parents drew near to the same altar rail. There were no dry eyes, and the words could scarcely be spoken, but their force was there: "Preserve thy body and soul unto everlasting life." This time also it was a last communion, but we did not know it. —*Rev. George E. Talmage*

Roosevelt told me: "The Salvation Army is doing great and good work [on World War battlefields] among the boys. My son's regiment was without a chaplain for a time, and your Atkins was asked to fulfill the duties, and a brave chaplain he turned out to be, marching and marching with the boys right up to the firing line. My son told me that chunks of flesh were taken out of his shoes, but he would not leave the boys—he was always at call, night and day."

Then, tapping his fingers on the table and looking into blank space as if he wanted to conquer the mysterious, he said: "My other boy left part of the family blood on the battlefield." —*Commander Evangeline Booth*

[Francis Cutler Marshall, commanding officer of TR's son, wrote to his wife, dated HQ 2nd Inf. Brigade, Montabaur, Germany, Jan. 7, 1919:]

I had, last night, the sad duty of telling Colonel Ted Roosevelt of the death of his father. We had been visiting together at my quarters during the early part of the evening. I had had a letter from his father, acknowledging one I'd written him of our final operation before Sedan, and he came to see it. We spend many such evenings together. He left about ten—and at ten-thirty I had a phone [message] from the Chief of Staff, reading me the news of Col. Roosevelt's death! I ordered my car and went out to the young Colonel's billet—six miles away—and told him…. And then we went together to his brother's— Kermit, a captain in the 7th—where I left him.

"To My Brother"

I loved you for your loving ways,
The ways that many did not know;
Although my heart would beat and glow
When Nations crowned you with their bays.

I loved you for the tender hand
That held my own so close and warm,
I loved you for your winning charm
That brought gay sunshine to the land.

I loved you for the heart that knew
The need of every little child;

I loved you when you turned and smiled,
It was as though a fresh wind blew.

I loved you for your loving ways,
The look that leaped to meet my eye,
The ever-ready sympathy,
The generous ardor of your praise.

I loved you for the buoyant fun
That made perpetual holiday
For all who ever crossed your way,
The highest or the humblest one.

I loved you for the radiant zest,
The thrill and glamour that you gave
To each glad hour that we could save
And garner from Time's grim behest.

I loved you for your loving ways,—
And just because I loved them so,
And now have lost them,—thus I know,
I must go softly all my days.

—Corinne Roosevelt Robinson, 1919

Mrs. Roosevelt, sitting at a table beside him, completed the solitaire she was playing and was about to leave the room when he looked up from the book he was reading and said, à propos of nothing, "I wonder if you will ever know how I love Sagamore Hill."

At five in the morning he was dead. *—Hermann Hagedorn*

138

JAMES MONTGOMERY FLAGG

CHAPTER VI

Theodore Roosevelt and Humor: The Joy of Life

> The Plaintiff's lawyer asked the judge to direct Roosevelt to refrain from frequently breaking out in smiles and laughter. The judge denied the motion, saying he could not direct a witness to speak in anything other than his habitual manner.
> —*Newspaper clipping,*
> when Roosevelt was defendant in a libel trial, 1915

If one were to count and compare the number of photographs of Theodore Roosevelt where he is somber, serious, or perhaps fiercely delivering a speech, versus images of him smiling or laughing…one would be surprised by the relative paucity of the ebullient TR.

Yet that is how he has been bequeathed to the generations (it is hoped with the added assistance of this anthology). Mount Rushmore? One of four great stone faces. The several postage stamps that honored him with his visage? Some of them displayed a mien of such fierce determination that people might have been afraid to lick the reverse side. The official White House portrait by John Singer Sargent, and other formal portraits? Roosevelt the confident, Roosevelt the dignified, Roosevelt the country squire…but scarcely images of Roosevelt the jolly.

He was jolly, in fact almost constantly joking with friends, teasing and cajoling, making allusions and comic references. Cartoonists caught this aspect of TR, and it was their output we appreciate. (Of course, depicting the hyperactive Roosevelt was their virtual sustenance for years!)

Roosevelt was the most caricatured president in American history. Cartoonists of daily papers and weekly magazines—always looking for material before the impending deadlines, anyway—knew a good subject when they saw one. And what they saw (or learned from their print-reporters) was that Theodore Roosevelt was a man of boundless joy, spirited good will, visceral optimism, and the confident intellectual's greatest weapon: humor that welcomes, disarms, and enchants.

Abraham Lincoln, a hero of Theodore Roosevelt, surely was the most sagacious of presidents. He probably was the most original humorist—as opposed to a man with a sense of humor, or who enjoyed laughing—and plausibly could have been a print humorist if he had not followed politics. Lincoln enjoyed reading humorists Artemus Ward and Petroleum V. Nasby, even at restive cabinet meetings, even during the height of the Civil War's crises. For all of Lincoln's fondness for parables and ironic lessons, he is also assumed to have required the psychic solace of humor.

TR used humor as a weapon, as great thinkers and debaters do—making points, exposing contradictions, explaining his thoughts with clarity. It surely was an essential element of his persona, but he employed it in the way that great minds of the past did. We think of Aesop's fables, Christ's parables, and Lincoln's stories. Effective communication, covered in the amiable soft cover of good humor.

But uncountable observers noted too that Roosevelt simply loved to laugh, and it came as naturally and as often as a person draws breaths. One-liners, implausible for a man at the dawn of the twentieth century, were his personal lingua franca.

Regarding the claim that Theodore Roosevelt was the most caricatured of all presidents, and likely of all Americans of any pursuit, several factors are dispositive. Other presidents received attention, but commentary frequently addressed their policies. When presidents were addressed, Uncle Sam or the elephant or donkey were surrogates—iconic figures like the dour Mr. Prohibition, or New Deal bureaucrats in caps and gowns, or Mr. Bomb during the nuclear era. Every generation's version of John Q. Public substituted for presidents of the day in many cartoons.

But TR was as irresistible to a cartoonist as candy is to a child. Given the choice between a traditional old Uncle Sam or an iconic elephant, especially when the subject of the cartoon exuded good humor and inviting features…cartoonists joined writers in trying to depict Theodore Roosevelt himself. During the Roosevelt presidency, the figure of Uncle Sam generally enjoyed a vacation as the cartoonists' iconic character.

Other reasons that TR was depicted so frequently are related to technology. As his career advanced, the ability to reproduce drawings in newspapers and magazines evolved from primitive chalk plates to awkward woodcuts to photo-engraving that allowed pen and ink drawings to be transferred to printing plates. Growing prosperity in the Gilded Age enabled the spread of literacy, popular journals, and classes of cartoonists, commentators, and critics. Add these ingredients to the final recipe—the most animated, colorful, and interesting personality of his time—and it was a grand dessert for the tasting.

Roosevelt's toothy grin, his bushy mustache, and his *pince nez* spectacles were low-hanging fruit for cartoonists. When TR gifted cartoonists with a Rough Rider uniform, the Big Stick, and a Bull Moose mascot, he was the cartoonists' gift that kept on giving, equally to supporters and the opposition press.

The actual few photographs of a laughing Theodore Roosevelt were seared into history's memory and are exceptions that prove the rule. Probably his most famous "face" was captured in 1916 when a photographer was setting up equipment for a formal portrait. Whatever evinced the hearty laugh in the close-up on Sagamore Hill's front lawn tempts viewers to smile too. Another candid caught TR on horseback after a train brought him to a Western town. In his element, in his environment, in his enjoyment of the moment—laughing, no doubt loudly.

Thanks to a few photos, many cartoons, and the happy impressions as collected here, we can see why Theodore Roosevelt was called The Happy Warrior before that title was bestowed on politicians of a later era.

Roosevelt's personality extended beyond his love of laughter. He possessed a love of humor, the incorporation of which permeated conversations and interactions. He sought out press humorists, a profession so common in his day that they had a large, formal association. Among those TR cultivated were Finley Peter Dunne ("Mr. Dooley"); Joel Chandler Harris of the Uncle Remus stories; Mark Sullivan; Brander Matthews;

and E. S. Martin; all of whom had "other" lives and literary pursuits but also were editorial writers for prominent publications.

With some humorists—for instance Mark Twain and H. L. Mencken—their opposition to Roosevelt's policies and their cynical regard for his democratic persona, prevented even an opening for friendship or cama- raderie. Among political cartoonists, TR had enduring friendships with "Ding" Darling, Homer Davenport (who originally was a bitter critic while working for the Hearst papers), and John T. McCutcheon of the *Chicago Tribune*. The latter artist virtually was the official cartoonist of the Bull Moose campaign and had shared several days on African safari with Roosevelt as the leader of his own expedition.

Despite their seeming transitory lightness, there is substance in the art forms of cartoon commentary and political caricature. Cartoons comprise the most understandable visual guides to our history, its issues, and consequences of public policy. Not yet fully appreciated as essen- tial resources for historians—and still far from being fully collected and annotated—they have inherently valuable and irreducible elements, especially so in Roosevelt's own time.

Political cartoons have to be accessible, as well as easily and imme- diately understood; for all their potential cleverness, they had to make important points using signs, symbols, iconography, and caricatures; they invariably persuaded or dissuaded readers, a heavy assignment for one drawing seen for a minute or so; and they were expected to be (but not always required to be) funny. An imposing checklist. Political cartoons had an additional obligation in Roosevelt's day; when a large percentage of newspaper readers were illiterate, or semi-literate, the demands were great upon artists to manage likenesses, situations, and presentation of issues.

A famous series of cartoons was the "Willie and His Papa" panels by F. Opper of the Hearst newspaper chain. These popular cartoons, collected in a book, depicted the Trusts as Papa, and President William McKinley's *éminence grise* Mark Hanna as the household's nursemaid. The president was little Willie, and playmate Teddy was dressed in a little soldier's cos- tume as he rode a wooden horse in the corner of every drawing.

Further to that point is evidence ensconced in the Prints and Photo- graphs Division of the Library of Congress; a blessing that such treasures, not ephemeral but very revelatory, have survived. There are White House scrapbooks of political cartoons, clipped from newspapers large

Colonel and Mrs. Roosevelt loved humor. I recall that Opper, the cartoonist,
once sent a book of his cartoons. One of the Opper cartoons pictured little Willie
McKinley and Teddy Roosevelt, the latter dressed in his Rough Rider suit.
Mr. Roosevelt laughed in his heartiest manner over this cartoon. He showed it to
Mrs. Roosevelt, and they laughed at it together. Mrs. Roosevelt took the book,
and kept coming back to show the Colonel another one, and would say:
"Theodore, you must see this one!" Then they would have another laugh.
—George William Douglas

and small from every part of America. A Washington newspaperman, reportedly, regularly gathered cartoons from around the country (some delivered to the White House directly), dated and marked them. The cartoons and journals were both supporters and opponents of President Roosevelt. They were pasted in scrapbooks which have been preserved.

TR likely took the pulse of the nation in this unique fashion, as he gauged the public's moods or reactions to his policies. And we can imagine that his own pulse increased as he laughed and laughed at the cartoons every day.

Whether initiating good humor and joking with virtually every person he met or enjoying the humor of others—even at his own expense—that is something disarming about a person. Simultaneously, it demonstrates self-confidence and a lack of pretension. To people who encountered TR, it was not peripheral but a basic aspect of his personality.

* * *

Mr. Roosevelt was never nettled by the cartoonists. Several times [when clipped cartoons arrived at the White House] I was present when handed to the President. Mrs. Roosevelt and some of the children would be there. They would open the batch of clippings and look them over and pass them around and have a good laugh over them. Mr. Roosevelt himself always enjoyed them immensely. A number of the original drawings of these cartoons were sent to him and they were hung on the walls of the library, and quite a few were hung in his study at Oyster Bay. —*James Amos*

At one time he was out riding [in the Badlands] and stopped for luncheon at the house of a woman who had a great reputation for making buckskin shirts. She was a good deal of a character who was living in a wild bit of country with a man who had shot the man she lived with before. He might have been her husband, for all I know, and might not. Theodore always carried a book with him wherever he went, and was sitting in a corner reading, with his legs stretched out. The woman, who was getting his dinner, stumbled over his feet.

She told him to move that damned foot.

He said that he thought that was a perfectly proper way for a lady to ask a gentleman to move, but that he had never happened to hear it put that way before. However, he said he moved the foot and what was attached to it and waited until he was called to dinner, which proved to be excellent; paid for it; and left as quickly as he could. He did not want to be in that woman's way again. —*Bill Sewall*

[Despite being a strictly observant Christian, the ways of a High-Church Catholic funeral mass were foreign to Roosevelt. However, his sense of humor survived, perhaps to silently test the decorum of his Military Aide.]

We drove to St. Patrick's Church in the open landau, passing through great crowds who had been attracted to the neighborhood by the published statement that the diplomatic corps would attend the services in uniform and that the President would be in attendance likewise. St. Patrick's Church is the most imposing Roman Catholic church in the district and is located on Tenth Street, between F and G, in the thickest shopping settlement of the city.

By the time we reached the church the edifice was already filled to overflowing with all the diplomatic corps and members of fashionable society which the Austrian Embassy had invited to be present. Everybody was in his best, the women vying with each other in their gowns and hats and the ambassadors, ministers, and attachés in full court uniforms. The two front seats on the left side of the aisle were reserved for the President and his aides, so he occupied the first and I the second, sitting just behind him. The Austrian Ambassador was across the aisle, and his wife looked like a gorgeous bird of paradise in electric, glittering colors. The dean of the diplomatic corps and his wife, Baron and Baroness des Planches, sat with them, and back of them came the rest of the corps according to rank, while social Washington sat back of us.

The procession of clergy and choristers up the aisle was a grand pageant. Signor Falcon, the Papal delegate, was present in gray and purple, with a long train held up by boys in red....

As we sat down a priest brought the President the printed programme. After looking over it he turned to me and whispered:

"When I see the length of this programme I regret my letter on the liberty of religious observances."

A few minutes later he caught a glimpse of Baroness von Hengelmüller, and with a twinkle in his eye he leaned back and said: "Archie, I hope you will not be so ungallant as to remind the Baroness of [Queen Victoria's] coronation [in 1838] and to ask her if the last sixty years has not passed like a dream to her."

These long waits sitting by himself, knowing himself observed by everyone, really get on his nerves, and he simply has to talk.

He thinks of the most ridiculous things and the more solemn the occasion the more ridiculous the things which suggest themselves to his mind.

The procession stopped further conversation and we had to center all our attention on the programme to keep up with the good Catholics who were supposed to know when to kneel and when to sit and when again to stand. The President kept his eye on the Austrian Ambassador, whom I soon found to be entirely misleading in the observances of church etiquette. At one part of the service the Ambassador, the President, and myself were the only persons standing and I had to touch the President to make him sit down. In commenting afterward on this he said: "If you had not touched my elbow, I should have gone on following the Ambassador, although realizing that he was leading me at times into blind alleys. When I see him again I shall denounce him as a heretic in disguise."

I saw that Madame Jusserand was the best posted Catholic present, and I followed her lead, and when it was time to kneel I would do so, at the same time giving the President a slight touch on the arm, which very soon he learned to respond to with such agility as to deceive anyone who might be watching him. At one part of the service when the censer was brought to the Cardinal to fill, one of the priests attending him coughed and then sneezed. I knew the President was dying to laugh. On leaving the church the first thing he said after getting into the carriage, while bowing to the applauding populace on the streets: "Archie, a priest who can't stand incense must be about as useless as a naval officer who gets sick when he goes to sea."

A little later he said: "If my dear old [Dutch Reformed] grandfather could have seen me there to-day he would have met me at the door and offered me poison and a pistol to choose my own form of death. It would never have occurred to him that I should not have been killed instantly for the salvation of my soul." —*Archie Butt*

[A story from TR's own childhood:]

Sometimes the children were allowed a little latitude of extemporaneous prayer. On one occasion Theodore availed himself of this liberty to a large degree.

His mother had disciplined him in some way for some misconduct, and Theodore thought unjustly. And so, when he came to his prayer before going to bed, he broke out in a request that God would bless the Union Army and give it success [and "crush" the Rebel forces]. He gave his mother this piece of his mind under the pretense of prayer, because he knew that she was a pronounced Confederate, and he took this means of getting even with her. She was so full of humor that she turned her face away so that he might not see her laugh. —*Ferdinand Iglehart*

There is nothing in human beings at once so sane and so sympathetic as a sense of humor. This great gift the good fairies conferred upon Theodore Roosevelt at his birth in unstinted measure. No man ever had a more abundant sense of humor—joyous, irrepressible humor—and it never deserted him. Even at the most serious and even perilous moments if there was a gleam of humor anywhere he saw it and rejoiced and helped himself with it over the rough places and in the dark hour. He loved fun, loved to joke and chaff, and, what is more uncommon, greatly enjoyed being chaffed himself. His ready smile and contagious laugh made countless friends and saved him from many an enmity. Even more generally effective than his humor, and yet allied to it, was the universal knowledge that Roosevelt had no secrets from the American people. —*Henry Cabot Lodge*

His humor is so elusive, his wit so dashing, and his thoughts so incisive that I find he is the hardest man to quote I have ever heard talk. His style of narration is so peculiarly his own that it is hard to reproduce it. In fact he does not reproduce it himself in writing. He cannot follow himself with pen in hand.

In conversation he is a perfect flying squirrel, and before you have grasped one pungent thought he is off on another limb whistling for you to follow. I can do all he does physically; I think that is one reason why he finds me agreeable to have about him; and I can follow him at times in conversation, even adding my share; but let him have the reins once between his own teeth fairly and squarely and he simply runs riot with the conversation. —*Archie Butt*

I must tell you of an incident which the President related in connection with the swimming of the Potomac by himself, the French Ambassador [Jean Jules Jusserand], and General [Leonard] Wood, some time ago. It had been my impression that they had swum the river with their clothes on, but the President said they did not, that they stripped, and just as they were going into the water, he noticed M. Jusserand had kept on his hands his kid gloves. The Ambassador was waist deep when the President saw him.

"Heavens, Mr. Ambassador," the President called to him, "what on earth are you wearing your gloves for?"

The President says that he thinks the Ambassador simply forgot to take them off, for he looked at them as if he did not know he had them on, but with a shrug of his shoulders he simply said, naively: "Oh, I feared we might meet some ladies, Mr. President." —*Archie Butt*

[Archie Butt was a native Georgian, and he recorded in a letter to his mother a dinner conversation with his senator, Augustus Octavius Bacon, a Democrat:]

We had a pleasant homelike evening. The Senator cannot abide the President as President, but likes him as a man. He truly believes that the President has no respect for the Constitution, while others like Clay, his colleague from Georgia, think the President one of the greatest men in the world and with a profound respect for the Constitution. So after all it depends on one's viewpoint. Bacon's hobby is the Constitution, and he is always on the watch for someone who has not the same respect for it as he himself has.

He told us the story which was told on him after the last inauguration. He was one of the committee to attend the President when he took his oath of office. On reaching the White House reviewing stand, he said the President turned to Senator Lodge and said:

"Lodge, did you see Bacon turn pale when he heard me swear to support the Constitution?"

"On the contrary, Mr. President," Bacon replied, "I never felt so relieved in my life!"

At luncheon he told us of some of his ornithological excursions on the White House grounds, how people would stare at him as he stood gazing up into the trees like one demented. "No doubt they thought me insane." "Yes," said Mrs. Roosevelt, "and as I was always with him, they no doubt thought I was the nurse that had him in charge." — *John Burroughs*

When a woman from Jacksonville, Florida, was presented to President Roosevelt in his office, she announced:

"Mr. President, I have come all this way just to see you. I have never seen a live President before."

"Well, well," was the reply, while the woman looked shocked, "I hope you don't feel disappointed, now that you have seen one. Lots of people in these parts go all the way to Jacksonville to see a live alligator." —*George William Douglas*

At a state dinner when he was President a woman guest noticed with apparent disapproval that he refused a cigar.

"Why, Mr. President," she remonstrated. "Don't you smoke?"

"No, madam," he replied, "but I like to go to prize fights. Won't that do?" —*Carleton Case*

Great men…even when quite keenly alive to humor which affects others, are apt to have their sense of humor chilled when it begins to stray within their own precincts. This was never the case with Theodore Roosevelt. He was as quick to laugh at himself as at another when there was genuine humor in the situation. This is one of the salient qualities, rare and fine, which made him so sympathetic as a companion. —*Henry Cabot Lodge*

To me, the clearest mental photographs of Roosevelt are taken from his humorous side. When I visited Sagamore Hill, he would stalk up and down the veranda, hands [clasped] behind him, his every faculty concentrated on the nonsense verses [for which Wells was famed] that he requested me to teach him. As soon as he had mastered one and tucked it away in his vast memory, he would chuckle like a schoolboy and say: "That's all right! Now teach me another!" — *Carolyn Wells*

It gave great scandal to many reverent Senators to see the way in which such successors of Leatherstocking as [Badlands friends] Abernathy and Sewall went to the White House and got the President's ear for hours at a time. Before Senator Hoar had come to know Mr. Roosevelt as he afterwards did, he went to the White House to remonstrate with him for appointing Ben Daniels marshal of Arizona. Mr. Hoar was one of the most dignified and sedate men in the Senate.

"Mr. President," said Mr. Hoar in horrified accents, "do you know anything about the character of this man Daniels you have appointed to be marshal of Arizona?"

"Why, yes, I think so," said Mr. Roosevelt, "he was a member of my regiment."

"Do you know," said Mr. Hoar, impressively, "that he has killed three men?"

The President was scandalized. "You don't mean it," he said.

"It is a fact," said Mr. Hoar.

The President was thoroughly indignant. He pounded his fist on the table. "When I get hold of Daniels," he said, "I will read him the riot act. He told me he'd only killed two." —*Newspaper clipping*

I am tempted to tell you of more jokes, for he loves them dearly so long as it hurts no one's feelings. Two timid parsons expressed the hope that "he would not embroil us in any foreign war."

"What," cried the President. "A war? With me cooped up here in the White House! Never, gentlemen, never!"

I wonder what the parsons thought when they caught their breath. His fun sometimes takes the form of mock severity with intimate friends. —*Jacob Riis*

He was in good humor, and someone started him on the subject of Pittsburgh and New York. Forgetting that Mrs. [Cornelius] Vanderbilt was the center of the [social] set he despises, he said: "While Pittsburgh is vulgar and common, it is not so sordid as New York. Our worst influences come from New York, not from Pittsburgh. Edith, my dear, why are you frowning at me? Oh, I see, dear Mrs. Vanderbilt, Edith seems to include you in that category I am about to denounce. You see, I know you better and think more highly of you than my excellent wife does, but for fear I may be led into an indiscretion about some in-law, or rather out-law, of yours, I will change the subject."

Which caused a good laugh, and no one enjoyed it more than Mrs. Vanderbilt. —*Archie Butt*

His irrepressible and buoyant humor enabled him often to see the comic side of the controversy. He once recalled a Cabinet meeting, when he was reporting his executive action—which he described briefly as "the taking of Panama"—and appealing for an endorsement of its legal and constitutional character, one of the Secretaries—I think it was Attorney-General Knox—exclaimed ironically: "Oh, Mr. President, do not let so great an achievement suffer from any taint of legality!" —*Hermann Hagedorn*

His sense of humor seldom deserted him…. After one of the cabinet meetings, when I was waiting for him, he came in chuckling. "My friend," he said very solemnly, "I have used real cuss words today, and perhaps committed sacrilege." He added that he had been obliged by etiquette to write an official letter to the new Pope, and that one of the members of the Cabinet had said, "Do you think the American people will stand for your calling the Pope 'His Holiness'?"

"Very well," he replied, "do you think they would like me to call him 'You — — fool'?"

"But," he added, "I said worse than that; I won't repeat it; and the member of the Cabinet agreed that the American people would hardly expect me to use such language to the venerable gentleman at Rome." —*Maurice Francis Egan*

Wednesday I lunched at the White House and saw Admiral and Mrs. Cowles. The latter is a sister of the President and, I think, was the only one of the children born in Georgia. President Hadley of Yale was there; Henry Cabot Lodge and his beautiful wife; Mr. Mills, the father-in-law of Whitelaw Reid [publisher of the *New York Tribune*, and later Ambassador to the Court of St. James], and one or two others. Just a family luncheon such as you or anyone might have! The President amused us all by reading a letter from someone to the effect that it was reported in New York that in order to emphasize his imperial way of living he was using gold knives, forks, and spoons, while his family used only silver and old broken china. —*Archie Butt*

Among the stories that I told [at a White House dinner] was one of sixteen lions that were seen emerging from a cave on Juja Farm. At the time certain congressmen were irritating the President considerably and, when I had finished my tale, he turned to Congressman Mann, who sat at his right, and said: "Congressman, I wish I had those sixteen lions to turn loose on Congress."

"B-but, Mr. President," queried the congressman after some hesitation, "aren't you afraid that they might make mistakes?"

With a snap of his teeth Roosevelt replied: "Not if they stayed long enough."

So he really originated the cry with which the Senate crowd retaliated when he departed for Africa: "America expects every lion to do his duty." —*Carl Akeley*

It was at that visit that, after a thorough inspection of the premises, the President asked the lad [Riis's son] what he thought of the White House.

"Pretty good," said he. "But I like better to ride up and down in the elevator at the hotel." It was his first experience with an elevator, and he made full use of it.

The President considered him thoughtfully a moment. What visions of politicians and delegations passed before his mind's eye I know not; but it was with almost a half-sigh that he said: "So would I, my boy, sometimes." —*Jacob Riis*

[After reports were published of TR being thrown by his horse into a creek, Archie Butt recorded the president's comments:]
"I do not mind so much being dumped out of my saddle, but Mrs. Roosevelt has made me promise not to get killed until after the 4th of March [Inauguration Day, when he would leave the presidency], and Ethel would be distressed, as the next winter will be her only chance to give a party in the White House."

[In 1904, the great Catalonian cellist Pablo Casals was invited to perform at the Roosevelt White House (he returned almost sixty years later to perform for John F. Kennedy). The performance of Bach's suites might have been the performance cited here:]
One of [the President's] Dakota friends went to Washington to renew his acquaintance with Mr. Roosevelt soon after he became President. While he was there he attended a musicale at the White House. At the close of the programme—classical music only had been played—someone asked the man banteringly how he had liked the entertainment. "I am afraid," he replied dryly, "I'm afraid it was a spell too far up the gulch for me."
The President, who heard the pertinent criticism, laughed heartily, turned to the man's wife, and saved the situation by remarking, "You'd better take care of the captain's pistol. I know that out in his country they shoot the fiddler when he doesn't play the tunes they want!" —*George William Douglas*

Father was very near-sighted, and I recollect our amusement [visiting the St. Louis World's Fair in 1904] when he paused to admire some statue, saying to the large group that was in tow that he considered it a particularly fine Diana. [It] happened to be Apollo. —*Alice Roosevelt Longworth*

I have got the President very much interested in Ty Cobb, the famous baseball player from Georgia. I told him I had given Ty a dinner at Clarence A. Edwards's house. He wanted to know all about him and the others whom we had invited to meet Ty.
Ty is only twenty-two years old and neither drinks nor smokes, and neither did any of the ball players who were there. That interested

the President greatly, as he saw in this the perpetuation of the game in this country and its higher development.

Yesterday at tennis when I tried to get a smash over the net I landed the ball on the President's head. "If you would emulate your statesman Ty more in placing your hits, your partners would be in less danger," he laughed. —*Archie Butt*

One night in camp he told us the story of one of his Rough Riders who had just written him from some place in Arizona. The Rough Riders, wherever they are now, look to him in time[s] of trouble. This one had come to grief in Arizona. He was in jail. So, he wrote the President, and his letter ran something like this—

"Dear Colonel, I am in trouble. I shot a lady in the eye, but I did not intend to hit the lady; I was shooting at my wife." And the presidential laughter rang out over the tree-tops. —*John Burroughs*

Another instance of his enjoyment of chaffing himself that I often like to think of occurred in the early days of my editorial association with him. We used to meet at a weekly [*The Outlook* magazine] round-table conference in which Roosevelt regularly took part. These meetings were generally held on Mondays at eleven o'clock in the forenoon.

One Monday morning he went to Brooklyn with some friends to inspect some model tenement houses in that borough, and did not reach the conference until between twelve and one. When he came in he was full of his experience and began to tell us about it. He had gone quietly and wished to avoid any publicity, "But," said he, "for some reason or other which I do not quite understand, the people recognized me, especially the children, and a crowd of the latter gathered around me."

We all smiled, for it should be explained that his characteristic feature, which was always seized upon by the newspaper cartoonists, was a mouthful of unusually fine and white teeth, which he unconsciously displayed whenever he laughed or talked emphatically.

Noticing the smiles on our faces he at once added, "Yes, I suppose there is something distinctive in my physiognomy. I remember that when I was running for the vice-presidency I had to speak in a Western town where the crowd in the hall was so dense that the officers in charge had great difficulty making a way for me through the packed audience to get to the stage where I was to speak. Mr. Dooley's comment was (Mr. Dooley as every contemporary American knows is the newspaper pseudonym of one of our most delightful and accomplished humorists): 'And thin along came Teddy Rosenfeld and bit his way to the platform!'" —*Lawrence F. Abbott*

In June 1910, the Roosevelt party arrived in London very early in the morning, having traveled from Berlin during the night. Mr. Roosevelt went to Dorchester House where he was the guest of Ambassador Whitelaw Reid, while I took up my quarters in a nearby hotel. Immediately after breakfast and after having removed some of the stain of travel, I went round to Dorchester House and by ten or eleven o'clock was engaged with Colonel Roosevelt over a great pile of accumulated mail.

It was a good deal of a task and one that was usually irksome to Mr. Roosevelt, although he performed it faithfully. A knock at the half-open door, accompanied by labored breathing, showed that somebody was there in a state of suppressed excitement. I said "Come in," when one of the liveried, silk-stockinged footmen—a typical English flunky—entered and announced in an evidently awe-struck voice...for kings were not in the habit of calling on private citizens at ten o'clock in the morning: "The King of — — — — is below, sir."

Mr. Roosevelt, of course, had to go down, not only because it was a king, but because it was a monarch for whom he had formed a real respect and friendship during his journey through northern Europe. Nevertheless, as the Colonel rose he threw down his pen, with a mixture of annoyance (at being interrupted) and amusement, and exclaimed: "Confound these kings; will they never leave me alone!" —*Lawrence F. Abbott*

During the journey through Europe the English king, Edward VII, had died, and Mr. Roosevelt was appointed by Mr. Taft as special ambassador to the funeral. One of the things he had to do while in London was to attend the elaborate public ceremonies of this funeral. Captain Bentley Mott, then our Military Attaché at Paris, was assigned to Mr. Roosevelt as his personal attaché in the performance of his ambassadorial duties.... The arrangement had to be made...for Mr. Roosevelt's part in the solemn and splendid procession which proceeded through vast crowds from Buckingham Palace to Windsor. As Secretary to Mr. Roosevelt, I was called into the conference.

Captain Mott felt that Colonel Roosevelt should ride a horse, dressed in the conventional long riding trousers, frock coat, and high hat. The Earl of Dundonald and Commander Cunninghame Graham... regretted that the Earl of Norfolk, the prerogative of whose family was to have charge of all English coronations and royal funerals, was insistent that Mr. Roosevelt should wear "ambassadorial dress"—this being, according to American precedent, a swallow-tail evening suit.

... [Colonel Roosevelt] came, the matter was laid before him, and he said: "Why, Mott, I appreciate your thoughtfulness, but I am here as an ambassador not to do what I like but what the English people like as the contribution of my country to the respect which the world is paying to the memory of the King. If the English people want me to, I'll wear a pink coat and green-striped trousers!"

The result was that he did wear American evening dress and rode in the procession in a carriage with M. Pichon, the French Ambassador, these two, I believe, being the only foreign representatives who were "commoners." Mr. Roosevelt told me that during the long drive he had all he could do to appease M. Pichon, because according to the exacting rules of precedence, their carriage had been placed after that of the King of Siam. This question of precedence gave Roosevelt no end of amusement....

He told me that at the funeral banquet given to the foreign representatives in Buckingham Palace the evening before the procession and ceremonies at Windsor—a dinner that he somewhat disrespectfully referred to as "the wake"—the Kaiser told him an anecdote of precedence connected with the funeral. It seems that two royal personages of eastern Europe—I think one was from a Balkan kingdom and the other from an Austrian principality—met with their private cars or saloon carriages at Vienna to take the Orient Express to Paris and London. They quarreled as to whose rank entitled him to be first on the train, but the aide-de-camp, let us say of the Balkan personage, was clever enough to get his master's car coupled directly on the engine.

The Austrian, therefore, had, willy-nilly, to take second place. Then came the regular dining car of the train. When dinner was served the Balkan Highness sent his aide into the private car of the Austrian Highness with his compliments and might he pass through to the dining car? No, he might not. So he had to wait until the train came to a station, get out, walk around his rival's car into the dining car, eat his dinner, stay there until another station was reached, and then walk around his rival's car again into his own.

As the Orient Express makes very long non-stop runs it may easily be imagined that although the Balkan celebrity got the first place on the train it was not by any means the most comfortable. This incident Roosevelt recounted with the greatest glee. —*Lawrence F. Abbott*

The Progressive campaign of 1912, with its exhausting work and its depressing disappointments, was a severe test for any man. Roosevelt came through it with two of his marked and engaging personal qualities unimpaired—his capacity for friendship and his unquenchable sense of humor. —*Lawrence F. Abbott*

I think humor was the most lovable of Roosevelt's qualities. I am not sure but that it was the most important of his qualities. He could be stern; he could be severe; he was occasionally biting although never bitter; he had a certain touch of bulldog pugnacity; but underlying it all was a reservoir of humor, not a careless or indifferent humor, not a mere jocosity, but humor which has its source in a spirit of sympathetic and joyous understanding of men and things—a spirit of which Emerson said in a eulogy of Sir Walter Scott before the Massachusetts Historical Society: "What an ornament and safeguard is humor! Far better than wit for a poet and writer. It is a genius itself, and so defends from the insanities." —*Newspaper clipping*

[TR said he never wanted his descendants, nor history, to believe that he frequently was drunk. At great personal expense, he produced dozens of character witnesses to the trial in Marquette, Michigan; and the publisher presented no proof of his libels. Roosevelt accepted only the bare minimum allowed by state law—six cents.]

Few things in Colonel Roosevelt's later life are fresher in the public memory than his suit against a Michigan editor who accused him of drunkenness. The unfortunate editor, unable to produce a scintilla of proof, admitted his fault, and so far as the records go, the matter was disposed of. There was nothing developed, however, to show where the tale started or what foundation, if any, it might have had.

Colonel Roosevelt had an explanation. He gave it to us one afternoon in the trophy room in Oyster Bay, when passing the cigars around, he remarked that he would vouch for the quality. "They must be good," he remarked, "for they're some of Leonard Wood's. I never smoke myself, so I have to rely on the judgment of others."

"Did you ever smoke?" someone asked.

"There is where that story of my drinking started," he continued, not hearing the question, or ignoring it.

"You see, when I would decline a cigar, saying I did not smoke, folks would often ask, in a joking way, 'What are your bad habits?' In the same spirit I would reply, 'Prize fighting and strong drink.'

"Now it so happens that the Lord in His infinite wisdom elected to create some persons with whom it is never safe to joke—solemn asses who lack a sense of humor. I am very fond of that story of Sidney Smith's, who, playing with his children, stopped suddenly, saying, 'Children, we must now be serious—here comes a fool.' You know the kind he meant—those poor unfortunates who must take everything said to them literally.

"One of these to whom I made that remark said, 'Roosevelt, I hear, drinks hard.' The other fool replied, 'Yes, that's true. He told me so himself.'

"And so the story went on its travels. That is all there ever was to the talk of my drinking. From that start, it spread and spread until, in self-defense, I was compelled to take action to stop it." —*John J. Leary*

For a long time Colonel Roosevelt had been writing magazine articles to increase his income. He needed the money, and his earnings from that work were large. He said to me once with a grin of good-humor: "Let me give you one piece of good advice, O. K.; never have a daughter married, get shot, and prosecute a libel suit all in one year. They're all very expensive proceedings." —*O. K. Davis*

President Roosevelt frequently took a "shortcut" to the executive offices from the residence of White House, walking down a rear terrace. One day he found a policeman asleep while guarding the door to a back entrance. The President passed the sleeping guard, with a broad grin on his face. The man in charge of the grounds at the time, having learned of the incident, started to arouse and admonish the policeman, when the President raised his hand and exclaimed: "No! No! Don't wake him up—unless he snores." —*Newspaper clipping*

At one of Mr. Roosevelt's receptions two members of a receiving committee possessed rather old-fashioned ideas as to conventional dress and they appeared in plain business suits. The other members of the committee were dressed in Prince Albert coats and wore silk hats. The contrast was so startling that when the two businessmen, arm in arm, approached the President, he raised his hand and shouted: "Here come the aristocrats!" —*Carleton Case*

[*After the presidency, between the New Nationalism speech and his third-party campaign for the White House, TR was occasionally ostracized by his former colleagues and social set, as he confided to his doctor and friend Alexander Lambert:*]

"You don't know how lonely it is for a man to be rejected by his own kind. I have just come from Boston, where I attended a meeting of the Harvard Overseers. They all bunched at one end of the room away from me, and I stood all alone there except for one man, nice General Hallowell, who acted like a perfect trump, standing by me through it all, gnashing his teeth in rage at those other fellows. By George!…we were like a pair of Airedale pups in a convention of tomcats!"

In his capacity as contributor to the *Kansas City Star* the men on that paper say the Colonel was the most considerate of men to work with. He had nothing of the small man's pride in what he wrote.

"If you think any of my stuff is rotten," he said, "don't hesitate to throw it away. I always like criticism. Secretary Root was invaluable in my Cabinet because he was always ready to oppose my ideas. We used to go round and round, and when he didn't convince me I was wrong, he frequently convinced me that I would have to modify my position. John Hay disagreed with me. But he was too kind-hearted to say so. So he didn't help me so much." —*Hermann Hagedorn*

In his writings he was rarely humorous or ironical. In conversation he was habitually so. —*Jacob Riis*

Colonel Roosevelt liked new martial or sporting implements— things he could play with —as keenly as any boy. In 1906 the Mikado sent the President as a token of esteem a complete suit of samurai armor from the thirteenth century. The President excused himself to an informal caller for a moment. Off went his frock coat and on went the armor. Presto! He made a costume parade of one, up and down the corridors of the White House. —*Elihu Root*

Theodore Roosevelt is a humorist. In the multitude of his strenuousness this, the most human of his accomplishments, has apparently been overlooked. There is a similarity between his humor and Mark Twain's. At Denver, at the stock growers' banquet during his recent Western trip, Colonel Roosevelt was at his best. He made three speeches that day and was eating his sixth meal, yet he was in the best of fettle. You couldn't pick a hall full that could sit with faces straight through his story of the blue roan cow. He can make a joke as fascinating as he can the story of a sunset on the plains of Egypt. —*Homer Davenport*, cartoonist. Article in Philadelphia *Public Ledger*, 1910

Lunching informally with him one day in the White House, which had just been renovated and redecorated, I noticed a splendid set of animal heads around the frieze of the dining room. "Are those your trophies?" I asked.

"Not on your life," answered Mr. Roosevelt, "the place is too insecure. Why, the next man that lives in this house might be a vegetarian, and then my heads would go down in the cellar." —*Henry van Dyke*, author, clergyman, diplomat

[Theodore Roosevelt was a polymath, accomplished and respected in many areas of study. Yet he was a notoriously poor speller, and his handwriting was atrocious—both tendencies serving as the occasion of humor at his expense:]

Noticing the great diversity of handwriting of the several [cabinet] members, I remarked as I passed a paper to the president: "Some profess to be able to read character in handwriting."

While signing he replied, through set teeth, "I'd like to see anyone read my character in my signature."

No one laughed as quickly, or as heartily, as Mr. Roosevelt at Secretary Root's rejoinder: "Why! Mr. President, no one can read the characters in your signature." —*Leslie M. Shaw*

[Roosevelt was a particular fan of Joel Chandler Harris's Uncle Remus stories. In 1915, he visited Atlanta—always dear to him because his mother was born in nearby Roswell—and besides a meeting and a parade in his honor, there was scheduled a large but private luncheon. TR's only request was that Harris be invited too. Famously—and almost painfully— shy, the writer was surprised by Roosevelt's request:]

He stood and turned to "Uncle Remus" and said with a fiery outburst: "I am going to introduce you to this audience, and you must say something." Mr. Harris expostulated, insisting that he had never done such a thing in his life and that he would die before trying.... President Roosevelt, holding the arm of "Uncle Remus" with one hand as if guarding against his escape, proceeded to eulogize the great Georgian, concluding his remarks with the statement: "Presidents may come and presidents may go, but Uncle Remus goes on forever!"

[When Harris finished his words of appreciation for the great ovation] he turned to Mr. Roosevelt with the coy statement: "Mr. President, you have made me make an ass of myself, but I forgive you!" —*Clark Howell*

One day at luncheon [during the time when the European War raged] the Colonel was speaking of the need of universal military service, when he touched sarcastically upon the song entitled "I Didn't Raise My Boy to Be a Soldier." Whereupon Mrs. Roosevelt, whose husband and four boys would go to war if war came, remarked:

"I didn't raise my boys to be the only soldiers!" —*Hermann Hagedorn*

"... Satan always does find
not only mischief
for idle hands
but evil pleasures for idle moments.

If you don't fill up the hours
with something that is good
they will be filled up
with something that is bad.

Nature abhors a vacuum."

Theodore Roosevelt

At Y.M.C.A. of Albany, New York
11 February 1899

CHAPTER VII

Theodore Roosevelt: Man of Faith

History largely has overlooked the fact that Theodore (incidentally, "Gift of God" in Greek) was in very public and very private ways among the most observant Christians of American presidents.

Theodore Roosevelt knew the Bible, declared it the most important book for anyone to read, and he "stood at Armageddon" ready to do "battle for the Lord."

TR was so full of life that many Americans found it difficult to believe that his life could end, that his presence would be removed from everyday life and consequential affairs. TR had coped with the death of his father, his wife and mother (on the same day), his dissolute brother, and his youngest son in ways that were particularly sensitive. As attested by diary entries and the accounts of relatives and friends, Theodore Roosevelt turned to God in those moments.

An important aspect of TR is his fervent Christian faith, which permeated uncountable speeches, writings, and acts. His favorite Bible verse, frequently shared, was Micah 6:8 (echoed in New Testament verses as well), "What doth the Lord require of thee, but to do justly, and to love mercy, and to walk humbly with thy God?"

Roosevelt was a member of the Dutch Reformed Church. As a boy, he participated in missions work around New York City with his father, whether the charity was church-related or "personal," public or private—it was all God's work. TR taught weekly Sunday school classes during his four years at Harvard. Throughout his life, he wrote for Christian publications. During the White House years, Edith, a strong Episcopalian, invariably attended her denomination's church across Lafayette Park, the "Church of Presidents." The president himself, however, frequently walked a little farther to worship at a humble German Reformed church, the closest he could find to that "faith of his fathers."

Roosevelt called his 1912 bare-the-soul campaign speech announcing his political principles "A Confession of Faith." Later, he closed perhaps the most important speech of his life, the clarion-call acceptance of the Progressive Party nomination, with the words: "We stand at Armageddon and we battle for the Lord!" That convention featured evangelical songs and closed with the hymn, "Onward Christian Soldiers."

He titled one his books *The Foes of Our Own Household* (after Matthew 10:36) and another *Fear God and Take Your Own Part*. After Roosevelt retired from the presidency, he was offered university presidencies, editorship of major newspapers and magazines, and many other prominent jobs. He chose instead to become Contributing Editor of *The Outlook*, a small Christian weekly news magazine that was founded by Henry Ward Beecher. He accepted a salary approximately one-eighth of those offered by magazines like *Collier's Weekly* that had hoped to snag TR's services and celebrity. Roosevelt's first essay for the magazine, telling the public why he chose to associate himself with the journal, cited *The Outlook*'s "paying heed to the dictates of a stern morality," and its "inflexible adherence to the elementary virtues of entire truth, entire courage, entire honesty."

TR was invited to deliver the Earl Lectures at Pacific Theological Seminary in 1911, but he declined due to a heavy schedule. Knowing, however, that he would be near Berkeley on a speaking tour, he offered to deliver the lectures if he might be permitted to speak extemporaneously, not having time to prepare written texts of the five lectures, as was the custom for guest lecturers. It was agreed, and Roosevelt spoke for 90 minutes each evening—from the heart and without notes—on "The Christian's Role in Modern Society."

TR was not perfect, but he knew the One who is. The aphorism "Speak softly and carry a big stick" found its counterpart when Roosevelt "hid the Word in his heart" and acted boldly, as per Scriptural injunction. As a very young man, hunting in the Maine woods, he slipped away from his guides early every morning to pray and study Scripture; today that spot is commemorated as "Bible Point." His faith sometimes led him down paths that dismayed the orthodox: he regretted that "In God We Trust" was on coinage because he thought it encouraged irreverence. He remembered cowboys in the Badlands making disrespectful jokes based on the words.

He appointed the first Jew to a presidential cabinet. A special message he wrote on patriotism and prayer was affixed to millions of Bibles distributed to American soldiers as they sailed to Europe in World War I. For *The Ladies' Home Journal,* Theodore Roosevelt wrote an article, "Nine Reasons Why Men Should Go To Church":

"In the actual world, a churchless community, a community where men have abandoned and scoffed at or ignored their religious needs, is a community on the rapid downgrade.

"Church work and church attendance mean the cultivation of the habit of feeling some responsibility for others and the sense of braced moral strength, which prevents a relaxation of one's own moral fiber.

"There are enough holidays for most of us that can quite properly be devoted to pure holiday-making. Sundays differ from other holidays, among other ways, in the fact that there are fifty-two of them every year.

"On Sunday, go to church.

"Yes, I know all the excuses. I know that one can worship the Creator and dedicate oneself to good living in a grove of trees, or by a running brook, or in one's own house, just as well as in church. But I also know as a matter of cold fact the average man does not thus worship or thus dedicate himself. If he strays from church, he does not spend his time in good works or lofty meditation. He looks over the colored supplement of the newspaper.

"He may not hear a good sermon at church. But unless he is very unfortunate, he will hear a sermon by a good man who, with his good wife, is engaged all the week long in a series of wearing, humdrum, and important tasks for making hard lives a little easier.

"He will listen to and take part in reading some beautiful passages from the Bible.

"And if he is not familiar with the Bible, he has suffered a loss.

"He will probably take part in singing some good hymns.

"He will meet and nod to, or speak to, good quiet neighbors. He will come away feeling a little more charitably toward all the world, even toward those excessively foolish young men who regard churchgoing as rather a soft performance.

"I advocate a man's joining in church works for the sake of showing his faith by his works.

"The man who does not in some way, active or not, connect himself with some active, working church misses many opportunities for helping his neighbors, and therefore, incidentally, for helping himself."

* * *

[As a boy, TR was taught to listen to a sermon so that afterward he could reproduce its outline and discuss the legitimacy of its Scripture basis. And so he learned to test a preacher's effectiveness. His sister recalled:]

Every Sunday afternoon at five o'clock we had a Sunday School in our own home. Father presided as teacher and the children of our household formed the class. Each child had a personally owned Bible. All had attended church that morning and the first matter for discussion was the sermon we had heard. It was the duty of every one of us to bring in an abstract of that sermon, and the boy or girl who had the best one was highly praised by our father; that was a great prize. We would then look up the Scripture and the context would be explained, and we would discuss it freely, reading selections from our own Bibles. It was a cheery, happy hour, enriched by our father, who thus made sermon-hearing very attractive and profitable. —*Corinne Roosevelt Robinson*

The father and mother of Theodore were very careful in his religious instruction. They taught him that the Bible was the book of books; that talking to God was as real as talking to people; and that to be a consistent Christian was to be the greatest thing in life, and to include about every other thing. Family prayers led by the father were just as regular as the breakfast on the table, and the children were taught at a very early age that there was a real relation between them and the God of heaven. The mother taught Theodore at her knee the little prayer, "Now I lay me down to sleep," and other prayers as well. —*Ferdinand Iglehart*

Roosevelt began to memorize the Bible when he was three years of age and helped teach his own children to memorize in the same way. Mrs. Roosevelt told a friend that he carried the Bible so thoroughly in his mind that he could quote large sections of it. *—Hermann Hagedorn*

Theodore, then sixteen years of age, called at my study and said: "I have come to have a little talk with you upon a personal matter. I would like to become a member of the church. You know how strictly I have been raised religiously in Christian faith and [Reformed] denominational doctrine, and I feel now as if I ought to unite with the church. I feel that one who believes so firmly in the Bible and in Christianity as I do, should say so publicly, and enter openly into the active service of the church; to drill with the troops and fight in the battle-front with the soldiers of the Cross. To join a church now will do me good personally and will be in obedience to the express command of Christ. I want to be a witness for Christ; a doer of the word." *—Rev. Dr. James M. Ludlow*, Pastor, St. Nicholas Collegiate Reformed Protestant Dutch Church, New York, when sixteen-year-old Theodore desired transfer from membership in the Madison Square Presbyterian Church

When Mr. Roosevelt was only eighteen and came to my Maine camp he would go off by himself on Sunday to an isolated point and take his Bible so that he could read it without anyone bothering him. Because of this custom of Mr. Roosevelt, his fellow campers afterward called that spot "Bible Point."

He had a Bible on the ranch in the early days and read it regularly. He was an extensive reader of the Bible. I guess he found it, as I did, a source of real common sense. He would quote it frequently in conversation and always to fit the case in point. He read the Bible to find the right way and then how to do it. Some folks read it to find an easier way into heaven—"to climb up some other way."

He always carried a Bible or Testament with him in the early days. While on the ranch he had a Bible and frequently carried it with him and read it regularly. *—Bill Sewall*

[W. Emlen Roosevelt, his cousin and associate from boyhood, never thought of TR ever "doubting his faith in God":]
It was such a vital part of his being. Even as young men, when we would lie about in the woods resting during our hunting trips, he

United States
Civil Service Commission,
Washington, D.C.

Nov 27, 89

My dear sir,

'Of course a politician can be a christian; he will never do really first class work in politics unless he applies the rules of morality and christianity as rigidly in public as in private life.'

Yours truly
Theodore Roosevelt

would talk about God and related subjects in a perfectly natural way.
—*W. Emlen Roosevelt*

He was greatly offended when anyone dared to classify the Christian as on the same footing as the other religions of the world, for he considered it as the only true religion. And so in reviewing Kidd's *Social Evolution* he objects that "Mr. Kidd's grouping of all religions together is offensive to every earnest believer." —*Christian Reisner*

It seems like a paradox that this smart, rich man's son, with his fashionable equipment, his sporting habits, his posing as a prize-fighter and a star dancer, should be found teaching a Sunday school class, and a mission class at that. But the old house on 20th Street had gotten in its work on him so thoroughly that it was the perfectly natural thing for him to be regular in his attendance upon church, devoted in his religious habits, and engaged particularly in saving the souls of poor children. He was all through his life a paradox. The paradox is only a seeming contradiction and not a real one, so that the gay, young, rich sport at Harvard and the teacher in the mission school were not opposite at all, but the natural life of the one person.

We doubt whether in all American life there ever appeared such a paradox as he. From the beginning to the end, his life was full of apparent contradictions, which were not so at all, but in harmony with the same character. —*Ferdinand Iglehart*

"Why do you suppose, Edith, that they put in an extra hymn, and if they do put it in, why in the name of goodness don't they put in one which people can sing?"

"That is too funny," added Mrs. Roosevelt, "for they have added another hymn because they heard that you liked more singing."

"Did I ever say so?"

"Yes," said Mrs. Roosevelt, "you did in the presence of one of the choir last summer, so you have no one but yourself to blame."

"Well, then, please suggest to them if they do me the kindness to add more hymns to sometimes put in 'Jerusalem the Golden,' or 'Oh, Paradise, Oh, Paradise,' or something in which I can lift up my voice and praise." —*James Amos*

Theodore Roosevelt was a true Christian. He believed in God, and that all peoples must have faith, that a nation forsaking its religion is a decadent nation. He was a churchgoer, as an evidence of his faith and for purpose of worship. His life, his ideals, and his acts established his faith in God. He was a reader of the Bible. I have no recollection of hearing him take the name of God in vain. I believe that he gathered many of his ethical ideals from the Scriptures. His courage was maintained by his sense of righteousness and justice. He was clean in thought and speech; a man of broad sympathy, a sympathy limited neither by race nor creed. He was a doer of good works, and a strenuous advocate of those principles which are laid down in the Commandments. —*Leonard Wood*

[Roosevelt was a] professing Christian though not a theologian. He did not have a mind for philosophic argument. Results established facts for him.

He was never interested in the discussion concerning the Divinity of Jesus; he never had any occasion for doubting it. To him Jesus was a very real person. Moral courage is absolutely impossible without character, and he had an abundance of the former. He would never have wasted time going to church if it had been to him an empty form. —*Dr. Nicholas Murray Butler*

Mr. Roosevelt's creed? Find it in a speech he made to the Bible Society. "If we read the Book aright," he said, "we read a book that teaches us to go forth and do the work of the Lord in the world as we find it; to try to make things better in the world, even if only a little better, because we have lived in it. That kind of work can be done only by a man who is neither a weakling nor a coward; by a man who, in the fullest sense of the word, is a true Christian, like Greatheart, Bunyan's hero." —*Jacob Riis*

Mrs. Roosevelt likes such hymns as "Nearer, My God, to Thee" and "Art Thou Weary," while the President said his favorite hymn was No. 457, beginning "Christ Is Made the Sure Foundation." His second favorite is "Holy, Holy, Holy, Lord God Almighty." He also expressed great admiration for "Jerusalem the Golden" and "The Son of God Goes Forth to War."

For the first time I realized that I had no favorite hymn, but I think at my funeral I should like to have sung "Nearer, My God, to Thee." I have thought of it during the day and I believe that I shall take "Nearer, My God, to Thee" as my favorite. *[It is said by survivors of* The Titanic *that as the ship was going down Captain Butt ordered the band to play the music of this hymn.]* —*Archie Butt*

Mr. Roosevelt had a sentimental liking for the old-fashioned hymns and the old-fashioned religion. He always had a Bible in his study and he could quote from it very handily. I once heard him say that the man who didn't read the Bible was a fool.

There is one thing that ought to be said by a man who saw Mr. Roosevelt at very close range, who saw him in the privacy of his home, and of his own room, at his meals, in the midst of his family. Traveling, in conference with business leaders and politicians, in the midst of political battle. That is that Theodore Roosevelt was the most thoroughly Christian man I have ever met anywhere. —*James Amos*

[A letter was published by the General Secretary of the New York Bible Society saying that when he asked Roosevelt in the summer of 1917 to send through that society a message to the American troops going abroad, TR chose Micah's text as his message, which he wrote out in his own hand with this comment:]

He himself declared his faith in the closing words of his address to the Young Men's Christian Association in New York City the night before he surrendered his stewardship as Governor into the hands

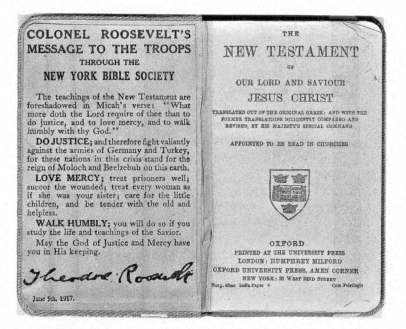

COLONEL ROOSEVELT'S
MESSAGE TO THE TROOPS
THROUGH THE
NEW YORK BIBLE SOCIETY

The teachings of the New Testament are foreshadowed in Micah's verse: "What more doth the Lord require of thee than to do justice, and to love mercy, and to walk humbly with thy God."

DO JUSTICE; and therefore fight valiantly against the armies of Germany and Turkey, for these nations in this crisis stand for the reign of Moloch and Beelzebub on this earth.

LOVE MERCY; treat prisoners well; succor the wounded; treat every woman as if she was your sister; care for the little children, and be tender with the old and helpless.

WALK HUMBLY; you will do so if you study the life and teachings of the Savior.

May the God of Justice and Mercy have you in His keeping.

Theodore Roosevelt

June 5th, 1917.

THE
NEW TESTAMENT
OF
OUR LORD AND SAVIOUR
JESUS CHRIST

TRANSLATED OUT OF THE ORIGINAL GREEK: AND WITH THE FORMER TRANSLATIONS DILIGENTLY COMPARED AND REVISED, BY HIS MAJESTY'S SPECIAL COMMAND

APPOINTED TO BE READ IN CHURCHES

OXFORD
PRINTED AT THE UNIVERSITY PRESS
LONDON: HUMPHREY MILFORD
OXFORD UNIVERSITY PRESS, AMEN CORNER
NEW YORK: 35 WEST 32ND STREET
Nonp. 48mo India Paper *   Cum Privilegio

---

of the people; and so let him stand before his countrymen and before the world:

"The true Christian is the true citizen, lofty of purpose, resolute in endeavor, ready for a hero's deeds, but never looking down on his task because it is cast in the day of small things; scornful of baseness, awake to his own duties as well as to his rights, following the higher law with reverence, and in this world doing all that in him lies, so that when death comes he may feel that mankind is in some degree better because he has lived." —*Jacob Riis*

Nothing better shows the even balance which Roosevelt kept than that while he was active in the gymnasium [boxing], he was also active in the Sunday School. He had joined the old church of his fathers, the Dutch Reformed, in New York, before going to Harvard. There being no church of his denomination in Cambridge, however, he took a class in an Episcopal Sunday school.

He had learned the spirit of service from his father. He must not live unto himself alone; he must feel he was doing something for others. He got along famously with his boys. When one of them came into the class with a black eye, the teacher questioned him earnestly about it. The boy explained, with manifest truthfulness, that his sister had been pinched by a boy who sat beside her. He had told the offender to stop and he would not stop, whereupon the gallant brother had fought for her.

"You did perfectly right," said Roosevelt, the muscular Christian, and he gave him a dollar as a poultice for the black eye. The class hailed this as a fine example of justice, and drew nearer than before to their teacher, for there is no way to get a firmer grip on a boy's heart than by taking his part in battle.

Some of the grave elders of the parish, however, hearing of the matter, were much displeased. In the end, Roosevelt left this field of labor and found a class in a Congregational Sunday school. —*Carleton Case*

I do not know of any other public man who has made so much use of the Bible texts and examples. He evidenced a wide acquaintance with it. —*James Morgan*

A few hours after Roosevelt's death, there came to me a well-known Broadway theatrical producer whose long career had acquainted him with disappointment in mankind and disillusionment, which breed cynicism. With tears in his eyes he complained to me most bitterly. He said: "It's fearful and amazing that all the world is now talking about the loss in Roosevelt's death. But all the world is missing the greatest loss of all—can't they see it? It was his faith in humanity! Why, he knew as much about men and women as I do, but—God bless him—he still believed in 'em!" —*Richard Washburn Child*

When he was in Emporia in 1912, Roosevelt came on Sunday morning. He was tired after a long, hard campaign; weary and over-strained. He needed sleep, but he got up and went to church and it was then that we had the talk about God and religion. He went to a very small church, I think the smallest congregation we have, the Dutch Reformed church. He did not let it be announced to what church he was going, because he wanted to avoid a crowd and be undisturbed as far as possible.

I went with him, and I remember this curious incident. He sang with his hands behind him, without the book, from memory, the entire hymn, "How Firm a Foundation Ye Saints of the Lord," and did not miss a word. I stood by him and was interested to see if at any time he would get to *da-da-ing* or *la-la-ing*, but no word escaped him. He was letter-perfect. There were few people in the church and no reporters. The reporters had all gone over to one of the big churches which had extended an invitation to the Colonel to be present. —*William Allen White*

Theodore Roosevelt was Governor, elected upon the pledge that he would rule by the Ten Commandments, in the city where, fifteen years before, the spoils politicians had spurned him for insisting upon doing the thing that was right rather than the thing that was expedient. Say now the world does not move! It strides with seven-league boots where only it has a man who dares to lead the way. Not necessarily at a smooth or even gait.

He knew what was before him, and as for the politicians, they were not appreciably nearer to the Ten Commandments than in the old days. They had not changed. They had fallen in behind Roosevelt because it was expedient, not because it was right. —*Jacob Riis*

[An entry in John Hay's diary of 1904 takes note, and makes a tongue-in-cheek suggestion, following President Roosevelt's impromptu remarks at a church service:]

June 21. The President returned from Valley Forge yesterday and we all congratulated him at the Cabinet meeting to-day on his sermon on Sunday. It seems it was entirely impromptu, Knox having asked him to speak only just before church time. [He] says the question what is to become of Roosevelt after 1908 is easily answered. He should be made a Bishop. —*John Hay*

[The legendary prize fighter and longtime world champion John L. Sullivan was one of many people led to the "straight and narrow" by Theodore Roosevelt. Sullivan repented of his bad habits after a career in the ring. The men remained friends, and Sullivan brought TR a gift before the African safari.]

The other day John L. Sullivan, who was in town, called on the President and presented him with a gold-mounted rabbit's foot, and the President brought him to luncheon. The President and Sullivan are really pals when they get together. The President says he is the cleanest prize fighter we have ever had, that he always fought squarely and never sold a fight.

The talk was all prize fighting, much to the disgust of Mrs. Roosevelt, and when one of the guests started to describe a prize fight at the table to-day Mrs. Roosevelt stopped him and said that she would not permit more than one prize fight discussion a season in the White House. —*Archie Butt*

[Regarding a "feeler" for TR to become Editor of a New York newspaper after the presidency, advanced by an Editor of The New York Times:*]*

Every day, at one o'clock, Delaney, a colored messenger employed at the Treasury Department, came over to the White House and shaved the President. There was a small room, between the President's private office and Mr. Loeb's office, which was always used for this purpose. There was, of course, no regular barber's chair, but Delaney did the best he could with a big arm-chair. The shaving hour was always a good one to see the President, for it gave the interviewer a better chance to say what he wanted to say in full, as the President, with his face covered with lather and Delaney's razor sweeping over it, was rather at a disadvantage as to talking.

I opened proceedings by handing a note to the President. He stopped Delaney's work and brought the message close to his face, as he always did when reading without his glasses. Then, as he got the purport of the message, he burst out laughing and jumped up from the chair. Waving the towel in one hand and the telegram in the other, he walked about the room and continued to laugh for a moment or two.

"This is the most extraordinary thing I have ever heard of," he said. "Why, O. K., I couldn't edit a paper. It's preposterous!"

Then he began to laugh again. Delaney stood there, with a grin on his face, waiting for the President to get back into the shaving chair. But the President seemed to be immensely amused by the proposition, and yet apparently he recognized the fact that there was a serious side to it....

"This is not what I want to do, and writing for *The Outlook* [a Christian weekly magazine of religion and commentary] is.

I want to preach. I have a good many sermons in me that I want to deliver, and *The Outlook* will furnish me a bully pulpit. —*O. K. Davis*

The President has two pews on the side aisle [of Christ Church in Oyster Bay]. He and Mrs. Winthrop and I occupied the first one, and Mrs. Roosevelt, with Kermit and Miss Ethel, occupying the one behind us. The President bowed his head in prayer just as all good Episcopalians do (this was Mrs. Roosevelt's faith) on entering church, and so did each of us. As the service proceeded I noticed that the President followed the service without the use of a Prayer Book, singing the chants, even going through the *Te Deum*, without notes, as it were.

He sang all the hymns and said the creed aloud. But I noticed that he did not bow his head in the creed nor did he at the Gloria. I suppose this was too much form for a member in good standing of the Dutch Reformed Church.

He has a poor idea of music, I imagine, for while he sang all the choral parts of the service, he was usually an octave lower than the choir in the hymns, but he did fairly well in the difficult Gregorian chants, much better than I who had sung in a choir at Sewanee, and I recognized the impossible formations of the syllables in the *Te Deum* and remembered, with a smile, how I used to work my jaws in it so that the precentor would not know that I was not singing. Well, the President got through it in the most wonderful manner. —*Archie Butt*

He was a man of great spiritual insight and development. His fights for the right were but the expression of his spiritual beliefs— such outward expressions required a great spirit to explain them. —*Dr. Alexander Lambert*

He was quicker than many of his contemporaries to perceive that evolution is not necessarily and exclusively Darwinian. Above all, he did not permit it to make a materialist of him. "The tracing of an unbroken line of descent from the protozoan to Plato does not in any real way explain Plato's consciousness." —*Edward Wagenknecht*

He compelled his body to obey him, so that without cessation because of pain or anything else he accomplished a wonderful amount of work. His great spirit dulled the cut of pain; it could not disturb him or check his activities. Such a conquering spirit gets its strength from but one source—faith in God. —*Edwin Van Valkenburg*, after a visit to TR in the hospital

He regularly took "communion" (observed the Lord's Supper) which is always recognized as the most intimate form of prayer.

Mr. Roosevelt lived the glad, free life of a conscious son of God. All who are fathers would say, "Well done" to such a son as Theodore Roosevelt—and our God is a Father. —*Christian Reisner*

There is yet one side of Theodore Roosevelt upon which I would touch, because I know the question to be on many lips; though I approach it with some hesitation. For a man's religious beliefs are his own, and he is not one to speak lightly of what is in his heart concerning the hope of heaven.

But though he is of few public professions, yet is he a reverent man, of practice, in private and public, ever in accord with the highest ideals of Christian manliness. His is a militant faith, bound on the mission of helping the world ahead; and in that campaign he welcomes gladly whoever would help. For the man who is out merely to purchase for himself a seat in heaven, whatever befall his brother, he has nothing but contempt; for him who struggles painfully toward the light, a helping hand and a word of cheer always. —*Jacob Riis*

Everybody knows that Theodore Roosevelt was intensely religious; that he did not hesitate, on all proper occasions, to announce publicly his faith in the fundamental doctrines of Christianity. He was a devoted member of the Dutch Reformed Church and attended its services regularly.

He told me that his firm faith in God, and his actual knowledge of Him had been the chief motive in his individual character and his public service.

Some think it smart and big to doubt. But the people of America believe. They want the human element in their heroes and the superhuman elements as well. They want them earth-born and born from above too. It will take a nation a long time to die which has as its heroes Washington, Lincoln, and Roosevelt, the crown of whose greatness was their goodness. —*Ferdinand Iglehart*

[Theodore Roosevelt, in a controversial—and unsuccessful—move, opposed "In God We Trust" appearing on coinage. He had witnessed incidents of cowboys in saloons making rude jokes from it, and moreover he felt it did not reflect appropriate reverence. Dr. Christian Reisner recalled another iconoclastic Roosevelt opinion about the matter of Church and State.]

He was just as frank...and as late as 1915 opposed a New York State bill making Bible-reading in the schools compulsory. He called it a fanatical move. —*Christian Reisner*

President Roosevelt was much criticized because he tried to take from the coins the words "In God We Trust." In a letter to a protesting clergyman he expressed the conviction that to put such a motto on coins worked no benefit, but positive injury, since it augmented an irreverence which was likely to lead to sacrilege. He felt that such a rich and dignified sentence "should be treated and uttered only with that fine reverence which necessarily implies a certain exaltation of spirit."

He agrees that the phrase should be inscribed on public buildings and monuments where it will carry the message of reverence. He affirms that since the phrase is used on commonly handled coins it becomes an object of jest and ridicule in word and cartoon, as, for example, "In 'gold' we trust." He concluded his defense by saying that he will restore the motto if Congress orders, but, "I earnestly trust that the religious sentiment of the country, the spirit of reverence… will prevent it." —*Christian Reisner*

Roosevelt's religion was simple, unostentatious, and genuine. He made no parade of it, neither did he ever conceal it. His addresses were sermons; they made free use of Scripture, which he employed with telling effect. He met the sorrows that came to him with a courage that belongs to sincere Christian faith. He lived and died a professed and earnest follower of Jesus Christ. —*Rev. William E. Barton*

My brother's knowledge of the Bible was as extraordinarily thorough as was his information on the history of his beloved country, that country to which he gave his time, his thought, and in the highest sense, himself. —*Corinne Roosevelt Robinson*

During the eight years Mr. Roosevelt spent in Washington as Vice President and President, he constantly attended Dr. Schick's services [at the German Reformed Church].

While Roosevelt was a member of his congregation, Dr. Schick said once to his friend, Dr. Albert C. Dieffenbach, that in case the President could not attend church he wrote a note to the minister or telephoned, expressing his regrets and giving reasons. He took part in the service with customary enthusiasm, reading the responses and singing the hymns with fervor. He listened with interest to the sermon, responded to special appeals with generous contributions, and participated in the Holy Communion and other special services. —*Edward H. Cotton*

Theodore Roosevelt was one of the most profoundly religious men this nation or any other nation ever had. He was one of the most powerful believers I ever saw; and one of the most prodigious religious actors I ever beheld. Religion is a science and an art. As a science it is a system of doctrines to be believed, as an art it is a system of duties to be performed.

Mr. Roosevelt had the science of religion down to a perfection in the most simple and sincere faith, in the cardinal doctrines of our religion, and he practiced it vigorously, as an art, in the multitude of secular acts. He believed firmly in knowing the will of God; but he put the heavy emphasis of his life on doing that will in everyday life, for after all religion consists as much or more in doing secular things, from a religious motive, as in doing the religious things themselves.

God has so planned it that we are to spend most of our time in so-called secular service; but the religious motive sanctifies it and makes all of life sacred. That was the theology and practice of Theodore Roosevelt. —*Ferdinand Iglehart*

He never paraded his religion or his faith, but both were very fundamental with him. —*Dr. Nicholas Murray Butler*

It was inherent in father to be reserved about the subject of personal religion. He claimed that actions "talked" in religion as in everything else. These told of his faith in a clear way. —*Kermit Roosevelt*

My brother seldom talked about doctrinal subjects in religion. He had a profound faith which he believed would show itself in his actions. In my judgment he led in an absolute and exact way the life that is laid down for a Christian. He believed that a Christian life was the one to lead. —*Corinne Roosevelt Robinson*

He had accepted the invitation to address the brotherhood, and the appointment was made for four o'clock. Invitations were sent to other congregations, and the [Oyster Bay] church was crowded, and thousands of people stood on the outside. The President came down from Sagamore Hill at the appointed hour, with his own little Bible, which bore the evidence of much wear....

He preached a real sermon to the brotherhood. His subject was that men must practice the religion which they profess, and that, if they do not practice it, they are self-deceived in counting themselves professors. He took as his main text James 1:22—"Be ye doers of the word, and not hearers only, deceiving your own selves."

During his sermon he had a slip of paper on which he had jotted down different texts, which he made the basis of the various divisions of his message. Someone in the audience saw that slip and asked Dr. Bowman if he could secure it for him as a souvenir, and the pastor wrote the President and received from him the following answer:

Dear Brother Bowman: I have taken pleasure in autographing the memorandum of those texts. With all good wishes, believe me, Faithfully yours.

(Signed) Theodore Roosevelt.

The memorandum of texts was as follows:

Matt. 7:1.

"Judge not, that ye be not judged."

Matt. 7:16.

"Ye shall know them by their fruits. Do men gather grapes of thorns, or figs of thistles?"

Matt. 25:37-40.

"Then shall the righteous answer him, saying, Lord, when saw we thee an hungered, and fed thee? or thirsty, and gave thee drink?

"When saw we thee a stranger, and took thee in? or naked, and clothed thee?

"Or when saw we thee sick, or in prison, and came unto thee and the King shall answer and say unto them, Verily I say unto you, Inasmuch as ye have done it unto one of the least of these My brethren, ye have done it unto Me."

James 1:27.

"Pure religion and undefiled before God and the Father is this: To visit the fatherless and widows in their affliction, and to keep himself unspotted from the world."

James 3:17,18.

"But the wisdom that is from above is first pure, then peaceable, gentle, and easy to be entreated, full of mercy and good fruits, without partiality, and without hypocrisy. And the fruit of righteousness is sown in peace of them that make peace." *—Rev. W. I. Bowman*

Mr. Roosevelt said…"Every sensible man believes in and practices religion." To take God out of consideration when viewing Mr. Roosevelt's life is to mislead the people and lessen the permanency of his influence. Without a religious training similar to that which he and his associates received and followed, there will be no leaders

of caliber and strength to succeed the present-day leaders; teachers and parents must realize that or fail at their task. The child without a religious training is unfitted to meet life's problems successfully.
—*Christian Reisner*

Military Hero

TR's service in the "Splendid Little War," the Spanish-American War, and his famous taking of San Juan Hill, added to the legend of the reformer-politician, cowboy, and zealous Police Commissioner. His Rough Rider persona was glorified through his lifetime; in movies of the 1920s and beyond; and in cartoons, dime novels, and even card games.

Theodore Roosevelt neither drank nor smoked, his face and persona were attached nevertheless to beer, whiskey, cigars, and countless other commercial products, never with his permission. Even cigar bands, breakfast cereal and other products carried his face, if not his endorsement.

Songs, Dances, and Show Tunes

TR was the subject of scores of songs, dances, and show tunes. His face adorned colorful covers and his personality inspired sheet music and popular songs.

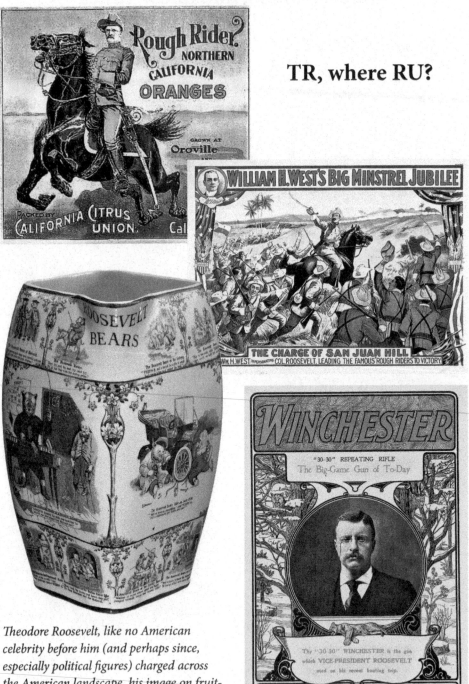

TR, where RU?

Theodore Roosevelt, like no American celebrity before him (and perhaps since, especially political figures) charged across the American landscape, his image on fruit-box labels; elaborate stage productions; kitchen items and houseware; and firearms.

Theodore Roosevelt had many publishers throughout his career, and in his early days was a part-owner in G P Putnam's Sons. But the majority of his many books were published by Charles Scribner's Sons. After he died, and before two sets of his Complete Works were issued in uniform editions, Scribner's promoted TR's books in special bookstore displays, categorized by their their themes, with pertinent photographs of Roosevelt.

CHAPTER VIII

Theodore Roosevelt: Intellectual, Polymath, Cognoscente

Not even excepting Thomas Jefferson or citizens like Benjamin Franklin the American Leonardo, Theodore Roosevelt stands in history as one of his nation's great minds, in capacity, catholicity, and accomplishments. But he wrote: "No man can reach the front rank if he is not intelligent and if he is not trained with intelligence; but mere intelligence by itself is worse than useless unless it is guided by an upright heart, unless there are also strength and courage behind it. Morality, decency, clean living, courage, manliness, self-respect— these qualities are more important in the make-up of a people than any mental subtlety."

A key to Roosevelt's insatiable curiosity and his intellectual motivation can be found in what he once said: "The capacity to be bored is an awful handicap."

When Theodore Roosevelt was Contributing Editor of *The Outlook* magazine, its president, Lawrence F. Abbott, once estimated that TR published perhaps 2.5 million words, and wrote a total of approximately 18 million words when his letters are included in the count. Roughly half a million words are in the *Theodore Roosevelt Cyclopedia*, a book of mere excerpts and passages.

Such things are hard to estimate, especially a century later as correspondence and miscellaneous writings are still being discovered. In the same manner, the number of books Roosevelt wrote and published is elusive, as some were compilations or collected speeches; but forty to fifty separate volumes is a reliable number.

Theodore Roosevelt probably wrote more books than many of his countrymen read (even today?), and probably more than many presidents had. And we must look beyond "words, words, words" as a primary determinant of sagacity or intelligence: Edward Everett spoke for two hours at Gettysburg, and Abraham Lincoln followed with a two-minute address. As with the lesson of such a comparison, posterity is blessed that Roosevelt generally wrote in colorful and memorable prose, seldom failing to assert and explain his points.

He agreed with Poe, regarding the mere accumulation of words, decrying "the mad pride of intellectuality."

As noted earlier, the intellect of Roosevelt was partly attributable to his eidetic memory and photographic memory—rare mental abilities infrequently gifted on the same person, but evidently so in TR's case. To his variety of intellectualism, he added an insatiable curiosity and a catholicity of interests.

Some of the many letters TR exchanged were unorthodox. This intellectual giant, for instance, had a problem spelling simple words (although he could generally master longer words and many scientific and biological terms). Also, Roosevelt had the handwriting of a child, a sloppy child at that, compared to standard penmanship of the Victorian era.

These peculiarities might have prompted Roosevelt, around 1906, to join the crusade for Simplified Spelling, a fad promoted by Andrew Carnegie, Brander Matthews, and others. It was basically "fonetic speling," an attempt to wash the vestiges of incompatible Germanic and Romance rules from American English. TR even ordered the Government Printing Office to adopt Simplified Spelling, but this was perhaps the shortest-lived of any Roosevelt reform: his Executive Order was rescinded by a recalcitrant Congress.

As a "literary feller" (as he called himself once when his livelihood depended almost solely on writing books), TR certainly was the most well-read of American presidents, Jefferson not excepted. While he was president, he wrote freelance, scholarly articles on a variety of subjects for general-interest and academic journals. He also wrote for children's magazines and popular weeklies. After leaving office, Roosevelt wrote lengthy art criticism of the famous Armory Show, where Cubism had its first major American showing. The essay was somewhat jejune, but it was informed, and of course, earnest.

When TR's son Kermit recommended to his father *Children of the Night,* an obscure book of poems, Roosevelt was so impressed that he wrote a favorable review for a major magazine, sought out the starving poet, and arranged for him a government job, with instructions to "think poetry first" and bureaucratic pencil-pushing second. Thus commenced the successful career of a major American poet, Edwin Arlington Robinson.

When Roosevelt was busy wrapping up myriad threads of his Administration's closing days, and planning the logistics of a major safari in Africa, he took a moment, not as a writer of books but as a reader, to encourage a fellow author. Kenneth Grahame worked for the Bank of England, but enjoyed a circle of readers who had read his books of childhood—really, adult books about the halcyon days and things of childhood, *The Golden Age* and *Dream Days.* Out of the blue it must have seemed to Grahame was the letter he received from America:

The White House, Washington,

January 17, 1909

Personal

My Dear Mr. Grahame—My mind moves in ruts, as I suppose most minds do, and at first I could not reconcile myself to the change from the ever-delightful Harold and his associates, and so for some time I could not accept the toad, the mole, the water-rat and the badger as substitutes. But after a while Mrs. Roosevelt and two of the boys, Kermit and Ted, all quite independently, got hold of The Wind Among the Willows [sic] and took such a delight in it that I began to feel that I might have to revise my judgment. Then Mrs. Roosevelt read it aloud to the younger children, and I listened now and then. Now I have read it and reread it, and have come to accept the characters as old friends; and I am almost more fond of it than of your previous books. Indeed, I feel about going to Africa very much as the seafaring rat did when he almost made the water-rat wish to forsake everything and start wandering!

I felt I must give myself the pleasure of telling you how much we had all enjoyed your book.

With all good wishes,

Sincerely yours,

THEODORE ROOSEVELT

... and so a modest British author was encouraged by a fan letter. (And Roosevelt's publisher, Scribner's, was encouraged to publish *The Wind In the Willows* in the United States.)

Roosevelt wrote many works on American history. Without setting out to do so, because they were written or assigned in random order over many years, he eventually covered the sweep of the entire national narrative, like pieces in a jigsaw puzzle. Several of his books, like *The Naval War of 1812* and the multi-volume *Winning of the West*, continue to be regarded as standard works in their field. Listed in general order of their place in the American story (not publication dates), they include: *New York City*; *Gouverneur Morris*; *The Winning of the West*; *The Naval War of 1812*; *Thomas Hart Benton*; and *Hero Tales from American History* (with Henry Cabot Lodge). Daniel Ruddy has assembled those puzzle pieces, portions of each book, into a seamless narrative, splendidly in *Theodore Roosevelt's History of the United States: His Own Words*.

Other random titles included a biography of Oliver Cromwell; the two-volume *Life-Histories of African Game Animals* with Edmund Heller; many collections about hunting and camping; and several anthologies of his articles, speeches, reviews, and essays.

A member of the American Academy of Arts and Letters, Roosevelt was also president of the American Historical Association, elected just one month after his exhaustive and contentious Bull Moose campaign for the presidency of the United States. He immediately prepared a memorable address, "History as Literature."

When he was "on fire" over a topic, like a preacher of the Jeremiah sort, Roosevelt sometimes was criticized for being, indeed, preachy. At Oxford University, the Archbishop of York pronounced the lecture "Beta Minus" but the lecturer "Alpha Plus." And his speech at the Sorbonne in Paris initially was met by remarks that it was commonplace, prosaic.

But that speech, which contained the "Man in the Arena" passage, has grown in respect through the years and today is among his most-cited sentiments:

"It is not the critic who counts, not the man who points out how the strong man stumbles, or where the doer of deeds could have done them better. The credit belongs to the man in the arena, whose face is marred by dust and sweat and blood, who strives valiantly...who knows the great enthusiasms, the great devotions, who spends himself in a worthy cause; who at the best knows in the end the triumph of high achievement, and who at the worst, if he fails, at least fails while daring greatly, so that his place shall never be with those cold and timid souls who have never known neither victory nor defeat."

Yet portions of Roosevelt's books can startle the reader. This man of so many different but characteristic thoughts and words occasionally had other "voices." Counter-intuitively, perhaps, Theodore Roosevelt could be introspective and philosophical, even poetic. To the poet Robinson, whose denizens of the fictional Tilbury Town often dealt with melancholia and sorrow, TR wrote: "There is not one among us in whom a devil does not dwell; at some time, on some point, that devil masters each of us. He who has not fallen has not been tested. It is not having been in the Dark House, but having left it, that counts."

In Africa and Brazil—even when nearly delirious with fever on the latter expedition, and always exhausted at the end of each day—he dutifully wrote in his diary, he wrote letters to home (even if he would arrive before the post did), and wrote chapters of magazine articles about his explorations. In each case, the articles became book chapters. But in longhand, covered in mosquito protection, wearing gauntlets, he wrote lengthy chapters—in duplicate or triplicate, in case the couriers would get lost or killed.

At home, TR usually dictated his letters and speeches. He is reported as sometimes having had two secretary/stenographers working simultaneously.

His practice as an executive, even during the presidency, was to prepare major messages far in advance of their delivery. In another example contradicting the stereotype of his supposed egomania, he routinely produced copies of that message or address to send home with trusted visitors, experts, pertinent allies, or government personnel, and friends.

He asked for suggestions, and required that nobody hesitate to contradict him. When comments came, Roosevelt enthusiastically discussed the matters and frequently altered, dropped, or added material.

Previous presidents wrote periodic messages and delivered occasional speeches, but TR was the first—as well as a great—communicator in the White House.

* * *

We rode or walked together every day, and we derived much pleasure and satisfaction from selecting our subjects and discussing their treatment. There never was a more delightful companion in the world than Theodore Roosevelt.

He had an unusually wide range of interests. He knew books and literature and loved them both. He had seen men and cities like Ulysses, and had the keenest interest in everything relating to our common humanity.

He had no taste for telling stories which existed solely to be pointed with a joke, and he never was in danger of drifting into anecdotage. But he had the rare and fascinating gift of the tale-teller where the merit lies in the art of narration, in the humor or sentiment which pervades it, and not merely in a jest which concludes it. —*Henry Cabot Lodge*

It made little difference into what channels the conversation turned. Sooner or later Father produced information that often startled students of the theme under discussion. He knew the species of Hannibal's elephants by the shape of their ears as shown on the Carthaginian coins of the period. He could recite "The Song of Roland" in the original French. He could tell you in detail the history of the heavyweight boxing champions. It was never safe to contradict him on any statement, no matter how recent you might feel your information was. —*Ted Roosevelt*, TR's son, from a magazine article

[Justice Edward Douglass White was asked to critique a draft of a presidential address and] went into detail and pointed out half-a-dozen passages which he thought Mr. Bryan would seize upon as material for effective Democratic criticism. The party broke up in gloom. Justice White went home and said to his wife, "We shall never be invited to the White House again. I've upset the apple-cart. The President read us his Message and I severely criticized it."

"Oh, my dear, what could have induced you to do such a thing as that!"

"I didn't want to," complained the Justice, "but he dragooned me into doing it!" For some time they felt perturbed about the incident, believing that their pleasant and friendly relations with Roosevelt had been interrupted if not destroyed. Two or three days later Mrs. White attended a state reception at the White House although another engagement prevented the Justice from accompanying her. As she approached the President in the formal line he stepped out of his place and literally "grabbed both her hands"—as the Justice expressed it—exclaiming: "Mrs. White, do you know your husband gave me the worst abuse the other evening that I have received since I've been President!" And then, just as she was wishing that the floor would open and swallow her up, he quickly added with his magnetic smile: "And the worst of it was he was absolutely right, *absolutely right!*"

Of course, Mrs. White reported this to her husband as soon as she got home and with relieved feelings they watched for the publication of the Message with some curiosity. When it appeared they found to their satisfaction that the criticized passages in the original draft had been completely modified in accordance with the suggestions of the Justice.

"Where," said the Justice to my friend in commenting on this incident, "will you find a more striking instance of open-mindedness in a great political leader than this?" —*Archie Butt*

Frequently he used to say to his advisers: "Prepare me a paper on the subject." In these papers the essence of a highly technical matter had to be condensed both clearly and accurately so that he could study it at his leisure and give a decision on it. These reports he would put in his inside coat-pocket, and often he would say: "I will take this home with me; come and see me about it tomorrow."

One day when, as his naval aide, I had presented him with such a memorandum upon a matter of vital concern to the Navy, he looked at the paper for a few minutes, slowly turning over the pages and pausing a short time at each, as though giving it a preliminary survey. Then, instead of putting it in his pocket, he laid it down and, in place of his usual formula, said abruptly: "All right; what have you got to say about it?"

Being of course disappointed at this apparently careless way of treating a subject of so great importance, I said:

"Mr. President, I intended that paper for your inside pocket. I think it would be best to postpone discussion of it until after you have read it."

President Roosevelt did not object in the least to plain speech as long as it was genuine, and perhaps he found my protest amusing, for he laughed and said, "But I have read it; I know everything in it."

It seemed incredible that he could have mastered so technical a matter in so offhand a manner; yet his subsequent discussion proved that he had. I once heard him say that he often "read" as many as three books in one evening. I do not doubt it. —*Rear Admiral William S. Sims*

As I think of him I remember him as the [first] president I ever met, as the only president who ever took that much interest in a poet— that I know of. There have been good presidents; good presidents are few and far between. He was one of our kind. He quoted poetry to me. He knew poetry. Poetry was in his mind; that means a great deal to me. —*Robert Frost*

A dead phrase became a political missile. There it lay. There it had always lain. Roosevelt stumbled on it, looked at it, roared, picked it up, hurled it at the right mark, and exploded it into fame. Everything became something else. There ceased to be any such thing as the commonplace. But when one had gone away from him one found that what he had really done was to make the world itself momentarily, immortally interesting. —*William Hard*

In our conversation I mentioned Edna Ferber. And the Colonel said, "Now that girl is doing splendid work! That Emma McChesney [the independent, entrepreneurial character of Ferber's early stories] of hers is a real creation! A real creation!" Some time after the Colonel's death I mentioned this to Edna Ferber.

"Yes," she said, "the dear man! That was just like him. He was the most encouraging person that ever breathed." —*Arthur Guiterman*

He greeted me with that delightful heartiness that was so characteristic of him. It so happened that I had written a story which had been published in the current number of *Harper's Magazine* and which he had to read on the ship on the way over. For some reason it had pleased him and he not only spoke of his satisfaction with it, but to my speechless astonishment he repeated word for word a bit of dialogue out of it that I suppose was ten lines long. Of course I could not have done it.

That is just an example of his extraordinary power of memory and the astonishing accuracy with which he could recall such things, including many, as in this case, that were not important. —*E. S. Martin*

He was rarely if ever trite, and must have been in complete accord with the thought of John Morley, that a platitude is not turned into a profundity by being dressed up as a conundrum. —*Joseph S. Auerbach*

In all the long and busy years of his presidency, if you wrote and asked him a question one day, the reply almost without exception would be received on the third day. Just as soon as a letter could get to Washington, he answered and returned; and all his letters had the personal touch, with characteristic corrections, or the impulsive postscript written with his own hand. —*Robert Bridges*

As President Roosevelt came down to breakfast at my house one morning, I expressed the usual hope that he had slept well. "To tell the truth," he replied, "I hardly had a chance. I looked around the room, as I always do, to see if it contained any book of importance which I had not read. I found a prose translation of Dante's *Inferno* which was new to me, and which was so remarkable that I had to read it through. This kept me up until five in the morning." —*Dr. Arthur T. Hadley*

President Roosevelt's favorite form of hospitality was the luncheon. Those who were privileged to be his guests heard him at his best at that informal meal....

When the president found a book he liked he would telegraph the author to any part of the country and invite him to lunch the next week, and the author would usually come. The president would garnish the table with a couple of his cabinet officers, and a few others. —*William Howard Taft*

No house in our family would be complete without [books]. They overflow every room. They are piled on the tables. They multiply with the fearful rapidity of guinea pigs. Catalogues and book stores fascinate us as a snake does a bird. These books range from first editions, vellum Horaces, Eliziviers, and Aldines, to autographed copies from the authors, guarded in a special glazed bookcase. —*Ted Roosevelt*, son of TR

When Brander Matthews [author, essayist, and professor of literature] lived on East 17th Street, he used to have the most interesting groups for luncheons on Saturdays during mid-winter months. When Rudyard Kipling was in New York, he was naturally a center of interest in these groups.

Kipling used to listen to [Theodore Roosevelt's] stories with undisguised amusement and would often offer comments upon them that were, in their way, as good as the stories themselves. Kipling and Roosevelt made an interesting pair. —*Dr. Nicholas Murray Butler*

[Roosevelt learned German as a child, living for months in Dresden with his siblings. He also managed French, knowledgeable about the ancient forms of each tongue. He spoke Italian and endeavored to read classical Greek and Latin.]

The President talked with great energy and perfect ease the most curious French I ever listened to. It was absolutely lawless as to grammar, and occasionally bankrupt in substantives; but he had not the least difficulty in making himself understood. —*John Hay*

In preparing to write *The Winning of the West*, he took great pains to search out and to use original materials; and in his prefaces and elsewhere he details his chief sources. He presents a few excursus on authorities, particularly in the Appendix to the original first volume, where he reprints some of the Indian speeches. In order to reach manuscript collections he made extensive journeys, particularly in Kentucky and Tennessee. —*Albert Bushnell Hart*

[Corinne Roosevelt Robinson] suggested that I send my quatrain ["Preparedness"] to her brother.

> *For all your days prepare,*
> *And meet them ever alike:*
> *When you are the anvil, bear —*
> *When you are the hammer, strike.*

He wrote back, thanking me and saying: "I shall not only live by these lines myself, but I will also teach my boys to live by them." —*Edwin Markham*

No more versatile man ever lived. There was hardly a subject of discussion on which he was not well posted, and on the numerous railroad and other trips I made with him, his tireless energy and activity were shown by the fact that he was never idle and that when he read, he remembered with that wonderful mind of his which seemed instantly to grasp essentials and never forget. He was a most omnivorous reader. —*John M. Parker*

[In his massive history *The Winning of the West*, Roosevelt] knows these people [many Indian tribes] sympathetically, not only because he has read the narratives of the white men who went among them, but because almost exactly a hundred years later he lived near similar Indians in the far Northwest. He excels in his sketches of some of the great leaders among them—Corn Planter the Iroquois, Logan the Mingo, Dragging Canoe the Cherokee, and McGillivray the Creek.

Never in his life did Roosevelt condone an act of treachery or murder by any race. He develops the murder of the kinfolk of [the Native American] Logan by worthless whites in a manner almost classic. He sees the gloom descend upon the noble chief like fate in a Greek play.

Then and now, much baseless sympathy has gone out to the Indians as driven from their ancestral lands by the insatiable white man. Roosevelt says on that point: "There were a dozen tribes, all of whom hunted in Kentucky and fought each other there, all of whom had equally good titles to the soil, and not one of whom acknowledged the right of any other; as a matter of fact they had therein no right, save the right of the strongest.... The white settler...does not feel that he is committing a wrong, for he knows that the land is really owned by no one." On the other hand, these were lands from which the Indians drew much of their food and clothing; and in large areas, such as the permanent villages of the Creeks and Cherokees, they had a kind of homestead title.

If there be a text to *The Winning of the West*, it is that the coming in of the whites was not to be stayed by any force in America. —*Albert Bushnell Hart*

For days at a time, when he was a young ranchman, he would roam the wilds alone with his pony, and his pocket editions of the classics, and the simplest and scantiest provisions. He slept on the prairie in his buffalo bag when the thermometer had fallen to sixty-five degrees below zero.

One night when he was out, a blizzard overtook him, and obliged him to seek shelter. Coming upon a cowboy, who was also fleeing from the storm, the two found a deserted hut, in which they took refuge. As they sat about the fire they had built, Mr. Roosevelt read *Hamlet* to his companion, who was an uncultivated son of the plains, but who was deeply interested in the tale. At the end of the reading he gave it as his enthusiastic opinion that "old Shakespeare savveyed [surveyed] human nature some." Mr. Roosevelt learned to take life everywhere as he found it. —*Carleton Case*

[Bishop J. L. Spalding of the Anthracite Coal Commission asked:] "Pardon me, Mr. President, but you astonish me that at your age you should have had the time in your busy life to read and remember so much as you do of ancient and modern literature." The President, blushing slightly, replied. "Bishop, I really am not entitled to much credit. I love books, especially those on vital subjects. I am blessed with a retentive memory, and I have more than some people do, as I require about five hours' sleep." —*Thomas H. Watkins*

Whatever one's preferences in politics might be, one's house was bound to the Republican interest when sandwiched between Senator Cameron, John Hay, and Cabot Lodge, with Theodore Roosevelt equally at home in them all, and [British diplomat] Cecil Spring-Rice to unite them by impartial variety. The relation was daily, and the alliance undisturbed by power or patronage, since [President] Harrison, in those respects, showed little more taste than Mr. Cleveland for the society and interests of this particular band of followers, whose relations with the White House were sometimes comic, but never intimate. —*Henry Adams*

He was very desirous of meeting William Yeats, the poet; but Yeats, who wandered in fairyland, was very hard to bring down to an exact date. The President hoped to arrange an appropriate party for him; but Yeats, lost in darkest Washington, did not appear at my club until very late on the night preceding the luncheon; consequently there was no great party.

The Roosevelt children, however, were there, with Mrs. Roosevelt—Archie apparently the most anxious to hear about the Irish fairies.

The Celtic poet seemed very happy, but he was silent. President Roosevelt beamed through his glasses, and tried to draw him out. Suddenly Yeats said, "It's the Little People we must consider."…

I said, "By the 'Little People' he means the Irish fairies."

It was President Roosevelt's turn to look astonished. "Mr. Yeats, have you ever seen an Irish fairy?" he asked, with a glint in his eye.

"Many times," Yeats said solemnly. "Sure, not only I, but every Irishman, especially the old ones that mow the hay in the twilight, have seen the Little People many and many a time; but they are not small insignificant creatures, like the English fairies; they are giants, the old gods come back again."

The President was bowled out, but the children found themselves on congenial ground. —*Maurice Francis Egan*

I had the pleasure of introducing to him both John Masefield and Edgar Lee Masters. The former motored with me to Sagamore Hill for luncheon, and afterward he spoke with interest of the way in which Colonel Roosevelt not only knew his poems from cover to cover, but was familiar also with the quaint pieces of almost unknown history upon which many of his stories in verse were founded.

My brother was deeply interested in Mr. Masters's striking "Spoon River Anthology," but earnestly exhorted him to show more of the beautiful side of life and more of the finer characteristics which he always maintained were to be found in human nature. After his first meeting with Mr. Masters he was anxious to have more talk with this poet whose power he gladly acknowledged; and the result was that visit to Sagamore Hill, which enabled Mr. Masters to paint Theodore Roosevelt at his home in so vivid a manner. —*Corinne Roosevelt Robinson*

"At Sagamore Hill"

 ... The talk begins.

He's dressed in canvas khaki, flannel shirt,
Laced boots for farming, chopping trees, perhaps;
A stocky frame, curtains of skin on cheeks
Drained slightly of their fat; gash in the neck
Where pus was emptied lately; one eye dim,
And growing dimmer; almost blind in that.
And when he walks he rolls a little like
A man whose youth is fading, like a cart
That rolls when springs are old. He is a moose,
Scarred, battered from the hunters, thickets, stones;

Some finest tips of antlers broken off,
And eyes where images of ancient things
Flit back and forth across them, keeping still
A certain slumberous indifference
Or wisdom, it may be.

    But then the talk!
...
    Time goes on,
The play is staged, must end; my taxi comes
In half an hour or so. Before it comes,
Let's walk about the farm and see my corn.
A fellow on the porch is warming heels
As we go by. I'll see him when you go,
The Colonel says.
    The rail fence by the corn
Is good to lean on as we stand and talk
Of farming, cattle, country life. We turn,
Sit for some moments in a garden house
On which a rose vine clambers all in bloom,
And from this hilly place look at the strips
Of water from the bay a mile beyond,
Below some several terraces of hills
Where firs and pines are growing. This resembles
A scene in Milton that I've read. He knows,
Catches the reminiscence, quotes the lines—and then
Something of country silence, look of grass
Where the wind stirs it, mystical little breaths
Coming between the roses; something, too,
In Vulcan's figure; he is Vulcan, too,
Deprived his shop, great bellows, hammer, anvil,
Sitting so quietly beside me, hands
Spread over knees; something of these evokes
A pathos, and immediately in key
With all of this he says: I have achieved
By labor, concentration, not at all
By gifts or genius, being commonplace
In all my faculties.
    ...

So, good-by
Upon the lawn at Sagamore was good-by,
Master of Properties, you stage the scene
And let us speak and pass into the wings!
One thing was fitting—dying in your sleep—
A touch of Nature, Colonel, you who loved
And were beloved of Nature, felt her hand
Upon your brow at last to give to you
A bit of sleep, and after sleep perhaps
Rest and rejuvenation; you will wake
To newer labors, fresher victories
Over those faculties not disciplined
As you desired them in these sixty years.

—*Edgar Lee Masters, 1919*

He talked of *The Spoon River Anthology*, and seemed to know it all, and some of it by heart.... He was to me as if we had always known each other. We sat down for two hours or more talking poetry, philosophy, hunting, fishing; talking of men and events and of the war, of life and fate and death.

If he had lived I believe we should have become fast friends, correspondents, and intimates. His death was a great loss to me and grieved me deeply. —*Edgar Lee Masters*

A man who does two thousand words of creative work day in and day out for every working day of the year is performing a portentous job from the brain-worker's point of view. If the estimate that Roosevelt produced eighteen millions of written words in his lifetime is at all reasonable, that alone would represent the work of thirty years of the lifetime of a literary man. Roosevelt had about forty years of active work, assuming that he began his productive activity when he published *The Naval War of 1812* not long after he had passed his twentieth year. Thus, in his forty working years he produced as a writer what in amount, at least, would have been a creditable fruitage of thirty years' labor by a professional man of letters who did nothing else but write.

Writing, however, was merely one of Roosevelt's avocations. —*Lawrence F. Abbott*

Colonel Roosevelt always disclaimed being a genius. He said with regard to the successful man: "The average man who is successful—the average statesman, the average public servant, the average soldier, who wins what we call great success—is not a genius. He is a man who has merely the ordinary qualities, who has developed those ordinary qualities to a more than ordinary degree." —*Hermann Hagedorn*

Mr. Roosevelt was a full man. Whatever anyone may think about his politics or political actions, no one will deny that he was a man of extraordinary cultivation, with distinguished attainment in numerous different lines. He was an indefatigable and omnivorous reader, whose remarkable memory caught and held the vast bulk of what he read. He had so developed the habit of concentration on what he read that all sorts of things could go on in the room about him without in the least disturbing him, or distracting his attention from his book or magazine. He was a highly competent judge, therefore, of the cultivation of other men. —*O. K. Davis*

Colonel Roosevelt was an amateur naturalist, and yet he was a naturalist of splendid training. He had the keen eye and mind of the ideal naturalist and he was further aided by a phenomenal memory such as few men possess. He found infinite joy in studying wild animal life in its native haunts, and the least of his pleasure in killing it. His greatest pleasures lay in seeing and learning, thereby proving him an ideal naturalist.

Many of his statements on the subject of his explorations and discoveries were twisted and ridiculed by hostile and ignorant critics. His enemies made great fun of the River of Doubt, the uncharted stream he traced to its source in the South American wilds. But the facts remain that he rendered a great service to the science of geography by locating it exactly, and that the Brazilian Government named it after him, Rio Teodoro [sometimes Rio Roosevelt].

Incidentally, I believe that his exposure and trials on that Brazilian trip led to his death. —*Carl Akeley*

When he promised a manuscript for a certain date, that promise was kept absolutely, no matter what intervened.

When he returned from the Spanish-American War and landed at Montauk, he sent word to [*Scribner's* magazine, where Bridges was editor] that he wanted to talk about his proposed story of the Rough Riders. Just before he started on that expedition he had said, "If I come back, you shall have the first chance at anything I write."

It was, therefore, on the first afternoon after he returned to his home at Oyster Bay that, on the lawn at Sagamore Hill, we talked over the book which developed into *The Rough Riders*. It was all perfectly clear in the Colonel's mind. He knew the grand divisions of his story, although he had not written a line. There were to be six articles, and the date was set for the delivery of the first one so that the serial could begin in the magazine promptly.

Very soon he was nominated for Governor of New York. I said to him one day: "I suppose this will interfere with your dates for *The Rough Riders*?"

"Not at all," he replied; "you shall have the various chapters at the times promised."

As everybody knows, he made a vigorous campaign for Governor of New York, and was elected, and inaugurated in the following January. Notwithstanding this arduous and exciting time, he fulfilled every promise, and the book was delivered on time. —*Robert Bridges*

[A record of the way Roosevelt employed his time was made by a man who accompanied him on his tour of the country as a candidate for the Vice-Presidency in 1900. It is the schedule of a day's occupations:]

7 a.m.—Breakfast.
7.30 a.m.—A speech.
8 a.m.—Reading an historical work.
9 a.m.—A speech.
10 a.m.—Dictating letters.
11 a.m.—Discussing Montana mines.
11.30 a.m.—A speech.
12 n.—Reading an ornithological work.
12.30 p.m.—A speech.
1 p.m.—Lunch.
1.30 p.m.—A speech.
2.30 p.m.—Reading Sir Walter Scott.
3 p.m.—Answering telegrams.
3.45 p.m.—A speech.
4 p.m.—Meeting the press.
4.30 p.m.—Reading.
5 p.m.—A speech.
6 p.m.—Reading.
7 p.m.—Supper.
8 to 10 p.m.—Speaking.
11 p.m.—Reading alone in his car.
12 p.m.—To bed.

—George William Douglas

My personal visit [to the White House in 1902] was made on the evening of the day on which he returned from his comet-like trip in the Carolinas. He had got back to Washington in the morning after five days of soul-wearying travel, still more wearying speech-making and function-holding, and the ceaseless strain of social and every other sort of exciting experience. Almost any other man would have gone to bed and put business aside for one day at least.

Mr. Roosevelt had gone to his desk, instead, to clear off the work accumulation of nearly a week. He then held an important Cabinet meeting, received many official and other callers who had vexing business matters to discuss, made several appointments to office, and attended to a multitude of other trying affairs. Yet, when I desired to withdraw on the ground that he must be well-nigh exhausted, he cheerily answered:

"Oh, no, I'm not at all tired. In fact, I never feel much of weariness. Light a cigar. I want to talk with you about an historical point which you criticized some years ago in one of my books."

Fortunately I was sitting at the time in a well-armed easy-chair… otherwise I think I might have fallen. Think of this busy man, ceaselessly engaged with strenuous public affairs, still remembering that poor little criticism of mine, years after it was written! The criticism concerned a minute detail of very small consequence in any case, yet so earnest and sincere is this man, and so "strenuous" in all that he does, that he remembered the point perfectly, and mentioned it now only because he was interested to explain to me how he had been led into the insignificant little error. —*George Cary Eggleston*

He unites the qualities of the man of action with those of the scholar and writer—another very rare combination. He unites the instincts and accomplishments of the best breeding and culture with the broadest democratic sympathies and affiliations. He is as happy with a frontiersman like Seth Bullock [of Deadwood, South Dakota] as with a fellow Harvard man, and Seth Bullock is happy, too. —*John Burroughs*

I said to him: "Theodore, if you are not careful, you will dry up mentally. Most office-holders allow details to occupy their attention and cease reading." A few days after that I received a note from Mr. Roosevelt in which he said, "I reviewed my reading after you spoke to me about it and on the way to Oyster Bay, I made a list of the books I could remember having read during the past two years."

The list, which he made from memory, contained nearly three hundred titles and authors. Among them were *Herodotus*, *Æschylus*; *Euripides*; six volumes of Mahaffy's *Studies of the Greek World*; Mahan's *Types of Naval Officers*; Nicolay's *Lincoln* and two volumes of Lincoln's speeches and writings; Bacon's *Essays*; five of Shakespeare's plays; *Paradise Lost*; two of Maspero's volumes on Early Assyrian, Chaldean, and Egyptian civilizations; Dante's *Inferno*; Lounsbury's *Shakespeare and Voltaire*; *Tom Sawyer*; Wagner's *Simple Life*; various books on the Boer War; Pike's *Through the Sub-Arctic Forest*; London's *Call of the Wild*; Fox's *The Little Shepherd of Kingdom Come*; Wister's *The Virginian*; and so on. The list when perused seems almost unbelievable. His mental alertness and furnishing were not an accident. —*Dr. Nicholas Murray Butler*

When he was President he sent for me, and taking me into his library, opened a drawer in his desk, lifted out a complete manuscript, put it on the desk, and said in effect: "It isn't customary for Presidents to publish a book during office, but I am going to publish this one."

We then went over together the complete manuscript of *Outdoor Pastimes of an American Hunter*. Some of these papers had been written before. Other chapters were the product of his hunting trips in Colorado and Louisiana while President. The book was ready for the printer, title-page and all.

To him the making of a book was a delight. He knew all the machinery of it, and he read his proofs with the accuracy and industry of an expert. —*Robert Bridges*

1904, May 8. The President was reading Emerson's *Days* and came to the wonderful closing line: "I, too late, under her solemn fillet saw the scorn."

I said, "I fancy you do not know what that means."

"O, do I not? Perhaps the greatest men do not, but I in my soul know I am but the average man, and that only marvelous good fortune has brought me where I am." —*John Hay*, diary entry

It was during delightful conversations that I came to know Theodore Roosevelt well, and to feel more and more the depths of his spiritual nature, his love for righteousness; his sane power of making compromises not ignoble when a good end required it; his plasticity of mind; his versatility and concentration; his power of using all that was valuable in other men; and his indomitable energy and courage.

There seems to be a wide-spread impression that he was uncontrollably impetuous, fixed in his opinions, unmanageable even by those persons whose opinions he ought to respect. Nothing can be more untrue than this. It is impossible to conceive of a man more willing to give up his opinions when those opinions were proved to be unfounded, or when the objection to those opinions was put in a way which attracted or pleased him.

He loved a good phrase and he was charmed by an apt literary allusion—it could not be too recondite or involved or pedantic; but if one opposed him and could put one's opinions into a compact sentence, he was always likely to accept the new point of view heartily, and

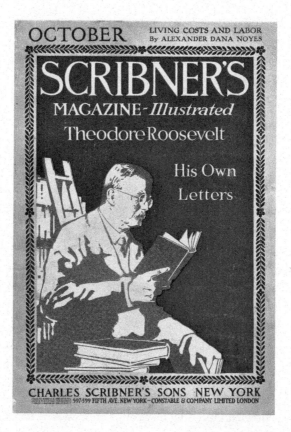

even enthusiastically. All his friends knew this very well. —*Maurice Francis Egan*

The literary work that he best enjoyed was writing his *African Game Trails*. The whole book, even the preface, was written by his own hand, word for word, in triplicate, in the very heart of Africa. One of the men who was with him said that no matter how arduous the day in the hunting-field, night after night he would see the Colonel seated on a camp-stool, with a feeble light on the table, writing the narrative of his adventures.

Chapter by chapter this narrative was sent by runners from the heart of Africa. Two copies were dispatched at different times. When he got to the headwaters of the Nile one of the chapters was sent from Nairobi and the duplicate was sent down the Nile to Cairo. These blue canvas envelopes often arrived much battered and stained, but never did a single chapter miss. —*Robert Bridges*

He was a voracious and omnivorous reader. It is impossible to estimate the amount of Roosevelt's reading but it must have been phenomenally large for he read all sorts of books, modern and ancient, at all sorts of times and with almost unbelievable rapidity.
—*Newspaper clipping*

I noticed his habit of reading a book rapidly while talking with his visitors, without the slightest distraction from the subject in hand. In this way he acquired much useful information, and relieved the *ennui* which most presidents must feel. TR had a remarkable ability in rapid reading, sometimes being able to grasp a paragraph or even a whole page, very much as the average man reads words or sentences.
—*Samuel McCune Lindsay*

When he reads he has such powers of concentration that he hears no noise around him and is unable to say whether people have been in the room or not. He is fondest, he says, of history and biography, and when he goes to light literature he wants ghost or detective stories.
—*Archie Butt*

He read while waiting for trains and for people to keep appointments and when driving in his automobile to the city. I have seen him pick up a book surrounded by a roomful of talking and laughing friends and in a moment become so absorbed in it that he had no more knowledge of what was going on about him than if he had been in a cloister cell.

During the railway journey from Khartum to Cairo on the tour of 1910…a special dinner was to be served one evening in the private saloon dining car placed at Roosevelt's disposal by the Governor-General of the Sudan. This dinner was to be attended by some important officials and other guests, who had taken the train at one of the stations we passed through. It was therefore essential that the company should assemble at the table promptly, but when dinner was announced Mr. Roosevelt was nowhere to be found.

I searched the train for him and finally discovered him in one of the white-enameled lavatories with its door half open where, standing under an electric light, he was busily engaged in reading, while he braced himself in the angle of the two walls against the swaying motion of the train, oblivious to time and surroundings. The book in which he was absorbed was Lecky's *History of Rationalism in Europe*. He had chosen this peculiar reading room both because the white enamel reflected a brilliant light and he was pretty sure of uninterrupted quiet. —*Lawrence F. Abbott*

President Roosevelt loved a good book, and it made no difference whether the book was old or new. In a letter he wrote me just before his death, he rejoiced over the fact that Kermit had written a poem in praise of [Portugal's national poet] Camões, whose ancient volume he had cherished in many voyages. He was constantly recommending books to me, and I returned the compliment.

Once, when he was going West, he asked me to send him something I liked. It was almost hopeless to find anything he had not read but I made up a packet of Lady Gregory's plays, William Yeats's poems, some verses by Tom Daly, and, I think, Douglas Hyde's *Songs of Connacht*.

When he came back, his mind was full of the Celtic sagas; he had, as it were, torn the essence of the Celtic spirit from its body. "I find," he said, "in the pagan Celtic literature an ideal of romantic love which I supposed had only come in with Christianity."

As an amateur in Celtic literature I was soon left behind in President Roosevelt's rapid advance in his Gaelic studies. One day I said to him, "You must concentrate your ideas of Celtic literature in an article, which I shall ask you to publish in the *Century Magazine*."

He promised. Time passed; there was a period of political turmoil; tremendous rows in the Senate—I think Senator Chandler was leading a revolt there—and one day at lunch he said to me, "I will give you your article to-day; it is for the *Century*. Look it over."

"But, Mr. President," I said, "how could you find the quietness of mind to write a paper like this when you and the Senate seemed to be on the verge of an open war?"

"It was just the time for quiet and interesting work," he replied, "it took my mind off that caterwauling."

When the article came out, splendidly illustrated by Leyendecker, he sent me, on Washington's birthday, the original of the beautiful picture of Queen Maeve, with an inscription. —*Maurice Francis Egan*

We were not always climbing and often had good long stretches when I would ask questions and get him started on any subject which presented itself to my mind. For instance, I told him of going into the second-hand book stores in London and once asking a big book man what American author had the largest sale in England; and how he had told me Edgar Allan Poe was now and always had been the biggest American seller.

"I am not surprised," said the President. "He is our one super-eminent genius. In spite of the persistent effort to belittle him, and I must say it has come largely from New England, he still remains the most eminent literary character we have produced. I do not think that the New England school has tried to belittle him because he was not from New England, but their rules for literature are so adjusted that it will not permit of such an irregular genius as Poe.

"Even as sane a man as [Oliver Wendell Holmes, Sr.] declared Poe to be one-fifth genius and four-fifths guff. If any man was ever about five-fifths genius, that man was Poe. The next most eminent literary man I think we have produced is Hawthorne, in spite of the fact that I do not care for him and seldom read him." —*Lawrence F. Abbott*

Was there ever such a man before? How he knew all the facts, or where he gathered them, I cannot imagine. I have been studying almost for a lifetime on the very subject on which he was talking, and yet he seems to have gone deeper in three weeks' preparation than I almost in a lifetime.

It seemed to me Colonel Roosevelt was practically a specialist in everything. The first time I saw him he discussed two things that I believed I knew more about than any other person in America, and he certainly knew more about those things than anybody else I have talked with.

I have talked frequently with professors in American universities whose special province it is to deal with the history and literature of Iceland, and I don't think one of them had the feeling of Icelandic literature nor the grasp of Icelandic history that Roosevelt did. I don't know anybody in America from whom he could have borrowed them, because I never met anyone else who had them. He probably was a pioneer in this as in many other things. The same spirit of discovery probably took him into Icelandic history that took him into the Brazilian jungle. —*Vilhjalmur Stefansson*

He was no pedant. He liked novels and stories of adventure and books of humor, but he wanted them to be written by men of intelligence and skillful workmanship. Books of travel and exploration especially appealed to him although he was not interested, as he once told me, in mere biography. —*Archie Butt*

It had long been Colonel Roosevelt's habit to write to some confidential friend, at the time, in full detail, about every event of any importance in which he was concerned. The publication of some of his letters [edited by] Joseph Bucklin Bishop has disclosed something of the extent to which he carried this practice, and has revealed the length and detail of such letters. They form an invaluable and practically complete informal record of the events of his official life, and constitute an unexampled source of authoritative information for future historians. —*O. K. Davis*

One of the brightest of the newspaper men who went with him on his long Western trip said to me, when they were back East: "I don't think any sane man could be with him two weeks without getting to like him; but the thing that struck me on that trip was the way he grew; the way an idea grew in his mind day by day as he lived with it until it took its final shape in speech. Then it was like a knock-down blow." —*Jacob Riis*

The President has the greatest power of concentration I have ever seen. When he is reading or thinking he does not seem to hear anything which goes on about him. Once when we got into a discussion and became rather loud and then got to laughing I suggested that we would disturb the President. Mrs. Roosevelt said it made no difference to him, that he would not hear us; and so we paid little attention to him after that if he was reading.

Doctor Rixey and I carried on a conversation about him once in chairs next to his and he did not even hear us, not even when we mentioned his name. I got a good deal of pleasure from merely watching him on this trip. —*Archie Butt*

He never leaped before he looked. But it never took him long to look. —*Dr. Lyman Abbott*

His marvelous executive ability was due in great part to the habit he had formed of constant industry and of perfect concentration of mind. Many people can accomplish a creditable amount of work if undisturbed and if allowed to work consecutively at one thing. Mr. Roosevelt could not only work without being sensitive to disturbances, but he could turn rapidly from one thing to another, compass each fresh situation, and bring to bear his whole power of decision.

I have seen him for many hours at a time working at his desk in the White House offices, dealing with a great number of matters that were of vastly different degrees of importance. It need not be said that things which for one reason or another could not be settled were not rashly disposed of merely for the sake of clearing his desk. But if the case was in hand, he did not hesitate.

He was never groping in the valley of indecision. His was neither the parliamentary temperament nor the judicial temperament, but it was in the highest sense that of the executive. He could lay out his work and perform it. —*Albert Shaw*

CHAPTER IX

Theodore Roosevelt:
Patriot and Activist

*Perhaps—until America's recent rediscovery of the "Man in the Arena"
speech—there was no more iconic and oft-quoted credal statement
associated with Theodore Roosevelt than: "Aggressive fighting for the
right is the noblest sport the world affords."*

Theodore Roosevelt equated patriotism with family values: each an
essential impulse and related to each other. "Patriotism stands in national
matters as love of family does in private life. Nationalism corresponds
to the love a man bears for his wife and children," he said. Translated
to policy, he considered himself the heir of Whigs and Abraham Lincoln and policies of Manifest Destiny expansionists, favoring a "National
Policy" of a strong government and a strong Chief Executive.

To Roosevelt, Nationalism was not a concept or policy of bullies and
boors, but rather a positive evocation of a culture's heritage. In his nation's
case, he savored the patrimony of Western civilization and values; seeds
planted in a rich, welcoming soil.

The consistency of his viewpoints was remarkable. Opinions he
formed, and observations he made, in his twenties on subjects as dis-
parate as naval strategy and social justice were often indistinguishable
from—and as sound as—those he advocated at the end of his life.

When he formulated a package of new policies to meet new challenges in 1910, a logical step between the reforms of his presidency and the Bull Moose platform of 1912, he chose to name the program the New Nationalism. America First was a concept TR promoted, applicable to the new loyalties of individual immigrants and to matters of State in world affairs. In its muscular aspect, a Roosevelt watchword was "If I must choose between righteousness and peace, I choose righteousness."

But in a revealing story, the famously ebullient patriot was not blindly confident of American advancement as an automatic thing; he knew that indolence was a historical product of prosperity, and that societal concord had softened many nations' "soldierly virtues." Roosevelt entertained the writer H. G. Wells at Sagamore Hill and candidly shared a gloomy assessment of the challenges facing America in the future, and the peoples' possible response. He grabbed Wells by the lapels and passionately said (probably as much to himself): "But, it…is…worth…the…fight!"

It is possible that TR's father was again the inspiration for his activism, as he was an example of charitable impulses. His father's example informed much of TR's subsequent life.

In truth, labels like "activist," even "Progressive," describe Theodore Roosevelt and the warp and weft of his life less well than the label "Reformer." Even terms like Liberal and Conservative are subsumed by the reformer's impulse to test, improve, and pass along the elements of a healthy society, an honorable nation. It is scarcely acknowledged in view of twentieth-century debates and instant-categorization, that TR's "Progressivism" was markedly different from that of Woodrow Wilson and other liberals of the time. It is the latter's philosophy, not TR's, that largely informed politics, legislation, and regulations of the subsequent century.

The summation of Theodore Roosevelt's essence as an engaged patriot can be provided by TR himself, obliquely. In his *Autobiography* he described his favorite cartoon and shared his pride in cartoonist Everett Lowry's assessment. It bespoke Roosevelt's vision of Patriotism and Nationalism, reformism and activism in practice—not that of a perfervid crusader, but of a secure, confident legatee of the "essential home values":

"There was one cartoon made while I was President, in which I appeared incidentally, that was always a great favorite of mine. It pictured an old fellow with chin whiskers, a farmer, in his shirt-sleeves, with his boots off, sitting before the fire, reading the President's Message. On his feet were stockings of the kind I have seen hung up by the dozen in Joe Ferris's store at Medora, in the days when I used to come in to town and sleep in one of the rooms over the store. The title of the picture was 'His Favorite Author.' This was the old fellow whom I always used to keep in mind. He had probably been in the Civil War in his youth; he had worked hard ever since he left the army; he had been a good husband and father; he had brought up his boys and girls to work; he did not wish to do injustice to any one else, but he wanted justice done to himself and to others like him; and I was bound to secure that justice for him if it lay in my power to do so."

* * *

"My rule," [Roosevelt said to me], "is a simple one: Do the best you can, with what you have, and do it now." —*George Shiras III*

"They will say, most likely, that it is made up of platitudes," he told me when he had finished [writing a speech], referring to his newspaper critics; "and so I suppose it is. Only they need to be said just here and now."

They did need to. The Ten Commandments are platitudes, I expect; certainly they have been repeated often enough. And yet even the critics will hardly claim that we have had enough of them. —*Jacob Riis*

Theodore's first handicap was the asthma; the second handicap was the fact that he was born in a rich man's home. He is the first very rich man's son who ever became President. All virtue does not inhere in those that are poor or in moderate circumstances, nor is all vice to be found in wealth, but the fact is that out of poverty and moderate financial circumstances, in this free land of great opportunity, have come most of our successful men. There is a feeling of self-dependence, and industry, so necessary to success which is demanded by it. —*Ferdinand Iglehart*

When he entered public life he found this nation sunk in a sordid materialism, due to our amazing prosperity as a nation, which had somewhat obscured the great ideals to which the republic was dedicated. Roosevelt, in the spirit of an ancient prophet, preached the higher life, both for nation and for individual. —*James M. Beck*

He was a remarkable executive, partly because he knew how to handle men and get them to work…he was the busiest man I ever knew, and yet he never seemed to be hurried. —*Lawrence F. Abbott*

He poured into my heart such vision, such ideals, such hopes, such a new attitude toward life and patriotism and the meaning of things, as I had never dreamed men had. —*William Allen White*

"I am charged with being a preacher. Well, I suppose I am. I have such a bully pulpit," said Mr. Roosevelt, referring, of course, to his great political audiences. He was afraid, however, in claiming to be a preacher, of being counted presumptuous or of seeming to lay claim to a peculiar abundance of an artificial piety which some people believe should characterize the preacher. —*Christian Reisner*

He came to my office one day when I was out and left his card with the simple words written in pencil upon it: "I have read your book, and I have come to help." That was the beginning. The book was *How the Other Half Lives*, in which I tried to draw an indictment of the things that were wrong, pitifully and dreadfully wrong, with the tenement homes of our wage-workers.

It was like a man coming to enlist for a war because he believed in the cause, and truly he did. Now had come the time when he could help indeed. Decency had moved into the City Hall, where shameless indifference ruled before. His first thought was to have me help there.

For two years we were to be together all the day, and quite often most of the night, in the environment in which I had spent twenty years of my life. And these two were the happiest by far of them all. Then was life really worth living, and I have a pretty robust enjoyment of it at all times. —*Jacob Riis*

"Thank God for a Man!"

Thank God for a man! There was need
    In this much-doubting day
Of one that could fashion a deed
    As a sculptor the clay,
Undaunted by shadows of ill
    That the dawn might reveal,
Strong-heartedly laboring still
    For a noble ideal.

Direct in the candor of youth
That is clear as the sky,
He cleaves with the bright edge of Truth
Through the mask of the lie.
Endowed with the zeal that survives
And the courage to see
All things as they are, yet he strives
For the good that must be.

What matter the scurrilous sneer
And the buzz and the hum!
We know him: Wise, steadfast, sincere;
And the young men to come
Shall broaden the pathway he trod
And the work he began
Shall bring to fulfillment. Thank God
For His gift of a man!

—Arthur Guiterman

Theodore Roosevelt had his faults, certainly he did, for he was human; only one man ever lived who was without fault, and He was God. It was the singularly human element, that was liable to err, that made him so immensely popular. A faultless angel could never have gotten elected to any office which Colonel Roosevelt ever filled. The people want someone like themselves, capable of getting mad once in a while when it is necessary, and of fighting desperately when a just cause arises. *—Ferdinand Iglehart*

Mr. Roosevelt expressed a desire to see, first hand, what the [Salvation] Army was doing for the relief of the homeless and hungry. At that time we had allotted part of our floor space at our National Headquarters in New York on West 14th Street to some light work for the weaker sex. As Mr. Roosevelt passed into the building his quick eye caught sight of a delicate girl at work. Her earnings were just enough to keep her invalid widowed mother and other members of her family from actual starvation. A distressed expression crossed his face.

"The solution of the problem," he said, "is in finding employment, not giving charity." Correcting himself, he added, "For the present, of course, it is the only thing to do."

As he walked up a flight of stairs, in a voice that vibrated with enthusiasm he exclaimed, "Back to the land!" [*and other slogans of the movement's mission to establish farms for the urban poor.*] —*Commander Evangeline Booth*

I marched the Christian Endeavorers and the Methodist ministers to the support of Roosevelt in the fight between him and his wicked partners in the Police Board. That was not plotting, though they called it so, but just war; a kind of hold-up, if you like, in the plain interests of the city's welfare. But "the system" Roosevelt was called to break up. I shall not attempt to describe it. The world must be weary of it to the point of disgust. We fought it then; we fight it now. We shall have to fight it no one can tell how often or how long. —*Jacob Riis*

[The keystone of] Roosevelt's character was his ambition. And his ambition—the one great, ever-active purpose that, lying nearest to his heart, was the mainspring of his life—was to set an example before Americans, and especially youth. Always he saw himself in every public performance mirrored in the heart of youth. This reflection kept him always young. He was forever imagining himself as a man of the highest ideals, derived from good birth and liberal advantages, demonstrating to the youth of his country what such a man can do in politics in all honesty, without soiling his hands, for the betterment of American life and the progress of the world. —*William Allen White*

As Washington was known as the father of his people, and as Lincoln was known as the savior of his people, so my brother will be known as the brother of his people. —*Corinne Roosevelt Robinson*

"If I have anything at all resembling genius, it is a gift of leadership." Then he added, with a serious air: "To tell the truth, I like to believe that, by what I have accomplished without great gifts, I may be a source of encouragement to American boys." —*Julian Street*

Aristotle called mankind "political animals"—and no faunal naturalist ever understood that animal better than Theodore Roosevelt. —*Brander Matthews*

We took night trips together to see how the police patrolled in the early hours of the morning, when the city sleeps and policemen are most needed. They earned for him the name of Haroun-al-Roosevelt, those trips that bore such sudden good fruit in the discipline of the force.

They were not always undertaken solely to wake up the police. Roosevelt wanted to know the city by night, and the true inwardness of some of the problems he was struggling with as Health Commissioner; for the President of the Police Board was by that fact a member of the Health Board also. One might hear of overcrowding in tenements for years and not grasp the subject as he could, by a single midnight inspection with the sanitary police.

He wanted to understand it all, the smallest with the greatest, and sometimes the information he brought out was unique, to put it mildly. —*Jacob Riis*

Theodore Roosevelt was a veritable preacher of social righteousness with the irresistible eloquence of faith sanctified by work. —*Jane Addams*

Roosevelt is to the mind what the tuning fork is to the ear. When one wishes to strike the true note of Americanism, he needs only to touch Roosevelt as the choirmaster touches his tuning fork. —*Elizabeth Ogden Brower Wood*

Roosevelt's campaign for the reform of the police force became the moral issue of the day. It swept the cobwebs out of our civic brains, and blew the dust from our eyes, so that we saw clearly where all had been confused before: saw straight, rather. We rarely realize, in these latter days, how much of our ability to fight for good government, and our hope of winning the fight, is due to the campaign of honesty waged by Theodore Roosevelt in Mulberry Street. —*Jacob Riis*

I first met him in 1897...We walked home together after the dinner, covering many miles of Washington streets, deep in interesting conversation. It was until well after midnight that we separated. We talked over many things...indeed, we found so much in common that from that day our association became a close and intimate one, and a friendship began which strengthened as the years went by. Our moral standards were similar, as were our religious convictions. —*Leonard Wood*

I remember that evening in the camp when the regiment stood in front of him, and the parting came [after the Spanish-American War]. I can hear him say now as he did then:

"Remember when you go out into the world tomorrow, for nine days you will be regarded as heroes, and then you will have to take your places as ordinary citizens. You will be judged then for what you are, what you do as men, not as to what you have been." —*Major W. H. H. Llewellyn*

When the war began I was like the rest; I deplored your [leaving your office] in the Navy [Assistant Secretary] where you were so useful and so acceptable. But I knew it was idle to preach to a young man. You obeyed your own "demon," and I imagine we older fellows will all have to confess that you were in the right. As Sir Walter wrote: *One crowded hour of glorious life is worth an age without a name.*

You have written your name on several pages of your country's history, and they are all honorable to you and comfortable to your friends. It has been a splendid little war; begun with the highest motives, carried on with magnificent intelligence and spirit, favored by that Fortune which loves the brave. —*John Hay*, written after the Spanish-American War while Hay served as Ambassador to the Court of St. James

[William A.] Miller was an assistant foreman in the government bookbindery. He was discharged by the public printer, upon the demand of organized labor, on charges of "flagrant non-unionism,"

"BOY! THERE'S NOTHING LIKE HIM IN HISTORY"

he having been expelled from Local Union No. 4 of the International Brotherhood of Bookbinders. His discharge was in defiance of the civil service laws, and the matter having come before the President, he ordered that he be reinstated. In doing so he pointed to this finding of the anthracite coal strike commission which organized labor had accepted:

"It is adjudged and awarded that no person shall be refused employment or in any way discriminated against on account of membership or non-membership in any labor organization, and that there shall be no discrimination against or interference with any employee who is not a member of any labor organization by members of such organization."

"It is, of course," was the President's comment, "mere elementary decency to require that all the government departments shall be handled in accordance with the principle thus clearly and fearlessly enunciated." But there are people who do not understand, on both sides of the line. Seventy-two unions in the Central Labor Union of the District of Columbia "resolved" that to reinstate Miller was "an unfriendly act." The big [labor] leaders, including Mr. Gompers and Mr. Mitchell, came to plead with the President. Miller was not fit, they said.

That was another matter, replied the President. He would find out. As to Miller's being a non-union man, the law he was sworn to enforce recognized no such distinction. "I am President," he said, "of all the people of the United States, without regard to creed, color, birthplace, occupation, or social distinction. In the employment and dismissal of men in the government service I can no more recognize the fact that a man does or does not belong to a union as being for or against him than I can recognize the fact that he is a Protestant or a Catholic, a Jew or a Gentile, as being for or against him." —*Jacob Riis*

A cultivated but unassuming Negro, Mrs. Minnie Cox, a woman of excellent repute, was postmistress of Indianola, Mississippi. She had for some years been doing her work to the general satisfaction of the townspeople when without warning, the "hoodlum element" in the town, as Roosevelt described it, decided that she must go. Under the direst threats, she fled with her family.

[President] Roosevelt closed the post office. If the people of Indianola had no sense of decency, let them go for their mail to the next post office, five miles away.

He was bitterly denounced, not only in the South. But the post office remained closed until it became obvious that the Colored postmistress would not return under any conditions. —*Hermann Hagedorn*

At our meeting [with the trustees of the Tuskegee Institute] which had been called for the purpose of electing a successor to Booker T Washington, Mr. Roosevelt sat and listened to everything that the other trustees had to say for more than an hour. He then said in his most emphatic manner, striking the table with his fist, "Gentlemen, I sincerely believe that it is as important that we select the right man to succeed Booker T. Washington as it would be to select the right man as president of the United States!" —*Julius Rosenwald*

The unusual combination of physical and moral courage with an active mentality not only had built around him an enormous popularity, but was in danger of creating in the public mind a super-man. No one would so have deplored this as Roosevelt himself, and it may be said of him that from the beginning to the end of his career he made no attempt to foster this delusion. —*Mary Roberts Rinehart*

In a letter to [George Otto] Trevelyan [TR] recounts the visit of three "back-country farmers," who, after much effort, had succeeded in getting to him and explained that they "hadn't anything whatever to ask." They came merely to express their belief "in me" and "as one rugged old fellow put it, 'We want to shake that honest hand.' Now, this anecdote seems rather sentimental as I tell it [but] they have made me feel that I am under a big debt of obligation to the good people of this country." He coveted the confidence of the people. —*Christian Reisner*

Many have asked the secret of Roosevelt's wonderful hold on the public and his ability to carry a crowd with him. Presumably the question will be discussed long after those who heard him have crossed the Great Divide, and with as wide, if not as great, a difference of opinion as when he was in the flesh.

His own explanation may be given in one word: "Sincerity." This, he maintained, was the real secret, though he admitted that other qualities in his speeches were contributing factors. The discussion in which the Colonel declared himself on this point came one night when he and a party of three were returning to New York from a red-hot Roosevelt meeting—two meetings, in fact, one in a hall, the other outside.

It was precipitated by a remark by A. Leonard Smith of *The New York Times*, to the effect that the Colonel "certainly had that crowd."

"What seemed to get them?" asked the Colonel. It was a question none in the party could answer, for the crowd, like most Roosevelt crowds, was enthusiastic from the start, and one could not say that this, that, or the other point had been the most effective. Smith ended this phase of the discussion by declaring the Colonel "always got the crowd."

"Isn't it because the crowd always knows I am sincere?" asked the Colonel. "I think it is. Otherwise—bah!" (this with a wave of his hand) "It surely must be that in the years I have been in public life, folks have always found me sincere. Men do not always agree with me; in fact (this whimsically) many have been known to differ with me very seriously; but my worst enemies do not, I believe, question my sincerity.

"My speeches would never get over if people did not believe I was sincere. An orator, which I am not, would get a crowd, perhaps, but he could not hold them if he lacked sincerity, or if the people thought he did. We have all seen orators come and go, but none ever retained a hold on any perceptible part of the public who at least did not carry the impression of sincerity.

"I have never hesitated to say a thing because it might be unpopular any more than I have ever found it at all necessary to say things I did not believe merely because they might be popular. In the end, as Emerson says, truth, however unpleasant, is the safest traveling companion. I have never found it at all necessary to pussyfoot or indulge in pleasing sophistries to hold any crowd.

"On the other hand, I have never hesitated to tell folks unpleasant things I thought they should be told, any more than I have been afraid of hecklers." —*John J. Leary*

I spent the last night at Sagamore Hill with the President and sat until late talking on every subject under the sun, or rather the moon, for it flooded everything. I shall always remember this visit with the greatest pleasure. The individuality of each member of his family is indelibly impressed on my mind....

The President...predicted, that last night we were together, that we should have war with Japan, not as soon as it was suggested as being in his mind, but he said it would be sure to come.

"No one dreads war as I do, Archie," he said. "As President I would go far to avoid it. The little that I have seen of it, and I have seen only a little, leaves a horrible picture on my mind. But the surest way to prevent this war with the East is to be thoroughly prepared for it." —*Archie Butt*

[*On making speeches in the 1910 off-year election, despite advice to stay aloof:*]

"That is what I am going to do whether we win or whether we lose. If we win, I shall probably be accused of plotting some deep schemes of personal political advantage. If we lose, I shall certainly be accused of being a sorehead and a bad loser. But you boys [assembled reporters] will know the truth...."

There were always some newspapers pounding him. He illustrated the situation, perfectly, one afternoon in conversation with me in his room at *The Outlook* offices. It was on the sixth floor.

"There are only two elevators in this building," he said, "and I must use one or the other of them. If I go down by the side elevator, that is evidence of furtiveness. If I go down in front, that is proof of ostentation." —*O. K. Davis*

[*TR's entourage at the Bull Moose convention in 1912 included his nephews Nicholas Roosevelt, George Roosevelt, and Teddy Douglas Robinson.*]

We managed to wedge our way through the shrieking mob out onto the street, which was a sea of cheering people. There followed one of the most thrilling events of my life. People packed their windows and lined the roofs, and were so thick in the streets we could hardly drive. Everyone was howling with delight, and cries of "Teddy!" filled the air. At the cross streets to each side as far as we could see people were wedged in. Everyone cheered, everyone was hurled along in the irresistible force of the delighted mob. Ahead rose TR, bowing to the right and left while the cheering continued. I have never before seen or felt such a thing. It was absolutely beyond description. All of us in the auto—even old Mr. Howland—cheered and jumped up and down, even standing on the seats. —*Nicholas Roosevelt,* from unpublished diary entry

After the applause had finally died down, someone started to sing the "Battle Hymn of the Republic." With one accord the great audience joined in the immortal words of the opening stanza:

He is trampling out the vintage where the grapes of wrath are stored.
He has loosed the fateful lightning of His terrible swift sword.
His truth is marching on!

From that moment, throughout the remaining two sessions of the [Bull Moose] convention, it was to all intents and purposes a religious gathering. —*William Draper Lewis*, writing of the Bull Moose convention, 1912

"America's Triumvirate"

Three masters among men our land has known:
A Washington, who came when Freedom spoke;
A Lincoln, like none else, and all our own;
A Roosevelt, the heir to Great-Heart's cloak.

Let dedicated currency and coins
Declare these as our peerage and our pride;
These are the sons of heroism's loins,
Of one who took Columbia for his bride.

Though each was born to lead a tragic day
As heroes must, unto its fabled place
With such a lineage, our nation may
Fear not the future outcome of her race.

Washington, Lincoln, Roosevelt,—what fame
Nobler than repetition of each name?

—*Isabel Fiske Conant*

[Frank] Harper [TR's personal secretary in 1912] was a young Englishman, with all the traditional respect of an Englishman for persons in authority, and he had not yet learned much about Colonel Roosevelt's ways with those around him. He seemed not even to have learned that the one thing which the Colonel always demanded of a friend was that he should fight for his own ideas. I doubt if there was any other way of so promptly losing Colonel Roosevelt's respect as to make him think that you were yielding your own judgment to him without a struggle simply because he was Colonel Roosevelt, and without regard to the merits of the proposition involved [*a trait that Harper soon overcame, as he became a trusted aide*]. —*O. K. Davis*

THE MOST INTERESTING AMERICAN

In 1914 an Englishman, a Frenchman, and several Germans told me that if Colonel Roosevelt had been the President of the United States at that time that the war in Europe would not have occurred; that the Kaiser would not have dared! —*Anthony Fiala*

When [the Great War] began, it brought to Colonel Roosevelt very little besides criticism and objection from sources which ought to have been among the first to support and applaud. Several times, during that period, when I saw him, he seemed as near despair as Theodore Roosevelt could come. Many of his old, tried friends gave him their customary eager support. But he knew he could rely on that always, and in this emergency it did not seem to count much with him.

He felt, with all the intensity of his intense spirit, the paramount necessity of a great stirring of the soul in the United States. He despised and hated the course of the Administration, and Mr. Wilson's success in leading the American people against what Colonel Roosevelt felt to be right, honest, and courageous brought him almost to the point of embittered desperation. —*O. K. Davis*

And, cowboys or dough-boys,
We'll follow his drum, boys.
Who never said, "Go, boys!"
But always said, "Come, boys!"

—*Arthur Guiterman*

One of the last things Mr. Roosevelt did before he died was to write a letter asking Congress to pass the Constitutional Female Suffrage Resolution. Thousands, if not millions, of people, who had been against woman suffrage or had been lukewarm on the subject, were stirred into enthusiastic approval because Colonel Roosevelt was so certain of the wisdom and practicability of this reform, which came in the adoption of the amendment by Congress shortly after his death, to the lasting benefit of the nation. —*Ferdinand Iglehart*

He was the subject of that vigorous controversy which always accompanies the leadership of a strong man who has the capacity to decide and the courage to act. His political course, during the last ten years of his life, curried such controversy to the extreme of violence. Yet it was a thoroughly consistent and understandable course. —*O. K. Davis*

226

Mr. Roosevelt, while a strict partisan, was above all a patriot. When he headed the Progressive ticket many Democrats voted for him. As a rule the rank and file of the Democrats of this country always had the highest respect for Mr. Roosevelt and large numbers of them loved him. At the time of his death the Democrats of the nation seemed to have suffered as deep sorrow as the Republicans. —*Ferdinand Iglehart*

As the train was coming east from Denver, after his stop there, it ran for a long time through the very sparsely settled section of western Kansas. It was a dark afternoon, with a rather hard rain falling. I was sitting in the Colonel's car talking with him about the events at Denver when I noticed a woman standing at the wire fence that ran alongside the track. She had a baby in her arms, and had protected him from the rain by throwing a part of her shawl over his head. About half a mile away was a small ranch house, where evidently she lived. It seemed that she had walked all that way in the rain, carrying the child, just on the chance of getting a glimpse of Colonel Roosevelt as his train swept by.

The Colonel was facing the other side of the track and did not see her. I touched him on the knee and pointed out the window. Instantly he took in the situation. He jumped to the rear platform and waved his hand to the woman. She saw him, and with both hands lifted the baby up toward the Colonel. There she held him until the train had rolled far down the track and was almost out of sight. Then she turned and started trudging back through the rain toward her house.

"By George!" said the Colonel, as he came back into the car and resumed his seat. "A thing like that gives you a lump in the throat. It makes me feel like a great calf. These people have such trust and confidence, and so often they think a man can do all sorts of things that no one can do." —*O. K. Davis*

He did not originate great new truths, but he drove fundamental old truths into the minds and the hearts of his people so that they stuck and dominated. —*Elihu Root*

"Whatever I do, old friend, believe it will be because after painful groping I see my duty in some given path."

So it was always with him. —*Jacob Riis*

"THE LONG, LONG TRAIL"

CHAPTER X

Theodore Roosevelt: American

Theodore Roosevelt's last speech—delivered by another
because he was too ill to attend a rally—concluded:
"We have room but for one soul loyalty,
and that is loyalty to the American people."

A remarkable aspect of Theodore Roosevelt's personality and accomplishments is that, more than a century after he left America's stage, he is honored, even revered, by people on both the right and left sides of the political spectrum. There is still enough TR to go around when people revere him even for what he did not do.

He was not "all things to all people," as many grasping politicians try to be; but in St. Paul's sense, Roosevelt appealed to common, elemental, communal values in people's souls: values, desires, and dreams. Consistency might be the hobgoblin of little minds, but regarding values it should be sought in public leaders—statesmen—and is rare enough in politicians. Certain principles are immutable; truth is not conditional; and societies are defined by their values. Theodore Roosevelt was not plagued by hobgoblins.

He was consistent in many things, a result of many factors, not least of all the patriotic and moral teachings of his father. Certainly, his views on many matters evolved—we should distrust anyone who does not grow—but they invariably were extensions of, not departures from, his native principles. He wrote a paper in college favorable to women's suffrage, and later in life he was the first major national politician to favor the extension (earlier than his wife and sisters; earlier than "progressive" Woodrow Wilson). He was largely indifferent to labor and living conditions in New York tenements until Samuel Gompers led him on a tour of Manhattan's Lower East Side. Thereafter he was, to and through his presidency, his party's most sympathetic advocate of labor.

Consistency and iconoclasm are rare partners, but they cohabited in Theodore Roosevelt. Similarly, he often adopted positions that threatened his political status. He invited Booker T. Washington to dine at the White House soon after he became president, a move met by widespread opprobrium; he appointed African-Americans to posts in the South despite White Southerners' opposition; in the early months of the Great War in Europe, Roosevelt argued for preparedness when the nation was in a pacific and isolationist mood, turning him for a while as a pariah.

TR boldly admitted to honoring, not disdaining, "practical" politics. In his view, practicality frankly included negotiation and compromise. He was sued by the boss of the New York State Republican Party after he charged "corrupt bargains" between the GOP and Democrats. William Barnes set out to prove that Roosevelt compromised in many similar ways through his entire career. In his defense, Roosevelt maintained that compromise was not a term of disparagement as long as motives were high and one's integrity was preserved. (Barnes lost the case. And he was the Republican leader only a few years later who advocated strongly for TR's nomination as president in 1920.)

Explaining his idealism as a value tempered by "practicality," TR advised, "Keep your eyes on the stars, but your feet on the ground."

Contemporary Roosevelt partisans, particularly if they are Constitutionalists, might be wary of the Regulatory State he originally constructed; however, TR plausibly would regard it as a Frankenstein's monster today. On the other hand, some politicians cloak themselves in his mantle when not justified. He was cited, during recent healthcare debates, as having favored National Health Insurance...which he never had. He advanced the power of the State, but bitterly denounced socialism. It became a creed of some followers—whom he called the "lunatic fringe."

Roosevelt was creative when he regarded his policies as essential to prevail. When his authority was not renewed to declare lands as federally protected parks and sanctuaries, he and Gifford Pinchot worked until midnight on deadline day, signing orders to preserve many such areas. When Congress declined to approve and fund the good-will circumnavigational cruise of the Great White Fleet, he ordered the warships to sea nonetheless, and dared Congress to deny provision for fuel and supplies.

A further caution, perhaps, to "Originalists" is the account of President Roosevelt's conversation with a friendly senator he wished would accept a Supreme Court nomination, as he was a great expert on the Constitution. "Why, you have two of the nation's greatest experts on the Constitution right in your cabinet—Taft and Root!" TR is supposed to have replied ruefully, "Yes, but they don't always agree with me."

Just as a healthy democratic republic is not a perpetual-motion machine, leaders like Theodore Roosevelt are American exceptions and blessings. As a president he could be considered the "Great Anticipator": there is no way to count—although the instances might be many—how many social difficulties, political crises, and international problems might have arisen, even in subsequent generations, but for his foresight and actions.

After TR's death and the immediate flurry of biographies and memoirs, his presence in the national consciousness somewhat receded. In part, the reason might have been the new issues and conditions of the following decades—the Roaring Twenties, the Great Depression, World War II—even the person of his fifth cousin as president. TR even became as much of a caricature in plays and movies, as he was honored as a consequential leader.

But a good man cannot be kept down.

Gradually his America has remembered and honored and—one prays—is learning from this Most Interesting American. Choosing one word to define Theodore Roosevelt is an open question, but ultimately the question is futile. However, in the days following his death, it was a cartoon in The New York Times that answered the question, very possibly as TR would have been most pleased.

Edwin Marcus's cartoon showed the goddess of history striking descriptions under Roosevelt's name—President, Soldier, Statesman, Historian, Explorer, Naturalist, Orator—and writing, instead, American.

* * *

Roosevelt was the greatest preacher of righteousness in modern times. Deeply religious beneath the surface, he made right living seem the natural thing, and there was no man beyond the reach of his preaching and example. In the sight of all men, he lived the things he taught, and millions followed him because he was the clear exemplar of his teaching.

Unless we may except his Conservation Policies, Roosevelt's greatest service during his Presidency was the inspiration he gave young men. To them he was the leader in all they hoped to be and do for the common good. The generation which was entering manhood while he was President will carry with it to the grave the impress of his leadership and personality. —*Gifford Pinchot*

He lived, and he lived abundantly, he lived exuberantly, with all his universality, within submissions. He submitted to the continuing life of the individual and of the family and of what is greater than the family. And to that greater thing he gave his supreme submission. He gave it to the greatest cause he could perceive. He gave it to America. —*William Hard*

[In the multi-volume *The Winning of the West*] are generalizations which Roosevelt derives from his own experience in the plains and mountains, we have an expression which suggests another literary value to the great story which he tells. He is not merely a scholar looking at these people from a distance, he is himself among them as hunter and trailer. He is neighbor to these settlers hewing their clearings out of the everlasting forest. —*Hamlin Garland*

We probably have never had a President who responded more freely and heartily to the popular liking for him than Roosevelt. The crowd always seems to be in love with him the moment they see him and hear his voice. And it is not by reason of any arts of eloquence, or charm of address, but by reason of his inborn heartiness and sincerity, and his genuine manliness. The people feel his quality at once. —*John Burroughs*

He was my friend, and the friend of all humanity. He opened my eyes, and put hope in my heart, as no other living man had ever done before. Being an ignorant man—without even a common school education—I sought only for truth, and, by heaven, I found it in him. —*An anonymous Colorado contributor to the Roosevelt Permanent Memorial Committee, 1919*

The King of Italy, Victor Emmanuel III, was the first of a considerable company of European monarchs that Mr. Roosevelt met on his tour. It was quite apparent that the kings liked him. At all events, after the formal and punctilious hospitalities had been fulfilled, they all, without exception, went out of their way to show him personal attention. There was something about his personality that attracted them.

European kings have not always had an entirely happy time even in days of peace. Their relations with their fellowmen are necessarily circumscribed and often artificial. With Roosevelt it was as though they said to themselves: "Here is a real man that we can meet, talk to, and associate with as men, not kings. He won't kowtow to us and he won't embarrass us." There was really an element of pathos in it.

When Mr. Roosevelt came home he was accused, during the Progressive campaign, by some of his silliest opponents, of an ambition to become king of America. His comment on these foolish critics was: "I know kings and they don't. A king is a kind of cross between a vice-president and a leader of the Four Hundred [high society]. I have been vice-president, and know how hollow the honor is. —*Lawrence F. Abbott*

He is gone. We cannot recall him; the thought of his loss is to those who knew him a gnawing pain. To try to console oneself by the remembrance of the great things he did, is useless. Other men have done great things, but there was only one Roosevelt. "He is a Man," the young King of Denmark said after they met; and I can say no more. May eternal Light shine upon him! —*Maurice Francis Egan*

My sister is the widow of a veteran of the Civil War. She was asked if she would like to meet a real live president of the United States. Her reply was:

"He's only a man."

Mr. Roosevelt was asked, over the 'phone at Sagamore Hill, as to whether he would receive her. His immediate response was:

"Bring the lady right up!"

When she arrived, President Roosevelt brushed aside all formality, and came out on the veranda to personally greet her, exclaiming:

"Delighted, my dear lady! I am proud to meet you, for you are the widow of a hero of a great war, while I only figured in a very small one."

Of course, the lady left Sagamore Hill filled with praises for Mr. Roosevelt, and she remained his ardent and life-long friend. Occurrences like these happened daily. —*Albert Loren Cheney*

There was a tough character with a prison record who joined the Rough Riders. He evidenced complete [transformation] in the army, and President Roosevelt later gave him an important office. Someone said to the ex-tough, "The President has taken an awful chance on you," and he replied, "No, the Colonel's confidence in me is what is going to keep me straight." —*William Loeb*

Roosevelt assailed the unrestrained Socialism then prevalent in France: "The deadening effect on any race of the adoption of a logical and extreme Socialistic system could not be overstated; it would spell sheer destruction; it would produce grosser wrong and outrage, fouler immorality, than any existing system." —*Christian Reisner*

It brings to mind the statement made by [French President] Clemenceau... "I cannot understand you Americans—you have the greatest statesman in the world living in your midst at Oyster Bay—yet you are looking for someone else to be your President." —*Vilhjalmur Stefansson*

We must take Theodore Roosevelt as we find him, with the virtue and vices of the deliverance of his message, but no one can read understandingly the record of his life and not feel that, according to his conviction—and we in should be quite unfair in failing to give this consideration due weight—the method employed was essential for the presentation of his cause. —*Joseph S. Auerbach*

He himself still lives. He lives, I may hope, to believe that he did not give its full proper place to the struggle of class. He lives, I may hope, to see that patriotism by itself is sacrilegious because it rends the body of Christ and tears His seamless coat. I may hope.

But plainly I see him striding on and beating the mist back with swinging elbows; and in the space beyond is the gravity of Washington and the fierceness of Jackson and the melancholy of Lincoln and all the riches of men in which we Americans are already so rich; and he turns his head on his shoulder; and he looks back; and I cannot hear him speak; but I can hear the thing that was his mark and the symbol of his meaning. I can hear the click of teeth with which he girded himself to all denial of things in himself that weaken and to all conquest in himself of things beyond; and I can hear him laugh.

And to the gravity of Washington, the fierceness of Jackson, and the melancholy of Lincoln I see added the timeless gaiety of Roosevelt. —*William Hard*

Roosevelt, like Lincoln, was in a true sense a preserver of our national unity. Lincoln saved us from section cleavage, Roosevelt saved us from class cleavage. He pointed out the road of straight Americanism where all could walk in amity towards the same goal. —*Calvin Coolidge*

The two figures at [Roosevelt's] side are guides symbolizing the continents of Africa and America, and if you choose may stand for Roosevelt's friendliness to all races. —*James Earle Fraser*, sculptor of the famed equestrian statue that stood for nearly a century at the Central Park entrance to New York City's American Museum of Natural History (of which TR's father was a founder). [Fraser was a student of Augustus Saint-Gaudens and likewise designed coinage, for instance the buffalo nickel. Fraser was sympathetic to Native American causes and is also known for his iconic lament for Indians' plight, "The End of the Trail."]

We who sat near him desired to hear him talk about himself and asked him many questions that would help us to gain some under-standing of this human dynamo, this composite man of the north and south, the east and the west, whom all respect, and none quite comprehend. And he was just as approachable on that subject as any other.

One of the party, calling attention to the fact that the New York *Sun* characterized his speeches as commonplace and platitudes, he gritted his teeth and said "*But I live them.*" He is just as willing to challenge any criticism of himself as to fight the battles of his country. —*William C. Deming*

I was taught by that dear little [grandmother] that in those days there were but two great men in the world; one was white and one was black. One was Theodore Roosevelt and the other was Booker T. Washington. While these appraisals by my grandmother were undoubtedly more instinctive and emotional than intellectual, they *were* sound and right. —*Dr. Ralph J. Bunche*

At the White House one day President Roosevelt came into his room, greeted me cordially, as was his custom, and then slipped over to another gentleman and greeted him. He brought that gentleman over to where I was, and said, "Dr. Iglehart, permit me to introduce to you Father ———, who has been doing very important work among the

Indians and has come to talk with me about it." And then, placing himself between us, he said, "Here's the great Catholic church, with its millions represented by this Catholic priest, on one side of me, and here on the other is the great Methodist church, with its millions represented by my old friend, and I am only a poor little Dutch Reform layman between the two."

The twinkle in his eye evidenced the fun that was always bubbling over within him. I replied, "No, Mr. President, you are not the poor little Dutch Reform layman between them. You are the great head of the nation and a Christian with a universal heart. You are large enough to belong to all the churches and all of us claim you as such, and we have reason to believe that you consider that all of us belong to you."

He warmed up instantly and answered, "My friend, you are quite right. I have the profoundest respect and warmest affection for all denominations, Protestant, Catholic and Hebrew. In my individual contact with men I have found the most splendid people imaginable holding these various beliefs, and in my public administration on all questions of moral reform, and those questions you know I consider paramount; the Protestant minister, the Catholic priest and the Jewish rabbi, and the millions that they represent, have vied with each other in sustaining me, and my arm has been as strong as the millions that they represent, in smiting evil and in building up the right. You can see how correct you were in saying that I belong to all of you and that all of you belong to me." —*Ferdinand Iglehart*

Pride in [his sons] became more and more manifest as reports began to come back from the front of their valor....

"I met Peter Dunne the other day [the humorist whose alter ego was Mr. Dooley]... Dunne said, 'Colonel, you want to watch out. The first thing you know they'll be putting the name of Roosevelt on the map.'"

He enjoyed the story and the laughs it raised, but he was never without the thought that the boys were in danger.

"Gray was right," he said, when Ted, Jr., was in a hospital. "You remember his line, 'the paths of glory lead but to the grave'? He is not dangerously hurt, but I cannot expect all will escape, I can only hope."

The end of the hope that all would return came to the Colonel one July night at Sagamore Hill. Phil Thompson, the resident correspondent at Oyster Bay, had called to ask about various matters, among them a cable message to the New York *Sun* from Raymond G. Carroll, one of its men at the front....

"I have here," he told him, "a cable message to the *Sun*. The censor has cut it some, so it is blind. It reads, 'Watch Oyster Bay for...' Have you any idea what it means?"

"Something has happened to one of the boys," he answered. "It cannot be Ted and it cannot be Archie, for both are recovering from wounds. It is not Kermit, for he's not in the danger zone at the moment. So it must be Quentin. However, we must say nothing of this to his mother to-night."

Confirmation of his fears came early the next morning. The Colonel took the blow exactly as one would expect him to.

"I must tell his mother," he said. —*John J. Leary*

[*Near the end of his life, when TR was wracked by old jungle fevers and myriad physical ailments, his sons were all fighting in France and he had been rebuffed by President Wilson from leading thousands of volunteers to fight in the Great War while the regular Army trained. A visitor reported:*]

I had just left his son at a hospital in Paris, and [Roosevelt] invited me over to lunch that I might tell him about it. On meeting him I remarked, "Colonel, I am glad to see you looking so well."

His reply was: "I feel like I'm a hundred years old and have never been young." —*LeRoy Percy*

His sudden and dangerous illness early in 1918 revealed at the same time both his own complete absorption in the battle he was waging and the dependence of a great part of the people on his vigorous leadership.

The Brazilian fever had seized him once more, complicated by a fistula and abscesses in his middle ears. One dusk in the beginning of February, he lay on a couch at the Hotel Langdon, where he generally stayed when he spent the night in New York, dictating to his secretary. His face was very gray.

"You are tired, Colonel Roosevelt," his secretary said. "Suppose we leave the rest of these letters until tomorrow morning?"

"No, we'll finish up tonight," he said, biting off the words. "When I was President I cleaned decks every day and I'm going to clean decks now."

He finished dictating. A minute later he fainted away with pain, rolling from the couch to the floor. The couch was drenched with blood.

A friend found him the next morning lying across his bed, evidently in agony. He believed that the end was not far off.

"I don't mind pain," he said, slowly and with difficulty, "when I'm only paying for something that I've had. I don't mind having to die. I've had my good time. I've had my full life." The eyes in the pallid face flashed suddenly. "But to think that those creatures will say that I'm out of the game!"

He was taken to Roosevelt Hospital [named, incidentally, for a benevolent relative from an earlier generation] for an operation on his ears. The surgeon in charge was frank. Only four similar operations had come under his personal observation; in every case the patient had died. "There are certain things I should like to live for," Roosevelt answered, quietly. "I should like to live to see my sons come back from France. But if it can't be, all right, doctor. I don't give a hang!" [After his ear operation, he lost balance and had to learn to walk again.]

It seemed that the whole nation stood breathless as it waited to hear whether Theodore Roosevelt was to live or to die. A rumor of his death flew through the city. Everywhere men gathered in groups and asked each other for the latest news about "T. R." A morning paper sent this challenge to the man fighting with the assailing shadows:

Theodore Roosevelt, listen! You must be up and well again. We cannot have it otherwise. We could not run this world without you.

He fought, and he won. A week later he was working in bed, dictating the keynote address he was to deliver in April at a Republican Convention in Maine.

He returned to the battle, declaring he felt "bully," and went West on a speech-making tour in which his hours on the public platform proved practically the only hours he did not spend in his state-room on the trains, fighting fever. An infection in his left leg gave him much pain. He admitted that perhaps it might be wise to restrict his public appearances.

Apprehension for the safety of his sons was always the background of his thoughts, though when he spoke of them it was the pride and never the fear that found expression. Archibald was wounded; Theodore was gassed and later wounded; Quentin fell fighting in the air, high over the German lines....

Republican politicians, preparing in the summer of 1918 for the presidential campaign of 1920, turned, with an accord which in 1914 would have seemed to them the ultimate impossibility, but which the facts of the situation now made inevitable, again to Theodore Roosevelt. In the New York State Republican Convention at Saratoga the men who had fought him most bitterly appealed to him once more for leadership.... Early in the autumn the Republican leader of one of the Atlantic states and a former Progressive leader of one of the Pacific states were seated with Roosevelt after dinner in the study at Sagamore Hill.

"Are you going to run for President in 1920?" asked the man from the East. Roosevelt, looking odd and unlike himself in his stiff white shirt-front and dinner-coat, with his right leg crossed over his left, answered promptly and without evasion: "Yes, I will run if the people want me, but only if they want me. I will not lift a finger for the nomination. I will not make a contest for it. It will have to come to me. It would be worthless on any other basis."

"Colonel, it will be yours, without strings, and on your own terms." The statement, on the surface, was rashly confident, but it was not without justification.

Roosevelt had throughout the war been the one outstanding figure in the Republican party, and now, at its close, was its acknowledged, undisputed leader. When, less than two weeks before the Congressional elections in November, the President issued an appeal for a Democratic Congress, it was inevitable that Roosevelt should be the one to answer him. In what proved one of the most powerful speeches of his career, Roosevelt drove the answer home. He struck, without mercy, blow on blow. His logic was clear, stern, and altogether relentless.... In the elections the Democrats were disastrously defeated. The Republicans returned to power in Congress with the man they had rejected and who had rejected them as their unrivaled leader.

Roosevelt's health was again causing anxiety. The abscess in his leg would not heal satisfactorily, and an attack of sciatica caused him much pain. He was forced to return to the hospital, and as week followed week and seemed to bring no healing, his friends became uneasy. The sciatica developed into inflammatory rheumatism. The prospect was set before him as not out of the range of possibilities that, like his gallant sister, Mrs. [Anna Roosevelt] Cowles, he might be condemned to spend the rest of his life in a wheelchair.

"All right!" he answered, after a pause. "I can live that way, too!"
—*Hermann Hagedorn*

Theodore Roosevelt was an unusual man for one so full of life and energy, and yet so gentle; the exponent of the strenuous life but always the perfect gentleman; quick of temper, but always under control. Would [that] we had more like him. —*Samuel McCune Lindsay*

Mr. Roosevelt died at Sagamore Hill at 4:15 Monday morning, January 6th, 1919, while he lay asleep.

The cause of his death was given as pulmonary embolism. Dr. William Gerry Morgan explained a pulmonary embolism as follows: "It is the passing of a blood clot into the pulmonary artery, then passing on until it reaches an artery too small to pass, thus cutting off the circulation."

For many months Colonel Roosevelt had been treated by the most eminent surgeons and medical men of the country, but it is said the malady baffled the skill of the physicians. While at the Roosevelt Hospital, Colonel Roosevelt had a number of serious operations performed. The belief is quite generally expressed that Mr. Roosevelt's system was filled with poison during the South American expedition....

The burial was in Young's Memorial Cemetery, on a beautiful knoll overlooking Long Island Sound. The plot was selected by Mr. and Mrs. Roosevelt directly after Mr. Roosevelt left the White House. —*Albert Loren Cheney*

Theodore Roosevelt is perhaps the greatest man in the world. To the European he typifies all that is essentially American. Abroad he is considered the greatest American. —*Jules Bois*

[On Saturday, January 4th, 1919, Theodore Roosevelt dictated a message that was read at a meeting of the American Defense Society at the Hippodrome, New York, on Sunday night, a few hours before he died. In this message, he again addressed the thoughts that had been burning in his mind, and this was his last ringing message to the American people:]

"There must be no sagging back in the fight for Americanism, merely because the war is over. There are plenty of persons who have already made the assertion that they believe the American people have a short memory, and that they intend to revive all the foreign associations which most directly interfere with the complete Americanization of our people.

"Our principle in this matter should be simple. In the first place, we should insist that if the immigrant who comes here in good faith becomes an American and assimilates himself to us, he shall be treated on an exact equality with everyone else, for it is an outrage to discriminate against any such man because of creed or birthplace or origin.

"But this is predicated upon the man's becoming in fact an American and nothing but an American. If he tries to keep segregated with men of his own origin and separated from the rest of America, then he isn't doing his part as an American.

"There can be no divided allegiance here. Any man who says he is an American but something else also, isn't an American at all. We have room for but one flag, the American flag, and this excludes the red flag, which symbolizes all wars against liberty and civilization, just as much as it excludes any foreign flag of a nation to which we are hostile.

"We have room for but one language here, and that is the English language, for we intend to see that the crucible turns our people out as Americans, of American nationality, and not as dwellers in a polyglot boarding house; and we have room for but one soul loyalty, and that is loyalty to the American people." —*Newspaper clipping*

Popularity has become the fetish of men in public life. They seek it now in every breath of popular sentiment. They bend to every ripple from any nook of their districts. Right for right's sake, alone, regardless of consequences, has almost ceased to be a motivating influence with them. Yet they prate about being "Roosevelt men."

The failure of present-day public men to grasp the fundamentals of popular leadership made clear by Theodore Roosevelt is the astonishing feature of American politics today.

And our world is none the braver, since Great-Heart was ta'en. —*O. K. Davis*

In every sense of the word he was one of the cleanest men I ever knew. He was utterly incapable of a dishonest thought; he was an American to the core, and his splendid patriotic life should be an inspiration for generations to come. —*John M. Parker*

[Citizens] know very well that they could wish no happier lot than for their children in the cradle to grow up to be such as Theodore Roosevelt. —*Newspaper clipping*

It is as though Bunyan's Mr. Great-Heart had died in the midst of his pilgrimage…. He was the greatest proved American of our generation. —*Rudyard Kipling*

[Edith Wharton, a friend of TR and a relative of Edith Roosevelt, wrote this poem upon Roosevelt's death:]

"With the Tide"

Somewhere I read, in an old book whose name
Is gone from me, I read that when the days
Of a man are counted, and his business done,
There comes up the shore at evening, with the tide,
To the place where he sits, a boat—
And in the boat, from the place where he sits, he sees,
Dim in the dusk, dim and yet so familiar,
The faces of his friends long dead; and knows
They come for him, brought in upon the tide,
To take him where men go at set of day.
Then rising, with his hands in theirs, he goes
Between them his last steps, that are the first
Of the new life—and with the ebb they pass.
Their shaken sail grown small upon the moon.

Often I thought of this, and pictured me
How many a man who lives with throngs about him,
Yet straining through the twilight for that boat
Shall scarce make out one figure in the stern,
And that so faint its features shall perplex him
With doubtful memories—and his heart hang back.

But others, rising as they see the sail
Increase upon the sunset, hasten down,
Hands out and eyes elated; for they see
Head over head, crowding from bow to stern,
Repeopling their long loneliness with smiles,
The faces of their friends; and such go forth
Content upon the ebb tide, with safe hearts.

Theodore Roosevelt: American

But never to worker summoned when his day was done
Did mounting tide bring in such freight of friends
As stole to you up the white wintry shingle
That night while they that watched you though you slept.
Softly they came, and beached the boat, and gathered
In the still cove under the icy stars,
Your last-born, and the dear loves of your heart.
And all men that have loved right more than ease,
And honor above honors; all who gave
Free-handed of their best for other men,
And thought their giving taking: they who knew
Man's natural state is effort, up and up—
All these were there, so great a company
Perchance you marveled, wondering what great ship
Had brought that throng unnumbered to the cove
Where the boys used to beach their light canoe
After old happy picnics—

But these, your friends and children, to whose hands
Committed, in the silent night you rose
And took your last faint steps—
These led you down, O great American,
Down to the Winter night and the white beach,
And there you saw that the huge hull that waited
Was not as are the boats of the other dead,
Frail craft for a brief passage; no, for this
Was first of a long line of towering transports,
Storm-worn and ocean-weary every one,
The ships you launched, the ships you manned, the ships
That now, returning from their sacred quest
With the thrice-sacred burden of their dead,
Lay waiting there to take you forth with them,
Out with the ebb tide, on some farther quest.

—*Edith Wharton, 1919*

245

I was in Paris, dining out, when the word came of his death. I was stricken, and later that night at a table in the sitting room of my apartment on the Rue de la Paix, I wrote:

Theodore Roosevelt is dead, and I have lost a friend.

Life goes on. Men still rise in the morning to the labor of the day. They eat and sleep and labor and love. They plan and hope and dream. But something vital has gone. Something fine. Something that seemed as though it could not die. Fearless, reckless, boyish Theodore Roosevelt has joined the army at last.

Along those distant trails he loved to follow, the break of day sees the smoke rising from the campfires into the cold morning air. The cow-men roll out of their bed-rolls, and the bell mare nickers as the string follows her toward the corral. The sun comes up, and along the trail the horses move sedately, breaking a path through the clean whiteness of the winter snow. The outfit draws out to let another by, and the word is passed from saddle to saddle:

"Bad news, boys. The Colonel is dead."

Early morning in the camps in France. The boys roll out, groaning and complaining. But the Armistice has come, and each day now is a new day, a day nearer home. The splashing of water, tin pans and cups and coffee, and:

"Say, fellows, have you heard the news? Teddy Roosevelt is dead."

In the crowded places men are sitting in conclaves. There are questions of boundaries and treaties, of payment and punishment. Voices are raised, speaking of a world re-made, new boundaries, new laws. But Theodore Roosevelt has gone to a new land, where the boundaries are Eternity and the law is Peace.

The world has lost a man, but I have lost a friend.

—*Mary Roberts Rinehart*

Death had to take Theodore Roosevelt in his sleep. If he had been awake, there would have been a fight. —*Thomas Riley Marshall*

We may admire a public man for the things he has accomplished, for his brilliant and versatile ability; we may trust him because we believe in the wisdom of his judgment; but our affection only finds root in his character. —*William Draper Lewis*

[*Translating from a French publication:*] It was my fortune to accompany him on this journey in a private car. He was not then President, for he had retired from office the year before; he was not a candidate for election. He was simply a private citizen; but everywhere people came in throngs to greet him. He was their man. I remember one night, while the train was rushing through one of the great central prairie states, I looked out of the window just before I went to sleep and saw in the lighted doorway of one isolated farmhouse a little family group gathered and waving a flag; as I watched, another farmhouse flashed by and there was another little group waving their salute. It was as if they had waited up to bid a welcome and a goodbye to a brother, though they knew in advance he would be unseen and unseeing.

And in the morning, I woke up very early; it was scarcely dawn; but as I looked out, the people were up and greeting their friend. All night long, apparently, these friends of Theodore Roosevelt whom he never saw, one family group after another, had been giving him their benediction.

Another day on this same journey stands out in my memory. It was a Sunday. Mr. Roosevelt had stated positively that he would make no speeches that day. The special train was to run from the morning until almost dusk without a stop. It had not run far when I heard a strange sound. It swelled suddenly into a confusion of voices and then subsided. I looked out.

We had just passed a railway station in a wide stretch of country. Around the station I saw a crowd of people. Where had this crowd come from? Every farmhouse for miles must have contributed its entire household. Again as we passed another station came the crescendo and diminuendo of the sound of voices. Mr. Roosevelt came out from his stateroom where he had been reading. He could not pass these friends of his, friends he had never before seen, but friends who had cared so much for him that they had driven for miles over the rough country roads, in all sorts of vehicles, simply in order to be beside the track as his train went by.

So thirty times that day the sound of cheering voices swelled, thirty times the train stopped, thirty times Mr. Roosevelt left his reading to be out on the rear platform and greet those who had for the most part never seen him, and had no hope of seeing him, but who came just to show their friendship. —*Willis J. Abbot*

Even at night, the crowds kept appearing at stations where the train was scheduled for a stop, and often, even when the train was not due to stop, the crowd would be there just the same. They waited until midnight and after, and not a few times, when the train stopped in the small hours, the crowd would gather about the Colonel's car and shout: "Teddy! Teddy!" Sometimes they added the plea, "Stick out your head. We want to see you." Occasionally the Colonel responded to these demands, and when he did there was always a wild cheering and jamming to get into better position just to see him. —*O. K. Davis*

They telephoned the doctor, but by the time he arrived, the end had come. When the doctor left, Mrs. Roosevelt, James Amos [TR's valet], and Charlie Lee, who had been coachman and later chauffeur, knelt by TR's bed and recited the Lord's Prayer. —*Nicholas Roosevelt*

[From a 1924 speech on "Roosevelt's Leadership," delivered by Herbert Knox Smith, Commissioner of Corporations in the Roosevelt Administration; member of TR's Tennis Cabinet; Progressive politician:]

Above all the pictures of him in my memory, one stays always clear as the most wonderful and imposing in its silent presentation of the leader and the led. I don't think he ever even knew of it.

He was making a long trip by boat down the Mississippi River, in 1907 I think. Governor Pinchot and I were on the steamer just behind him. The night was very warm and Mr. Pinchot and I took our mattresses out onto the open rear deck to sleep. But I didn't sleep, because of what I saw through the night.

On one long reach of the river, and then the same on the next, we would catch a point of light in the darkness ahead. It would grow to a flame, a fire of driftwood on the shore. As we would come abreast of it, there would be an American flag driven in the sand; and about it a quiet group of twenty, fifty, a hundred, five hundred, silently gazing to watch the passage of the sleeping leader.

All through the night, along the Great Stream in the heart of our land, those points of light twinkled far ahead, grew bright and near, shone abreast of their groups and the flag, and fell astern. We were never out of sight of them, as far as I could tell.

I doubt if he knew of it; perhaps he did.

But that night in its beauty, its steadily recurring points of light and love, its silence and its vastness, seemed somehow to me to carry, beyond the power of speech or pen, the heart and meaning of his leadership—the heart and meaning of our response.

Afterword

The title of this book, as I explain herein, is the same as a magazine article from 1915, transformed into a small book in 1916. Theodore Roosevelt's popularity was at a low ebb, partly because the American public regarded the European War differently than did the crusading Colonel. Among his friends were editors at *The Century*. The monthly magazine assigned reporter Julian Street to write an article on the plausible topic—Theodore Roosevelt as the most interesting American. It was a straightforward profile, laudatory with the hint of a presidential feeler as much as an element of rehabilitation.

Casting about for a title for this book (perhaps influenced by the persistence of Street's focus in my mind) I could not think of a better title. TR—*Most Famous?* Not really. *Most Celebrated?* Not "Most." *Most Popular?* A hollow encomium at any rate. Most challenging for this historian.

"Most Interesting" is arguable, however. I admire Benjamin Franklin, Thomas Jefferson, Abraham Lincoln, Thomas Edison, and others as well, in and out of civic life. But TR—in the fashion of his inclusion on Mount Rushmore—is as interesting as any American this nation has produced. "Interesting" is a valid though arbitrary criterion for scholarly focus, and, perhaps more importantly, as the reason for this chrestomathy (more than a mere anthology), explaining one of America's great natural resources, Theodore Roosevelt. A user's manual, so to speak, for the legatees of our American heritage, to appreciate our iconic figure.

There will be no more *précis* here. Why I thought this book neces-sary I explained in the Introduction and, implicitly, on every page. I have admired Theodore Roosevelt since boyhood (mine, not his) so in a sense this book took a year to produce, but fifty years to prepare and compile. My library has more than five hundred books about Roosevelt; and I own complete runs of the major magazines and the New York newspapers of his era. Thanks to the methodology I adopted, arbitrarily dividing TR's interests into ten parts, my library eventually looked like a Technicolor forest-bed on a dewy morn—volumes sprouting hundreds of colored Post-It notes to guide me.

I was surprised that after so many years and so many Roosevelt books, there has not yet been a book that has collected his contemporaries' impressions and recollections in this manner—not policy analyses nor political stratagems, but aspects solely of his personality. I am already at work on a Rooseveltian Table Talk collection—a time-honored but nearly extinct category of biography that once encompassed consequen-tial figures from Luther to Dr. Johnson to Hitler— that will properly deal with his private opinions on public issues.

I initially was surprised, and some readers might be, on what is *not* here. But there are Rooseveltian legends that are not true and I there-fore avoided. I expected that many of TR's intimate friends would yield much material, but often they did not. Some intimate friends of his were reticent to share the private aspects of TR's personality—the morsels for which we, today, hunger. Victorians generally were chary of revealing… anything of a personal nature to their friends, no matter how flattering or interesting.

Recently discovered tape recordings of friends and relatives, arranged decades ago with the best intentions, are almost vacuous. Their sterility is explained by factors ranging from vestigial Victorian rectitude to intimi-dation posed by new-fangled tape recorders. Therefore the quotations ironically say as much about the witnesses as they do about Roosevelt himself.

On the other hand, some of the seemingly superficial articles and books of the day—by casual friends, acquaintances, neighbors—were a cornucopia of impressions and revelatory small-talk. Hallelujah for per-ceptive, chatty, and generous folks.

Different people shared different impressions, of course. TR's wife Edith burned her correspondence (another convention of earlier social practice); but ministers, aides, valets, were voluble. Cowboy friends were either chatty or reserved. One sister, Corinne, shared much; another, Bamie, was formal, restricting her memories to accumulated correspondence—unfortunate for the purpose of this book.

During my life I was blessed to have met several of the Roosevelts. I first met his first child, nicknamed by an adoring public "Princess Alice," at the dedication of the Roosevelt Island statue in 1967. She was scurrying from the ceremony when President Lyndon Johnson began to speak, which gave me my first opportunity for a chat and to have my copy of her 1933 autobiography inscribed. I also knew Edith Kermit Roosevelt, granddaughter and conservative newspaper columnist. We both worked for the newspaper chain owned by William Loeb, son of TR's White House secretary. Edith, based in Washington, assisted me on research for investigative articles. Bill Loeb frequently celebrated his godfather, encouraging my own tributes and running front-page editorials on TR's birthday. And I knew Nicholas Roosevelt, TR's nephew, who presented me with a typescript chapter of his 1967 memoirs, and gave me access to his unpublished "Recollections of 1912."

So, given the factors of time (I was born thirty years after TR died) I came as close as someone of my generation could have come to Roosevelt himself. Among contacts and acquisitions, I have the unpublished *Recollections of Theodore Roosevelt* by Samuel McCune Lindsay, a Roosevelt associate who served him in several capacities.

In this book there are few professional historians represented. I sought the impressions of eyewitnesses, not analysts—people who conveyed the wonder and attraction of the man. Readers will find some quotations and passages that appeared in subsequent biographies and history books. But it was my goal to *start* with such words, and dig deeper for the first recorded incidences. Sometimes this yielded corrections to inherited anecdotes and memes.

(And I will mention here that a collateral goal of this book was to challenge the spate, I suppose well intentioned, of internet memes and dollar-store plaques that festoon the "wisdom" of TR. Too often they owe more to fortune cookies than to Colonel Roosevelt. There is a current mania for colorizing photos of TR and Princess Alice. And we see uncountable impersonators, some even bearing a slight resemblance to the Colonel. Even Abraham Lincoln, to choose another American icon, has not endured such homage, strangely.)

TR suffers today from a curious separation from reality; and neither colorized photographs nor impersonators properly can fill the gaps. A purpose of this book is to rescue him also from the stereotype of an eccentric fellow who happened to accomplish things. Let us restore Theodore Roosevelt as a multi-faceted and exceptional American who, by the way, accomplished many things during a crowded life. Again: his personality in the larger and best sense, his *interesting* personality. TR was a *gestalt* American if there ever was one, and that fact animated my work.

This book is scholarly, I hope to say, but not academic. It shares the main points and important events in Theodore Roosevelt's life; but I have declined footnotes, endnotes, superscripts, and such. All the speakers and writers are identified in their section, noting their relevance and appropriate connections. Some people are lost to history, but were quoted in newspaper articles (many clippings preserved in scrapbooks) or tributes at meetings of Roosevelt societies that proliferated after he died. Always I have sought people who shared some manner of personal encounters. I was obliged to discern what recollections were authentic.

Further words about scholarship. I occasionally have condensed paragraphs or lines of quotations, attempting to avoid a tsunami of ellipses, but never altering anyone's meanings. The majority of impressions shared in this book are laudatory; but I have attempted to steer clear of Scylla and Charybdis— hagiography and the censorious. Roosevelt was not immune to such extreme reactions, but, again, the purpose of this book is to illustrate what made him interesting, not controversial. Tributes and eulogies were tapped only when observers shared something perceptive or previously little known to history.

Similar to my choice of avoiding our present-day stereotypes of a man whose personality must not be allowed further to elude us, readers may confront aspects of TR's career by what is *not* here. For instance, during health-care debates of recent years, it widely was claimed that "Teddy" Roosevelt was a progressive who argued for a national health system. We note that he disliked being called Teddy; that his brand of progressivism is not the Wilson-FDR-LBJ-Obama variety that has coursed through America's veins for a century; and that he never advocated a national health-care scheme. Comments thereunto would be here if these things were otherwise.

Of sources, Roosevelt enthusiasts will not be surprised by the number of citations of Hermann Hagedorn, a minor poet who was TR's semi-official biographer; with Joseph Bucklin Bishop, a virtual scribe at the end of Roosevelt's life; and of John Hay, who knew Theodore Roosevelt's father when Teedie was a young boy, and died while serving as TR's Secretary of State. There is a general feeling that Hagedorn's career coasted in the wake of TR's popularity, but he is due a reevaluation; his works are revelatory, informed, and eminently readable. He frequently shared what came close to gossip, in historical contexts. The same might be said of TR's valet, James Amos, whose access to the private Roosevelt was significant. He shared more than master-and-servant clichés, not afraid to contradict celebrities and even TR's friends... inuring to our proper understanding. TR's lifelong friends Henry Cabot Lodge and William Howard Taft were dry wells, but his Military Aide Archie Butt was a rich mine, partly because he prissily shared what otherwise would have been outrageous gossip in letters to his mother and sister who swore themselves to discretion, and maintained it for two decades. Likewise we are blessed that cowboy friends and hunting companions generally combed their memories and could be prolix, even rambling. TR had a goodly number of godly friends and ministers shared interesting stories and dispositive revelations about TR's faith, a neglected and misunderstood aspect of his personality.

I should not have to explain that an essential element of what made TR *interesting* to his contemporaries was reflected in, and equally led by, what we call today "popular culture." In singular fashion, before or since, Theodore Roosevelt became a familiar figure in cartoons and buttons (not only the predictable political sorts); children's books; toys and games; postcards; music and song sheet art; animation and movies; fiction novels; unauthorized product affiliations for cigars, cigarettes, beer, cookies, rifles; and much more. We lift the curtain on these graphic and commercial footprints of the Most Interesting American. They are nearly as important as spoken or written impressions.

A watchword as I proceeded to collect the quotations and passages in this book (ultimately more than 500 of them, by more than 150 individuals) was to preserve the context of Roosevelt's life and times. For historians, that is, not moralists, critics, or essayists, this once was *de rigeur*. But "thanks" to Political Correctness, attutides and terms are sometimes canceled or even altered to propel historical figures into last week's environment. To preserve the flavor of previous times is now, too often, a neglected, even abused and scorned, practice. I am determined to present why Theodore Roosevelt was interesting to his fellow citizens—not necessarily why he should be interesting to us, today—although I am certain that such will be the natural result of this anthology.

The trend among 21st-century historians, I sadly observe, is the frequent judgments of historical figures against standards of the present. It is a useless, biased, and often evanescent approach. Real personalities and valuable lessons of history become lost in such Woke games that are contrary to the historian's calling.

Critics find it useful to understand Roosevelt, for instance—as they proceed to mis-understand him—by casting judgment on his attitude toward Blacks and Native Americans. Different times, different dynamics, and different attitudes (even if TR's attitudes generally were more "liberal" and responsible than most of his colleagues) make little difference to many modern historians. By failing to contextualize, they collaterally obscure facts and lessons. It is similar to Lincoln: figures of the 19th century are called out as hypocrites for not having lived in the 21st century. Another example is, from all people, my late friend Edmund Morris, the Pulitzer Prize winning biographer of Theodore Roosevelt.

I was flattered when Edmund sent me a note upon the publication of my Johann Sebastian Bach biography, and he called it superior to his *Beethoven*. He disagreed, however, with my emphasis on Bach as a man of faith, and wondered whether "one man's Christianity is another's 'air of another planet,'" and why Muslims and Buddhists can be "moved" by the Mass in b minor, except that Bach "transcended" religion. This seems to me a rather earnest rejection of sympathy for Bach's world (1685-1750). And he disregarded the stated thesis of my book—the first treatment of Bach's faith life—and its subtitle "Christian Encounters."

Morris might have known more about Bach than I did, but to think he knew more about Bach and his faith than Bach himself did is farcical. Half of Bach's surviving music (about twelve hundred works) is Christian; he chose, unlike his Saxon contemporary Handel, always to have ecclesiastical employment; and Bach frequently attested to his Christian faith, holding it more precious than musical composition itself.

So it should become a larger mission of history-lovers and historians—indeed, all responsible citizens—to contextualize the past as an essential component of understanding…processing…and building upon it for the future. It is my hope that this book will enable readers to do that. To understand Theodore Roosevelt. To discover why he was so compelling, in so many ways, to those around him, to his nation, to the world. And to posterity. Possessing as we do the records of his deeds, I hope this anthology will reveal the remarkable personal qualities of this Most Interesting American.

"I Wish I Were Like Him!"

Acknowledgments

"Acknowledgments" at the ends of books sometimes seem—or are—perfunctory; and their place in the editorial order of things carry unavoidable implications. But there are friends and supporters of this book whom I acknowledge as literally the encouragers and angels whose friendship, concern, material and moral support—including prayer support—saw this project through as much as I did myself. Bridgette and Kevin Ehly; my son Ted Marschall; Barbara Haley; Ray and Teresa Eves; Gordon Riddle Pennington; Bernadette Castro; John Olsen; Ted Hake; Mel Birnkrandt; Terry Brown; Feather Schwartz Foster; Barbara Marschall; Duane Jundt; Alan Neigher; Deborah Benaglio; Sarah Phillips; John Adcock; Mark Seifert; Rod Sullivan; Maureen Nestor; Gary Gervitz; Ivan Smith. My editors at Post Hill Press, Ashlyn Inman; and Alex Novak, who shepherded one of my previous TR books (*Bully!*, Regnery History, 2011), who has been typically brilliant, supportive, wise, innovative, and patient; not necessarily in that order.

I cannot neglect other friends of mine, past and present, and friends of TR whose interest (there's that word again) in Roosevelt as well as my oft-stated vision for a project like this must be acknowledged: Alice Roosevelt Longworth; Edith Kermit Roosevelt; Nicholas Roosevelt; William Loeb; Dr. Albro Martin; Dr. Charles McLaughlin; Edward Peter Fitzsimmons; William Newman; Edmund Morris; Ted and Lilly Baehr; Charles Basbas; Lynn McTaggart; Rangers Scott Gurney and Mike Amato; Ed Norton of Oyster Bay; Norm and Penelope Carlevato; Jó Hardesty Lauter; and Maury Forman.

People Cited in the Text

Willis J. Abbot, journalist; author; historian

Lawrence F. Abbott, publisher and editor of *The Outlook* weekly magazine; Roosevelt biographer; TR's secretary during his post-safari tour of European capitals

Dr. Lyman Abbott, Congregational minister; publisher

Henry Adams, descendant of two presidents; historian; author; essayist; writing in his autobiography *The Education of Henry Adams*, quoted herein, in the third person

Jane Addams, reformer; social worker; Nobel Peace Prize recipient

Carl Akeley, conservationist; pioneer nature photographer; taxidermist

Robert A. Alberts, a spectator quoted in newspaper clipping

Henry J. Allen, newspaperman; Governor of Kansas

James Amos, valet to Theodore Roosevelt

Joseph S. Auerbach, attorney; essayist

Rev. William E. Barton, D.D., LL.D, Congregational minister; lecturer on Abraham Lincoln

James M. Beck, US Representative from Pennsylvania; United States Solicitor General

William Beebe, naturalist; ornithologist; entomologist; explorer

Albert J. Beveridge, United States senator, Indiana; biographer of John Marshall and Abraham Lincoln

Joseph Bucklin Bishop, biographer; reporter

Jules Bois, French journalist; author; poet

Dr. Ralph J. Bunche, diplomat; civil-rights leader; Nobel Peace Prize recipient

Edward Bok, author, Editor of *Ladies' Home Journal*

Evangeline Booth, Commander, The Salvation Army

John Burroughs, naturalist; conservationist

Rev. W. I. Bowman, Pastor, Oyster Bay Methodist church

Berton Braley, poet

Robert Bridges, Editor of *Scribner's* magazine; writer; critic (as "Droch") for *Life* magazine

William Jennings Bryan, three-time Democrat presidential candidate, who attended the 1912 Republican convention in the role of newspaper reporter for the George Matthew Adams syndicate.

Nicholas Murray Butler, President, Columbia College, later Columbia University; Nobel Peace Prize recipient; President, Carnegie Endowment for International Peace.

Archie Butt (Captain Archibald Willingham DeGraffenreid Clarendon Butt), Military Aide to Presidents Roosevelt and Taft, also a friend of the Roosevelt family. Most of his recollections in these pages are from letters to his mother or sister

Benjamin N. Cardozo, United States Supreme Court Justice

Carleton Case, author and anthologist

Albert Loren Cheney, Editor of the *Oyster Bay Pilot*

Richard Washburn Child, newspaperman; novelist; diplomat

George Cherrie, member of the Roosevelt-Rondon Brazilian exploration team

Mrs. Ralph Stuart Clinton (the former Miss Amy Cheney), a secretary of Theodore Roosevelt at Sagamore Hill

Edward H. Cotton, author; biographer

Isabel Fiske Conant, poet

Calvin Coolidge, President of the United States

Dr. Frank Crane, Presbyterian minister; speaker; anthologist

Stephen Crane, naturalist novelist; short-story writer

Gordon K. Dickinson, MD, a spectator quoted in newspaper clipping

Sir Arthur Conan Doyle, author of the *Sherlock Holmes* stories

Richard Henry Dana III, lawyer; civil-service reformer

O. K. (Oscar King) Davis, Washington correspondent, *The New York Times*; later Secretary of the Progressive National Committee

People Cited in the Text

Homer Davenport, political cartoonist. Davenport drew the iconic cartoon of Uncle Sam with his hand on President Roosevelt's shoulder: "He's Good Enough For Me!" in 1904.

William C. Deming, author; editor; civil-service reformer

Chauncey Depew, U.S. Senator, New York State; president, New York Central Railroad; humorist and after-dinner speaker

Mike Donovan, prize fighter; author of *Ten Years Of Boxing With the President*

George William Douglas, Canon, Cathedral of St. John the Divine, New York City; author

Maurice Francis Egan, diplomat; Catholic journalist; author

George Cary Eggleston, author; editor

Charles W. Eliot, President, Harvard University

Joseph A. Ferris, camping companion, later manager of a Roosevelt ranch in the Badlands

Anthony Fiala, cartoonist; polar explorer; original member of the River of Doubt team

James Montgomery Flagg, cartoonist and illustrator

James Earle Fraser, sculptor

Robert Frost, poet

Hamlin Garland, short-story writer of Western themes; novelist

Samuel Gompers, labor leader, founder of the American Federation of Labor

Arthur Guiterman, poet

Dr. Arthur T. Hadley, President, Yale University

Hermann Hagedorn, poet; Roosevelt biographer

William Bayard Hale, reporter. *The New York Times*; Democrat Party publicist

Col. E. W. Halford, Editor, *Indianapolis Journal*; relative of President Benjamin Harrison

William Hard, reformer; journalist

Albert Bushnell Hart, historian

John Hay, Abraham Lincoln's private secretary; author and poet; Theodore Roosevelt's Secretary of State

Will Hays, Chairman, Republican National Committee at the time of Roosevelt's death; subsequently Postmaster General; motion picture "czar"

Billy Hofer, hunter and guide

Clark Howell, Editor, *The Atlanta Constitution*

Harold Howland, historian

Ferdinand Iglehart, D.D., Pastor, Park Avenue Methodist Church, New York City; author

Otto H. Kahn, banker; philanthropist; patron of the arts

Rudyard Kipling, poet

Dr. Alexander Lambert, President Theodore Roosevelt's personal physician

Lincoln A. Lang, Badlands rancher

John J. Leary, reporter, *New York Herald*, New York *Tribune*, New York *World*; winner of Pulitzer Prize

Sir Arthur Lee (1st Viscount Lee of Fareham), diplomat; politician; philanthropist

William Draper Lewis, Dean, University of Pennsylvania Law School

Samuel McCune Lindsay, sociologist; chairman, National Child Labor Committee; appointed Commissioner for Education, Puerto Rico, by Roosevelt. Passages here from unpublished manuscript, *Recollections of Theodore Roosevelt*, in author's possession

Major W. H. H. Llewellyn, commander of a company in the regiment of Rough Riders

Henry Cabot Lodge, U.S. Senator, Massachusetts; historian; longtime friend of Roosevelt

William Loeb, Roosevelt's White House secretary; father of the New England newspaper publisher of the same name

Alice Roosevelt Longworth, Theodore Roosevelt's daughter

Rev Dr. James M Ludlow, Pastor, St. Nicholas Dutch Reformed Church, New York City

Edwin Markham, poet

Francis Cutler Marshall, US Army 2nd Inf. Brigade, commanding officer of TR's son Ted in World War I

Thomas Riley Marshall, Vice President of the United States

E. S. Martin, Editor of the old *Life* humor and commentary magazine; essayist for *Harper's Monthly*; editorial writer for *Harper's Weekly*; fellow Harvard graduate of Roosevelt.

Edgar Lee Masters, poet; biographer; essayist

Brander Matthews, professor, Columbia University; critic; author

People Cited in the Text

James W. McCarthy, Judge, United States District Court, New Jersey

Major General Frank Ross McCoy, aide to President Roosevelt; subsequently President of the Foreign Policy Association

John T. McCutcheon, political cartoonist, *Chicago Tribune*, African expolorer; foreign correspondent; recipient of two Pulitzer Prizes

C. Hart Merriam, mammalogist; zoologist; ornithologist

Robert J. Mooney, Associate Publisher, *The Inter Ocean*, Chicago

James Morgan, pastor; quoted in newspaper clipping

Joe Murray, a local Republican politician in the Manhattan district where the twenty-two-year-old Roosevelt first ran for office

Dr. Henry Fairfield Osborn, paleontologist; geologist; President, American Museum of Natural History

John M. Parker, Progressive Party leader; Governor of Louisiana

George H. Payne, Editor, *The Forum* magazine

Edmund Lester Pearson, librarian; author; bibliographer

George Wharton Pepper, US Senator, Pennsylvania

LeRoy Percy, US Senator, Mississippi; planter; activist

Gifford Pinchot, first Chief of the United States Forest Service; Governor of Pennsylvania; conservationist

Thomas Brackett Reed, Speaker, U.S. House of Representatives

Dr. Christian Reisner, Pastor, Broadway Temple, New York City

Jacob Riis, reformer; reporter; pioneer photojournalist

Mary Roberts Rinehart, short-story writer; mystery novelist; publisher

Corinne Roosevelt Robinson, sister of Theodore Roosevelt

Rev. Geo. W. Roesch, Oyster Bay clergyman

Eleanor Alexander Roosevelt, daughter-in-law of Theodore Roosevelt

Franklin Delano Roosevelt, President of the United States

Kermit Roosevelt, son of Theodore Roosevelt

Nicholas Roosevelt, nephew of Theodore Roosevelt. Passages here from typescript manuscript in author's possession, and unpublished recollections and diary entries

Theodore Roosevelt Jr., son of Theodore Roosevelt

W. Emlen Roosevelt, cousin of Theodore Roosevelt

Elihu Root, attorney; statesman; US senator. New York State; Secretary of War; Secretary of State; Nobel Peace Prize recipient

Julius Rosenwald, philanthropist; President, Sears, Roebuck and Company

Bill Sewall, Maine hunting guide of the young Roosevelt; later manager of a Roosevelt ranch in the Badlands

Albert Shaw, journalist; Editor, *Review of Reviews*; historian

Leslie M. Shaw, Secretary of the Treasury; banker; Governor of Iowa

George Shiras III, U.S. Representative, Pennsylvania; conservationist; pioneer nature photographer

Rear Admiral William S Sims, advocate of naval modernization; commander of US naval forces in World War; subsequently President, Naval War College

Herbert Knox Smith, Commissioner of Corporations in the Roosevelt Administration; member of TR's Tennis Cabinet; Progressive politician

Vilhjalmur Stefansson, President, the Explorers Club

Henry L. Stoddard, Publisher, *New York Mail*; author; editor

Roger Williams Straus, son of Secretary of Commerce and Labor Oscar Straus; nephew of Nathan Straus (part owner of Macy's and eventual publisher of *Puck* magazine); father of the founder of the publisher Farrar, Straus and Giroux.

Julian Street, author; essayist

Bill Sewall, Maine hunting guide of the young Roosevelt; later manager of a Roosevelt ranch in the Badlands

William Howard Taft, Secretary of War; President of the United States; Chief Justice, United States Supreme Court

Rev. George E. Talmage, Rector, Christ Church, Oyster Bay

Booth Tarkington, novelist (the *Penrod* series; *The Magnificent Ambersons*; *Alice Adams*); recipient of two Pulitzer Prizes for Fiction

William Roscoe Thayer, author; editor; President, American Historical Association, 1918–1919

Jefferson Toombs, poet

George Turner, U.S. Senator (Populist), Washington State; member, Alaskan Boundary Commission

Henry Van Dyke, author; clergyman; diplomat

Edwin Van Valkenburg, Publisher, Philadelphia *North American*

Edward Wagenknecht, historian; literary critic

People Cited in the Text

Thomas H. Watkins, coal-mining executive; member, Coal Strike Commission

John S. Watson, convention delegate, quoted in newspaper clipping

Stewart Edward White, Western writer; novelist

Carolyn Wells, novelist; writer of humorous and nonsense verse

Edith Wharton, novelist; short-story writer; recipient of the Pulitzer Prize

William Allen White, editor; essayist

Owen Wister, novelist (among his books was *The Virginian,* which was dedicated to Theodore Roosevelt); short-story writer; essayist

Henry A. Wise Wood, inventor; newspaperman

Elizabeth Ogden Brower Wood, activist; early leader of the Women's Memorial Roosevelt Association

Leonard Wood, physician; Colonel, First US Volunteer Regiment (Rough Riders); Major General, US Army; military governor of Cuba; Governor-General of The Philippine Islands

Father John Augustine Zahm, Roosevelt's Brazilian companion prior to the expedition charting the River of Doubt (later named Rio Roosevelt)

About the Author

The *Most Interesting American* is Rick Marschall's seventy-fifth book and his third about Theodore Roosevelt. His primary field is American popular culture, and he has also written biographies, children's books, and Christian apologetics. A former political cartoonist, editor of Marvel Comics, and writer for Disney, he has taught at four universities including the School of Visual Arts and Rutgers. He has spoken overseas on behalf of the US Information Service of the Department of State. As a Theodore Roosevelt authority, Marschall has served on the Advisory Board of the Theodore Roosevelt Association, was Cartoon Archivist for the Theodore Roosevelt Center at Dickinson University, and is a contributor to the weblogs *Theodore Roosevelt* and *The Roosevelt Dynasty—Family, Fitness, and Faith.*